MOVERS AND SHAKERS

The Study of Community Power

MOVERS AND SHAKERS

The Study of Community Power

PHILIP J. TROUNSTINE
TERRY CHRISTENSEN

ST. MARTIN'S PRESS
New York

Library of Congress Catalog Card Number: 81-51863
Copyright © 1982 by St. Martin's Press, Inc.
All Rights Reserved.
Manufactured in the United States of America
65432
fedcba
For information, write St. Martin's Press, Inc.,
175 Fifth Avenue, New York, N.Y. 10010

cover design: Edgar Blakeney

typography: Suzanne Bennett

art: Clarice Borio

cloth ISBN: 0-312-54962-8
paper ISBN: 0-312-54963-6

Contents

Preface   ix

1   THE NEW COLLABORATORS: JOURNALISTS AND
    SOCIAL SCIENTISTS EXPLORE THE SUNBELT   1

Why Study Power?   1
Finding a Balance: Journalistic Stories Versus Social Scientific
Methods   2
    Journalism's Awakening to Social Theory and Research   3
    Theory Builders in Search of Communication Skills   4
The Study of Power: Where Two Disciplines Meet   6
The Rise of the Sunbelt   7
    A Shift in Regional Dominance   7
    The Sunbelt Attraction: More Than Sunshine and Resorts   9
    The Unexplored Sunbelt City   11
A Sunbelt City Close Up: San Jose, California   12
Notes   15

2   SOCIAL SCIENCE AND THE STUDY OF
    COMMUNITY POWER   17

Introduction   17
    What Is Power?   17
    The Community as a Unit of Analysis   20

Political Science and the Study of Power   21

   The Early "Positional" Approach to Power   21

   The Progressive Reform Era: Getting "Politics"
Out of Government   22

   Systems Theory and Behavioralism   23

Sociology and the Study of Power   24

   The Stratification Theory of Power   24

   The Elite Theory of Power   25

   The Reaction to Elitism   27

   The Pluralist Theory of Power   30

   The Reaction to Pluralism   32

Toward Synthesis   36

   The Community Power Continuum   38

Explaining Variation in Community Power Structure:
An Inventory of Criteria   40

   Size   40

   Diversity   40

   Economic Diversity   41

   Structure of Government   43

   Political Culture   45

   Summary   46

The Decline of Elites?   47

Carrying on the Research   50

Notes   51

3   A PRIMER IN POWER STRUCTURE STUDY

Advantages of the Reputational Method   54

   Pinpointing Who Really Does "Run the Show"   55

Choosing or Defining the Community to Be Studied   56

   Why Study San Jose?   57

Overview of the Method   58

   Establishing a Base List of the Influential   58

   Selecting Initial Informants   60

   Preparing a Questionnaire   61

   Seeking Subtleties of Power   62

   Tallying Responses   65

   Starting the Second Round   67

Drawing Out Additional Information   69
Encouraging Candor   70
Mapping Institutional Interlocks   72
Notes   77

4   FLASHBACK: A SHORT POLITICAL HISTORY OF SAN JOSE   78

The First Hundred Years: An Agricultural City   79
1880–1940: Emergence of a Commercial City   81
The Reformers   82
The Bigley Machine   85
1940–1979: Emergence of an Industrial City   86
I. The Internal Forces   86
II. Outside Forces: Stimuli to Growth   89
III. The Growth Machine At Work   91
IV. The Challengers: Growth Versus "Liveability"   99
A Corporate City of the Sunbelt   108
Notes   109

5   POWER IN A SUNBELT CITY   112

San Jose's Top Leaders   113
San Jose's "Top Ten"   114
The Interlocking Web   119
Club Membership   121
Institution Membership   121
Access and Influence   124
Leaders Rank Their Peers   128
Overview of Findings   129

Power of the Press: P. Anthony Ridder   131
A Publisher's Editor: Larry Jinks   136
Mayors May Come and Mayors May Go (But the Power of the Office Remains): Janet Gray Hayes   138
The Land-Use Patriarch: Albert J. Ruffo   142
Money (and an International Reputation) Talks, and San Jose Listens: David Packard   144
Mr. Chamber of Commerce: Ronald R. James   149
The Classic Behind-the-Scenes Influential: Halsey C. Burke   152

viii   Contents

Inherited Power and Prestige—and Knowing How to Use Them:
Glenn George   154
A Mover from City Hall to Congress, But Still a Shaker in San Jose:
Norman Y. Mineta   156
It's the Man and His Network, Not the Job: Frank Fiscalini   160
    Observations   162

Notes   163

6   THE CHANGING OF THE GUARD: POWER IN THE
   SUNBELT AND FROSTBELT TODAY   164

San Jose Today: A Power Structure in Transition   165
    Grassroots Gains: How Deep Are They?   165
    California's Political "Free-for-all"   168
    Changing Business Interests   169
San Jose's Future: What the Survey Suggests   172
    Testing Our Hypotheses   172
    San Jose in the 1980s   174
Sunbelt Versus Frostbelt: Diverging or Merging?   178
    Power Politics in a Traditional Frostbelt City   178
    Why San Jose Lacks a Traditional Elite   181
Power in Sunbelt Cities   184
    Yesterday: The Old Guard Elite   184
    Today: Power in Flux   187
    Tomorrow: The New Corporate Elites Versus the
    Grassroots   189
Last Words   192
Notes   193

Index   195

Preface

Movers and Shakers is a book about power. It introduces useful concepts and basic theories of community power, offers a method for discovering the powerful members of a community, and recounts our investigation of political power in a particular community, San Jose, California. The result, we hope, is not only an interesting and instructive analysis but also an invitation to readers to use the ideas and examples presented here toward an informed involvement in their own communities.

Both of the authors have a practical interest in local politics. One of us, Philip Trounstine, is a working journalist; indeed, our study began with his series of newspaper articles in the *San Jose Mercury*. Terry Christensen is a professor of political science with interests in urban politics and research methodology. Both of us are active participants in the political life of San Jose.

This book, then, is based on our commitment both to wider theoretical understanding and to political involvement. Chapters 1 and 2 provide a concise summary of theories of community power and methods for studying it. Chapter 3 explains the approach we used, the reputational method developed by Floyd Hunter in his seminal study of Atlanta, *Community Power Structure;* in effect, the chapter offers a step-by-step guide for conducting a study of the powerful. Chapter 4 presents the background, and Chapter 5 analyzes the results, of our San Jose study; we hope these chapters may serve as a model for the analysis of other communities. The final chapter places San Jose in a national context of population shifts and political change; it shows how our city is representative of many cities—particularly in the Sunbelt—and symptomatic of changes taking place across the United States.

The interviews involved in the San Jose study and in an earlier investigation of Indianapolis were granted in confidence. We appreciate the candor of those interviewed, and we continue to honor their trust.

We are grateful to Floyd Hunter, William Domhoff, Larry Gerston, Alden Campen, Dennis Poplin, and David Eakins for their careful reading and helpful suggestions; to Bob Woodbury, Carol Ewig, and Douglas Gower of St. Martin's for their patience and support; and to Gretchen Ray, Gail Yasutake, and Jenny Frediado for typing the manuscript. We also thank the editors of the *San Jose Mercury News* for permission to expand the original power structure study from the newspaper, and we thank the Political Science Department of San Jose State University and the Sourisseau Academy for research assistance that helped get our project started. Finally, thanks to Mary, Jessica, and David Trounstine, and to Don Chree.

Philip J. Trounstine and
Terry Christensen

MOVERS AND SHAKERS

The Study of Community Power

1

The New Collaborators: Journalists and Social Scientists Explore the Sunbelt

WHY STUDY POWER?

Political science, sociology, journalism, economics, psychology—today, these and other disciplines purport to teach us how societies operate and who runs them. Yet far too often, studying them at the college level is no guarantee a student will gain anything more than skeletal knowledge of the forces that actually shape our communities. One reason for this is that power, the fuel that feeds decision making, frequently is treated in college courses in one of two ways. Either it is regarded as a complex mixture of relationships that should be broached only by the most advanced students of social science, because only they have the intellectual tools needed to comprehend elaborate theoretical constructs; or it is dismissed as a force exercised almost exclusively within the formal structures established by law—the courts, legislatures, executive branches, and so on. Discussions of the power of corporations, certain elite families, the church, media, and other institutions may be sprinkled into our general educations, but, by and large, we are taught that basic decision making in communities occurs in the official structures we call government.

This book is dedicated to the proposition that ordinary people can

1

understand the complex workings of power in their own communities—which persons and institutions have it and how it is exercised—but not if power is sought out solely in formal political structures. Rather, if we hope to learn how decisions are made in our communities, we must know how to identify the varied sources of power that shape those decisions. Furthermore, we need to understand the historical, functional, and regional factors that may make the structure of power in our communities different from or similar to other communities.

With these goals in mind, we'll discuss in this book various theories about and methods of studying power and look in more detail at a particular method that researchers can use in their own communities. We'll talk about the historical development of community power, using a particular American city as a case study and examining the results of a power-structure study of that city. Finally, we'll draw some broad conclusions about the organization of power in all large cities—especially in terms of regional variance—and we'll compare our case-study city to other urban areas to highlight both similarities and differences.

FINDING A BALANCE: JOURNALISTIC STORIES VERSUS SOCIAL SCIENTIFIC METHODS

First, however, we should start with some understanding of the two different disciplines likely to have an interest in the study of community power—journalism and social science. Often, these disciplines have been at odds with one another. Journalists have regarded social scientists as armchair intellectuals writing ponderous papers in arcane journals. Social scientists, on the other hand, have viewed journalists as intellectual lightweights who have little regard for rigorous methods or significant social theory.

These are, like all stereotypes, narrow and inaccurate views. And those who accept them shortchange themselves. Social scientists who ignore popular journalism miss a rich source of anecdotal material that can add a human dimension to the generalizations they make. They also miss an opportunity to communicate their findings to a wider audience. Journalists indifferent to social science deny themselves access to theories that can explain the events they describe and to methods that will take them beyond their traditional interviews, observations, and occasional forays into public records. Although natural allies, both professions turn away needlessly from one another, from people with similar interests who can share ideas, findings, methods, theories, and frustrations.

Journalism's Awakening to Social Theory and Research

Before television supplanted newspapers as the medium by which most of us receive the news, Walter Lippmann, the philosopher columnist, wrote:

> Universally it is admitted that the press is the chief means of contact with the unseen environment. And practically everywhere it is assumed that the press should do spontaneously for us what primitive democracy imagined each of us could do spontaneously for himself, that every day and twice a day it will present us with a true picture of all the outer world in which we are interested.[1]

Much has changed in the sixty years since Lippmann's observation, including the rise of electronic journalism. Even so, the press remains the chief means by which we attempt to understand the world. Yet not until Philip Meyer's book *Precision Journalism* was published (1973) was there a serious attempt to provide journalists with some of the social-science tools necessary to advance beyond spontaneous observation.[2]

It is to Meyer's innovative book that most of the credit should go for first showing reporters they need not fear computers and statistics. In it he announced that social science had "leaped beyond armchair philosophizing" and was "doing what we journalists like to think of ourselves as best at: finding facts, inferring causes, pointing to ways to correct social problems and evaluating the efforts of such correction." Journalists, meanwhile, were practicing their profession as they had for decades, preoccupied more by objectivity and fairness than by concern for systematic study.

In the last ten to fifteen years, however, newspapers have begun to commit resources to systematic study and more reporters have found that social science research tools are valuable journalistic techniques. Although in many newsrooms reporters who conduct surveys or work with computers, census data, and other "academic" instruments are still regarded as oddballs, newspapers have nonetheless come a long way since A. J. Liebling, the *New Yorker* press critic, remembered:

> . . . a fellow who would come in from a football game and before sitting down at his typewriter ask the drunks to shut up so he could hear himself think. The boxing writer christened him "The Genius" and the warning was not lost on me. That fellow wound up on a faculty.[3]

On superior newspapers today, reporters and editors recognize the value of articles based on time-consuming, costly social science research methods. They may not lead to the indictment of a local councilman or exposure of a grievous injustice; however, these methods are being used for a simple reason: they can illuminate the background against which the news unfolds.

Still, demographic analyses, precinct-voting histories, campaign-finance studies, and other sociological investigations are not common fare in most newspapers.[4] Their efforts generally are limited to survey and voter-poll stories, particularly around election time. Despite the development of computer software packages that have made social-science statistical tests accessible to journalists, relatively little has been done along the lines of Meyer's own survey for the *Detroit Free Press* following the explosive 1967 riots there, or Donald Barlett and James Steele's computer analysis for the *Philadelphia Inquirer* of more than 10,000 criminal cases in that city's judicial system. For the most part, journalists still observe and write about current events, pausing when they can to analyze and explain. They focus on specific, contemporary individuals, institutions, and events—what social scientists would call the "surface."

Theory Builders in Search of Communication Skills

In contrast, social scientists deal in both past and present, often in hopes of predicting or at least preparing for the future. Their goal is less to describe than to explain. They endeavor to probe beneath the surface of events and the actions of individuals to find the forces that shape them and to discern social patterns. Journalists generally require only enough information to tell the story, but social scientists try to analyze events and put them in their larger historical and social context. Their investigative tools are aimed at explanation and theory building.

While the journalist generally is out to tell a story, the social scientist is attempting to test a theory. A theory is a framework for explaining a phenomenon. But simple as that definition is, building theories about human behavior is no easy task. Researchers make hypotheses (educated guesses) about how they think things might work and then develop a method of gathering data that will test their hypotheses. When they've gathered enough data and tested enough hypotheses, they have the building blocks for their theory. They understand and can explain a phenomenon, even predict what will happen in other similar cases, if their theory is correct. To do this, it isn't enough to tell a story about a particular event like a journalist does. Researchers have to look at many events and find patterns among them. Their methods must be rigorous, so that they can collect valid and reliable information, and they must minimize subjectivity. Ideally, any researcher, no matter what his or her personal bias, could use the same methods and hit upon similar findings because the methods are neutral and scientific.

Professional journalists also try to be "objective," but they understand that their methods impose some subjectivity that cannot be overcome, even though they may tell a story fairly and accurately. Their ability to be scientifically objective is limited in the end because the individual reporter writes or produces the story, filtering out some information, giving attention to other facts, finding an angle, selecting language that adds color, and so on. No matter how hard they try, reporters cannot escape their own perspectives, their personal experiences.

Social scientists try instead to develop a method—a set of questions or measurements—that permits evaluation of raw data without interference of the researcher's bias. The final filter is not the individual researcher but the method itself. Of course, social scientists are not always objective either. A researcher's personal bias may well creep in to slant the methodology, tailoring results to fit that bias. Because of this danger, it is necessary to inspect carefully the methods that social scientists use and to criticize their failings. Nevertheless, scientific methods are designed to overcome the subjectivity of the individual researchers, be they reporters or social scientists.

While the theories and methods of social scientists may be more sophisticated than those of journalists, they are often poorly communicated. Consider, for example, this important passage from a book that, by and large, is better written and more understandable than many in the field:

> Citizen participation is cooptative in nature when the activities of non-elites in decision-making and policy implementation are channeled toward the pre-conceived goals of higher authorities. From the latter's standpoint, the objective of cooptative participation is to evoke the participants' interest, enthusiasm and sense of identity with the goals of the enterprise in question. The technique can, of course, be made to serve the interest only of those who set the objectives. But cooptation, in its non-pejorative sense, is predicated on the assumption that both the general goals and the general means to attain them must, for the most part, be established by "experts," if the "best" interests of the participants and the community are to be served.[5]

Here is a concept that ordinary citizens need to understand—that they should be on guard when participating in public or private programs for which "experts" have set the goals because they are likely to be coopted. But unraveling this message is no mean task. Scholarly papers, journals and texts too often are dry and dull, mystifying simple truths by couching them in jargon.

Yet these theories and methods have contributed greatly to our understanding of the way we live. Public-opinion polling, demographic election analyses, economic studies, research on the impact of land use, welfare and integration programs all contribute to social science, journalism, and public policy. What social scientists can do, and do well, is to stand back from the flow of daily events to discover the source and direction of that flow and, delving beneath the surface, to offer deeper and more complete understanding.

Journalists, on the other hand, generally do a good job of keeping us informed about daily events. Some of the hypotheses that social scientists test are informed by stories reported by newspapers or television. Journalists also can contribute to the advancement of social science through their skills in communication. Their sense of what is "news," their use of rich anecdotal material to tell a story or explain an idea, can provide a means of getting social science findings out of the libraries and into the public forum, where these findings can affect public policy. Clearly, the two professions can be useful to one another.

THE STUDY OF POWER: WHERE TWO DISCIPLINES MEET

One area where the collaboration between journalism and the social sciences is ripe to begin is the field of power structure research. The media, drawn to investigating community power because it makes a good news story and touches on a part of political life that is poorly understood, have discovered their need for more professional and systematic research skills. And, as we have seen, the social sciences urgently need to communicate to a less restricted audience.

Some newspapers have published comprehensive studies of decision making and community power on the basis of extensive research and interviews.[6] A survey of the nation's major newspapers found more than two dozen had studied power in their communities. Most of these were impressionistic works, using casual methods that yielded inconclusive findings. But some conducted systematic investigations grounded on rigorous method.[7]

Social scientists, in the meantime, have spent decades studying power in hundreds of individual communities. Through these studies, our knowledge of how power operates has grown enormously. Furthermore, various methods of studying power have been devised and tested and compared with one another, extending our knowledge of ways in which power can be measured. Unfortunately, social scientists have made poor progress in making their findings accessible to the general public. Tending toward generalization and abstraction, many studies have named no names, and some have not even identified the cities being studied. Their work has been criticized archly by one of their own as "hardly rich in descriptive detail."[8] Moreover, some social scientists have become ensnarled in internecine debate over methods, leaving out the ordinary readers who most need to understand power in their communities.

So while journalists can deepen their work by learning how to use scientific methods, becoming aware of their own biases and how to control them, social scientists can expand the impact of their work by making it accessible to a wider audience. In chapter 5 we'll see how the study of community power can be made interesting, abounding with rich human detail and historical background. Lively writing need not be the enemy of social science.

Just ahead, in chapters 2 and 3, we will look at a method of studying power derived from decades of scientific experimentation that researchers, be they journalists or social scientists, can use to determine who has power in any given community. Chapter 3, in fact, is a do-it-yourself guide to community power investigations, a sort of cookbook for survey researchers. Chapter 2 sets the stage for our methodological recipe by tracing the history of community power theory and methods. Studying power is a tricky business for the novice; it's something like making a souffle—it helps to understand the theory behind the method, so if the souffle falls we know why, and what to do differently next time. To adopt any method without fully understanding its sources is a mistake. It is necessary to understand the roots of our methods in order to control their biases.

Before we move on to a step-by-step description of the power study format, however, we need to introduce a second important focus of this book, that of the emergence in America of its Sunbelt cities and the shape of power structures in these growing cities. One city from this broadly defined region, San Jose, California, will serve as a case study and model to illustrate many of the power-structure principles and survey methods we'll examine in chapters 2 and 3.

THE RISE OF THE SUNBELT

A Shift in Regional Dominance

Urban America has changed radically during the past two decades. Population growth and economic expansion, long characteristic features of the industrial cities of the North and East, have moved to the South and West. Here's how the President's Commission for a National Agenda for the Eighties summed it up:

> Between 1970 and 1978, the South gained a total of 2.8 million people, the West over 1.1 million, giving these regions of the country a growth rate that was more than double that in the rest of the nation. At the same time, the North-Central states lost nearly 3 million people, while the Northeast lost nearly 2 million. For the first time in the history of the United States, more than half the population now resides in the South and the West, and these regions are expected to continue to grow at the expense of the population in other regions.[9]

Nine major metropolitan complexes lost population between 1970 and 1980; all of them were in the Northeast and North-Central regions.[10] Most other metropolitan areas in these regions experienced only modest population growth during the 1970s. In contrast, ten major metropolitan areas, all in the South or West, grew at least twice the national growth rate. Even the slowest-growing metropolitan areas in these regions grew faster than the fastest-growing metropolises in the Northeast and North-Central regions.

While the nation's thirty most populous cities experienced an overall decline of 5 percent from 1970 to 1980, twelve of them increased their populations, and eleven were in the West or South. The largest relative gains were in San Jose, Phoenix, El Paso, Houston, San Diego, and San Antonio. The largest losses were in St. Louis, Cleveland, Detroit, and Pittsburgh.

Finance and corporate headquarters remain, for the most part, concentrated in the Northeast and North-Central regions. Indeed, despite the serious decay that has struck portions of the inner cities of these venerable regions, "the North remains dominant on all measures of economic performance and has lost ground to the South in relative terms only." But the *vitality* of urban America—measured by corporate investment as opposed to disinvestment—has shifted to the Sunbelt cities:

> The emerging interregional disinvestment pattern has favored the West and later the South at the expense of the Northeast and Midwest. Between 1960 and 1976, the capital stock in the South grew twice as fast as that in the Northeast. Between 1966 and 1979, the industrial Northeast and Midwest lost nearly 800,000 manufacturing jobs, while national expansion added 2.3 million total jobs elsewhere. For every 100 manufacturing jobs created by new plants in the the North, 111 were lost to some form of disinvestment. In the South, 80 manufacturing jobs were lost for every 100 added through new capital investment.[11]

Along with the capital investment and industrial growth have gone people, votes and power. Following the 1980 census, apportionment in the House of Representatives required a shift of seventeen seats. Of the ten states required to surrender seats only one, South Dakota, was a Western state.

Although, as noted, the North remains dominant in this regard, even the financial industry has seen shifts (the country's largest bank is headquartered in San Francisco). New corporate headquarters are more likely today to be established in Houston, Los Angeles, Dallas, or Atlanta than in Northeast or North-Central cities.

The Sunbelt Attraction: More Than Sunshine and Resorts

The Sunbelt is a band of states that runs from California to Florida. Its northern boundary might be a line drawn between San Francisco and Washington, D.C. Beneath that line is the boom. North of the line, except in parts of the West, is the bust.

There are many reasons for this shift in economic and demographic growth. The term "Sunbelt" suggests the obvious one: The weather is good in the region—the main attraction for retirees and tourists, mainstays of the Sunbelt economy. But climate and tourism alone cannot account for the phenomenal growth of the region. Economic and technological factors seem to be the prime stimulus to the Sunbelt's new vitality.

The Sunbelt has the good fortune of being the right place at the right time for the expansive sectors of the contemporary American economy. Repeatedly, the propelling force of the Sunbelt's rapid growth, as one commentator on the region puts it, "has been some sort of 'resource,' be it copper or petroleum, aerospace or electronics, range empires or agribusiness. The 'gold fever' has never left the Sunbelt; it has merely produced gold in different, often more feverish ways."[12] Natural resources—especially energy and agricultural land—have played pivotal roles in the Sunbelt's new gold rush.

But there's not much that's "natural" about the electronics, aerospace, and defense industries, and they, too, are at the heart of the region's economy. Why did they move to the Sunbelt? Because they had a choice. They were young industries, free to build new facilities where they could derive the greatest economic advantage. Furthermore, with few exceptions, they were spinoffs of larger corporations or new industries in search of the most advantageous locations. These they found in the Sunbelt. The climate was pleasant enough to attract workers from other regions, and there was a substantial underemployed work force already available. Even better, from the capitalists' viewpoint, labor unions were extremely weak; even today, "right-to-work" laws that outlaw union shops dominate the region except in California, Oklahoma, and New Mexico. Land was cheap, facilitating construction of inexpensive, low-rise buildings; cheap labor also reduced construction costs. Energy was also inexpensively available. The new industries, relying on highways and air transportation, did not need to be physically close to the transportation network of ships, barges, and railroads that were the backbone of heavy industry in the Northeast and Midwest. While less finance capital was needed to gear up new industrial facilities, the advantageous economic conditions also applied to the construction of housing for workers, millions of whom were able to attain the American dream of a single-family home on a parcel of their own land.

These essentially new industries concentrated in the Sunbelt. Federal policy encouraged the process, for much of the electronics industry and most of the defense and aerospace industries depend on federal contracts. Through these contracts, and by other means, "the federal government poured moneys into southern states while draining them from northeastern states."[13] According to the *National Journal*, there was "a massive flow of wealth from the Northeast and Midwest to the fast-growing Southern and Western Regions," with inequitable distribution of defense spending (on missiles, aircraft, radar-jamming devices, military computers) accounting for "nearly all the federal spending disparities."[14] Nor was defense spending the only way in which federal funds were inequitably distributed.

> If the distribution of total federal outlays is examined by region, the disparities (paced by person-oriented relief or national defense) between various regions grew between 1970 and 1976, with federal resources going disproportionately to cities in the South and West. Relief and human capital development outlays were the most inequitably distributed between 1970 and 1976, with portions of the Industrial Heartland receiving the least benefits.[15]

Industrial expansion in the Sunbelt was not *caused* by lucrative federal contracts, however. Rather, the region attracted new industries, which in turn drew federal spending, like a powerful magnet. Industry locates where it is convenient and profitable to locate. And as one authority on urban development has pointed out, in the choice of location, the Sunbelt cities "shared one thundering advantage over the older industrial cities":[16] free from encumbrances such as huge public assets invested in streets, sewers, and utility systems, they were not bound by previous land-use patterns or municipal debt. These rising cities could be built from scratch to meet the needs of new industries, which wanted decentralized locations for their plants and equipment.

The new Sunbelt cities wooed industry with aggressive self-promotion. They actively recruited new technology and federal spending. They were confident, optimistic, probusiness, progrowth, "can-do" people. They were boosters. And their boosting went beyond rhetoric. Federal, state, and local funds were spent to build the infrastructure—roads, sewers, water systems, and sewage-treatment plants—that the new industry needed. Almost literally, new cities were built and built to suit. Meanwhile, the cities of the Northeast and Midwest, saddled with massive fixed capital, could not readily adapt to the new conditions, and they began to stagnate.

The Unexplored Sunbelt City

The new cities emerged "by huge leaps, not by evolution," creating "a curious form of urbanization" in which "life and culture have been sacrificed to the most robotized forms of mass production, mass merchandizing and mass culture."[17] This is clearly the view of a critic, but most of us would agree that the Sunbelt has produced new urban forms—new economic arrangements, new social structures, and perhaps new political systems.

Yet surprisingly little is known about this new urban phenomenon. Our traditional image of cities has been based on those of the Frostbelt. Both social scientists and journalists have a strong Northeastern bias, and at least until recently, when they wrote about cities, they generally dwelt on the cities of the Frostbelt. When they wrote about the urban crisis, it was the crisis of the Northeast, the problems of the Frostbelt cities that fascinated them, not those of the Sunbelt. We don't know much about the way these newer cities function politically or socially or economically. It's about time we found out.

We do have some dramatic outward signs that tell us Sunbelt cities are different from the cities of the Frostbelt. First of all, most of them are growing, not decaying. Newer, they don't suffer the same problems of physical disintegration. Often more homogeneous, they may experience somewhat less ethnic and racial tension. They're generally more affluent. Unemployment, poverty, health care, and welfare are not nearly the massive burden they are in the inner cities of the Northeast and Midwest. The President's Commission for a National Agenda for the Eighties underscored these observations, much to the dismay of Frostbelt urbanologists, when it suggested that federal policies ought to accept as inevitable the economic decline of Northeast and Midwest cities, retrain and sustain the poor and uneducated people left behind in those cities, and develop a policy of "assisted migration" to the Sunbelt cities where jobs are plentiful.[18] That Sunbelt cities show up repeatedly at the top of lists of "most livable cities"[19] is really no surprise, even despite their emergent transportation, housing, and pollution problems.

Politically, Sunbelt cities are popularly seen as relatively open, freewheeling and volatile, and lacking entrenched organizations and leaders. Most have "reformed" structures of government, utilizing city managers, nonpartisan and at-large elections, and the initiative, referendum, and recall. Much of the industrial and financial wealth of these cities is controlled by corporations headquartered thousands of miles away, represented locally by branch managers and regional vice-presidents. And, as we've seen, many of the industries in the Sunbelt cities are heavily dependent on federal contracts.

What effect does all this have on community politics and power? Past studies, most of which focused on the older, traditional cities of the Northeast and Midwest, provide clues but not answers. In part inspired by the need to find answers to these questions, an urban power study of San Jose, California, was undertaken in 1979.[20] Commissioned by that city's newspaper, the *San Jose Mercury News,* this case study offers a beginning step down the road toward finding those answers, which someday, it is hoped, will end in a definitive analysis of the differences between the power structures of Frostbelt cities and the booming cities of the Sunbelt.

But we need not stop with examples from one Sunbelt city. In addition to reviewing the social science literature, a survey of ninety-five major newspapers undertaken by the authors identified twenty-three that had performed power structure studies in their communities. In Sunbelt cities, especially, fourteen newspapers found a need to find out and report shifts in their local structure of power. Some observations from these studies are contained in chapter 6. In general, a common thread runs through each of these Sunbelt cities: a power structure undergoing rapid change. As one Ft. Lauderdale observer noted: "Anything that happened here before 1970 is ancient history."[21]

A SUNBELT CITY CLOSE UP: SAN JOSE, CALIFORNIA

San Jose, the fastest growing major city in the United States between 1970 and 1980 (it grew 36 percent) is typical of cities in the Sunbelt. Like so many others, it was a relatively small agricultural community of

95,000 people until it began to boom thirty years ago. The Santa Clara Valley, in which it is located, was known by many then as the Valley of Heart's Delight because of its gentle climate and its thousands of acres of orchards. During the 1940s, the economy of the city was still based on the processing and shipping of the valley's produce.

By 1980, San Jose had become the seventeenth-largest city in the country, with a population exceeding 630,000 and sprawling over 160 square miles. An additional 600,000-plus people live in neighboring cities of Santa Clara County. (See map, p. 14.) The tranquil Valley of Heart's Delight had been transformed into "Silicon Valley," with electronics, aerospace, and defense industries replacing the farms and canneries of an earlier era. Today, only five of the twenty-five largest firms in the county are not part of the electronics-aerospace industry.

The transformation of San Jose and Santa Clara County was wrought by the silicon chip, a tiny bit of silicon on which thousands of items of information can be stored. It is the essential component of the high-technology industries that are changing almost every aspect of the way we live. Silicon Valley is now the ninth-largest manufacturing center in the United States. Profits are enormous, growth is phenomenal, and, although the booming labor market has slowed somewhat, it is estimated that the area's economy creates 40,000 new jobs each year. What a contrast with the faltering industries and declining economies of the urban Frostbelt.

The cities that have grown up with this new technology generally are modern and affluent. In the San Jose area the 1980 median family income was estimated at $27,000. Comfortable, single-family homes, with median value surpassing $120,000, fill the valley. Transportation is almost exclusively by automobile, and virtually every family has one or more cars. The urban complex is scattered, with employment and retailing in new industrial parks and shopping centers.

This success does not mean the area is free of problems. City services haven't kept up with growth. Traffic congestion and air pollution are serious, and the rising cost of gasoline is a threat to the region's transportation system. The substantial, largely Hispanic, minority community has not kept pace with the economic advances of the Anglo majority. And downtown San Jose, once a vital shopping area, is now a wasteland of empty parking lots, only recently edging toward redevelopment. Housing construction has lagged behind the demand created by the job boom, and the price of housing has begun to affect industrial recruitment. Businesses, once elated with the region, have begun expanding elsewhere.

At the heart of it all is the city of San Jose. Governed by the city-manager system, the city was long ruled by a small business elite. But

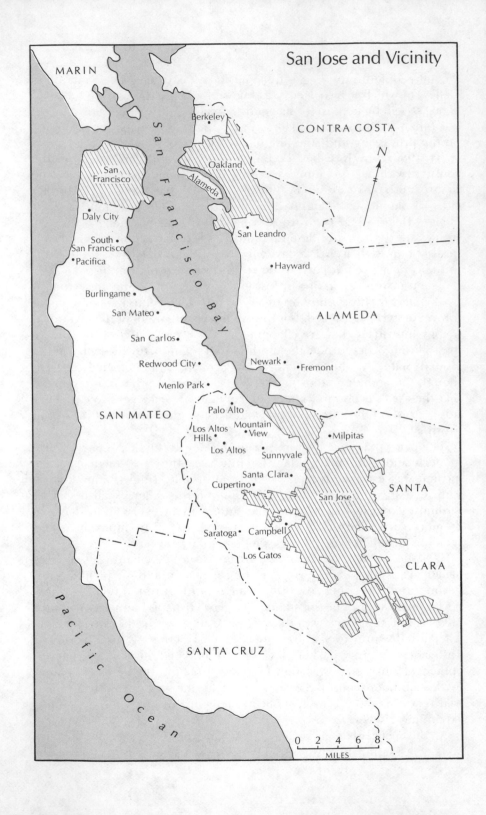

San Jose and Vicinity

MARIN

Berkeley

CONTRA COSTA

N

San
Francisco

San
Francisco
Bay

Oakland

Alameda

Daly City

San Leandro

South
San Francisco

Pacifica

Hayward

Burlingame

ALAMEDA

San Mateo

San Carlos

Redwood City

Newark

Fremont

Menlo Park

SAN MATEO

Palo Alto

Los Altos
Hills

Mountain
View

Milpitas

Los Altos

Sunnyvale

Santa Clara

Cupertino

San Jose

SANTA

Saratoga

Campbell

Los Gatos

CLARA

SANTA CRUZ

Pacific Ocean

0 2 4 6 8
MILES

the new arrivals have brought change with them and the challenge of a rival elite.

Chapter 4 tells the story of San Jose, from its founding to 1979, the year in which its power structure was first studied systematically. This history is important, for it typifies the kinds of demographic and political changes that have shaped the Sunbelt cities. These new cities may then be understood alongside their Frostbelt counterparts, where, as a study of the city of Indianapolis presented in chapter 6 will show,[22] historical developments have done little to alter the shape of the power structure. Historical differences and political, social, and economic conditions can then be compared and distinguished for Sunbelt and Frostbelt power structures, and the important similarities hiding beneath the surface can be rooted out.

Notes

[1]Walter Lippmann, *Public Opinion* (New York: Harcourt, Brace, 1922), p. 320.

[2]Philip Meyer, *Precision Journalism* (Bloomington: Indiana University, 1973), p. 4.

[3]A. J. Liebling, *The Press*, 2nd. ed. (New York: Ballantine, 1964), p. 73.

[4]The need for journalists to adopt social-science techniques is argued well and later detailed by Maxwell McCombs, Donald Shaw, and David Grey in their *Handbook of Reporting Methods* (Boston: Houghton Mifflin, 1976). "Behavioral science methodology makes possible a whole realm of description that is simply not feasible using the traditional interview or paper-and-pencil techniques of reporting." Furthermore, "news reporting is also enhanced by behavioral science methods that lead the reporter beyond description to explanation." p. ix.

[5]Peter Bachrach, Morton S. Baratz, and Margaret Levi, "The Political Significance of Citizen Participation," in Bachrach & Baratz, *Power and Poverty* (New York: Oxford University Press, 1970), pp. 206–207.

[6]See, for example, Franklin Dunlap, "One Man's City Hall," *Chicago Tribune*, 1972, or C. Frazier Smith, "The Shadow Government," *Baltimore Sun*, 1980. Also Mike Royko, *Boss* (New York: Dutton, 1971).

[7]Excellent examples include studies by Arnold Garson, *Des Moines Register*, 1976; Carey Gelernter and Paul Sweeney, *El Paso Times*, 1978; David Nimmer, *Minneapolis Star*, 1969; and Andrew McGill and Barbara Young, *Detroit News*, 1978.

[8]Raymond Wolfinger, "A Plea for a Decent Burial," *American Sociological Review*, vol. 27, p. 847.

[9]*Report of the President's Commission for a National Agenda for the Eighties* (Washington: U.S. Government Printing Office, 1980), p. 18.

[10]All census data taken from Daniel B. Levine, "What the 1980 Census Figures Show," remarks before the Conference on Urban Issues at the Washington Journalism Center, Washington, D.C., March 9, 1981.

[11]*Urban America in the Eighties*, report of the Panel of Policies and Prospects for Metropolitan and Nonmetropolitan America in the Eighties, one of nine panels of the President's Commission for a National Agenda for the Eighties (Washington: U.S. Government Printing Office, 1980), p. 42.

[12]Murray Bookchin, "Toward a Vision of the Urban Future," in David Perry and Alfred Watkins, *The Rise of the Sunbelt Cities* (Beverly Hills: Sage, 1977), p. 262.

[13]Robert Lineberry and Ira Sharkansky, *Urban Politics and Public Policy*, 3rd ed. (New York: Harper & Row, Pub., 1978), p. 61.

[14]"Federal Spending: The North's Loss Is the Sunbelt's Gain," *National Journal*, June 26, 1976, pp. 878–880.

[15]*Urban America in the Eighties*, p. 78.

[16]David M. Gordon, "Class Struggle and the Stages of American Urban Development," in David Perry and Alfred Watkins, *The Rise of the Sunbelt Cities* (Beverly Hills: Sage, 1977), p. 78.

[17]Bookchin, p. 262.

[18]*Report of the President's Commission for a National Agenda for the Eighties*, pp. 165–169.

[19]Arthur M. Lewis, "The Worst American Cities," *Harper's*, January 1975, pp. 67–71.

[20]Philip J. Trounstine, "Power in San Jose; Who Has It, Who Wields It," *San Jose Mercury News*, August 12–21, 1979.

[21]*Fort Lauderdale Sun-Sentinel*, February 19, 1979.

[22]Philip J. Trounstine, "Indy's Movers and Shakers," *The Indianapolis Star*, November 28–December 7, 1976.

2

Social Science and the Study of Community Power

INTRODUCTION

Most of us know intuitively that some people in our communities have more power than others. Most of us make assumptions about who these people are—elected officials, business leaders, bureaucrats, grassroots organizers, even journalists. Unfortunately, our assumptions, rarely based on methodical study and seldom tested, may or may not be on target.

Social scientists, on the other hand, have been examining the phenomenon of power for decades. Assessing power accurately and objectively through systematic study, to take us beyond our intuitive assumptions about specific communities, has been their goal. Their studies build on one another, as various researchers pose and test theories, criticizing and learning from each other and producing more sophisticated theories and methods in the process. Although no single theory or method has yet been accepted by all, the common goal is to advance our understanding of the complex and fascinating phenomenon of power. Reviewing earlier researchers' studies of power can help put our own work in its proper historical and theoretical context.

What Is Power?

Common sense suggests that *power* is the ability to make something happen—or perhaps to prevent something from happening. It is the

17

ability to control events, decisions, or behaviors. An accepted scholarly definition is "A can get B to do something he or she otherwise wouldn't do."[1]

Simple enough, but further thought suggests that power is a bit more complicated. It is, in fact, a multidimensional phenomenon. Awareness of this can help us to understand the complexity, and thus the difficulties, of studying power.

Consider, for example, the varied *sources* of power. *Physical strength* is one such source: human muscle, guns, and armies can make people do what they may not want to do. *Authoritative position* is another: both monarchs and mayors have the official authority to order people to do things. *Wealth* can be power: by controlling employment, spending, or lending, an individual exercises it. *Prestige*, a more subtle form of power, operates more by influence than by pointing guns, giving orders or withholding funds, but it may be just as effective. Often, those with authoritative positions or money also seem to have prestige. *Command of information*—about issues, the rules of the game, the other players, or strategy—is another source of power, particularly in our technocratic society. It is the power of expertise, exercised either by the experts or those who employ them. Similarly, *personal traits* such as exceptional talent, charisma, or oratorical skill may be sources of power. Our list could continue, but more important, as we inventory we should remember that the sources of power can be accumulated. If wealth or position bring prestige, so may either bring expertise, talent, and even charisma.

Another dimension of power is the *means* by which it is exercised. Some of the sources of power listed above imply their means. *Physical force* is most obvious: If someone puts a knife to your throat, you probably would do whatever you're told. *Institutionalized force* is another: If someone in a position of authority orders you to do something, you would probably comply. People in such positions—parents, police officers, tax collectors—have the ability to penalize you if you refuse. They may not need to use that ability, however, because most of us would obey them anyway. A more subtle means of exercising power than force or authority is *influence:* It means you do something others want you to do, not because they physically threaten you or have the power of the law behind them, but because you respect them or fear them enough to comply. You may also obey because they have skills in persuasion, or because you love or admire them and want to please them, or because you've been taught to accept their leadership. Influence, as we can see, can be a very subtle sort of power.

Influence and prestige, to a large extent, are the result of *socialization*, the process by which we are taught the basic values and acceptable behaviors of our society. Agents of socialization include parents, teachers, friends, co-workers, the media—virtually anybody or anything which communicates ideas to us. Among the ideas communicated are who has power and who should be obeyed and respected. This sort of power is based on a set of social cues that keep us in our place. Socialization is the inculcation of those cues. The greatest threat to established order is a breakdown in the process of socialization leading to rejection of the rules and the rulers.

Socialization is most complete when it has reached the state of *anticipated response*. An anticipated response is what happens when you do something you think others want you to do without being asked or ordered. Perhaps they don't even have to think about it. Certainly, *that's* power.

Clearly, having "power" is something more complex than A getting B to do something B wouldn't otherwise do. Power serves the social function of establishing and maintaining a system of order. Power is not randomly or individually applied. Patterns in the exercise of power emerge, forming a power *structure*.

Related to the means of exercising power, and particularly to the accumulation of power, are two additional dimensions: *scope* and *cost*. Each of us has some power, although some have more than others. For some, the scope of power extends to many issues as well as over time and territory. For others, the scope of power is narrow, applied only to a particular time, place, or issue. As students, we find that our teachers have inordinate power over our careers. But in the larger framework of the community, the same teacher may be only a minor figure at best. Similarly, for some the cost of using power is minimal. Perhaps only a word, a gesture, a signature on a check is necessary. For others, exercising what power they have may be an expensive effort. To many citizens, even minimal participation in politics—voting or joining a public lobbying group—may cost too much, whether in energy, in time, or in the psychological expense of challenging those they've been taught to respect and obey.

Power is multidimensional and not easily subject to definition. It can't be seen or smelled or touched. There is no machine, like a geiger counter, that can be pointed at an individual or an institution to measure their power. That is, in part, why there has been so much debate among social scientists about how to study it.

Efforts to define a phenomenon like power lead to theories, that is, sets of ideas about how something works. In this case, the theories have to do with who has power, how they get it, and what rewards power brings. But theories must have their basis in fact. The next step is to develop a method of collecting data to test the theory. If the method is objective, it will prove or disprove the theory. Unfortunately, it is often difficult to separate method from theory. Methods can be biased in such a way as to distort our findings and thus our theories. Perhaps we are so committed to proving our theory that in testing it we load the questions, pointing them towards a desired result. Or we may simply ask the wrong questions or use the wrong sources.

Because power is itself complicated, objective measurement is difficult. But if we are honorable researchers, we will do our best to make our questions and our methods objective, submitting them to the scrutiny of our readers.

The Community as a Unit of Analysis

Once we decide to study power, we must choose a unit of analysis for our examination, such as an institution (church, corporation, university) or some governmental entity (city, state, nation). Most students of power have focused on cities. They've used the term *community* to describe the unit of analysis because it is broader, referring not merely to the geographic territory of the city or to the governmental structure but to any and all social and political relationships in a place. All that is meant by the term community is some specific locality, a subunit of a nation or state. People in a community have certain things in common: economic interdependence, shared values, a means of communication, a governmental structure, and so on.

In the 1950s, when the formal study of community power began, defining a community was easier because cities were more clearly self-contained entities than they are today. But in the 1970s, suburbanization, freeways, and instant communications blurred the boundaries of communities. Federal and state intervention in municipal government diminished their autonomy. And their relative economic independence was dissipated by the replacement of home-owned industries with branch plants or offices of multinational corporations. All of these forces were particularly powerful in the sprawling new cities of the Sunbelt. But despite the forces of suburbanization and centralization, communities remain a useful subject for the study of power.

As Terry Clark, a professor and student of power, has observed, communities have been to social science what the fruit fly has been to biological science.[2] There are lots of them, they are convenient and accessible (after all, most of us live in one), they are less complex and more manageable to study than nations, and, even better than a fruit fly, they are often flattered to be studied. There are also enough of them to do comparative studies. In other words, communities have been handy laboratories for scholars. They are convenient for developing methods and testing theories; and what we learn from them helps us understand how power functions, not only in the communities themselves, but also in larger political entities.

Studying power in communities contributes to the development of our general understanding of power, but it also helps the residents of the communities studied understand their local political systems. Citizens should know who is exercising power and how. Public control of leaders is greater when they are known and visible; or, to quote a concise rule of thumb: "recognition of power limits power."[3]

Thus the task of students of community power is to map local power networks. By continuing to do such studies, we ensure relevant information for those with a practical interest in power as well as a greater understanding of changes in the possession and exercise of power over time. Communities remain the most convenient and productive unit of analysis for the attainment of these goals.

POLITICAL SCIENCE AND THE STUDY OF POWER

The Early "Positional" Approach to Power

The study of power is not new. Classical political thinkers from Aristotle to Machiavelli to Marx to Weber have theorized about it. Journalists have long been fascinated with the subject. But it was not until this century that researchers began to attempt systematic and empirical studies of power.

That may be surprising, since we might assume that political theorists have always spent their time chiefly studying power. That's true, however, only in a limited sense. For centuries, political theorists, especially in the United States, made their primary focus *government* rather than power *per se*. They concentrated on the formal structure of government and tended to ignore all the other quasi- or nongovernmental forces that made government operate. This structural bias produced an early political science that was legalistic and obsessed with studying constitutions, drawing organizational charts, and debating checks and balances and the separation of powers. Power was not altogether ignored, but the tendency was to deal only with its official application and to prescribe the best ways to formally distribute power in order to obtain the good society. In terms of power's multidimensional nature, traditional political scientists were apt to focus on *authority* rather than the other, more subtle manifestations of power.

Studies of community power by political scientists reflected such thinking, describing power in terms of the outward structure of government: the city charter, the office holders, their process of selection, and their powers. In the literature of community power studies, this is known as the *positional approach* because it focuses on those in formal positions of power—the visible, "legitimate" officeholders who are popularly and legally supposed to hold power. More sophisticated proponents of the positional approach might extend it to include those who hold formal positions in certain nongovernmental institutions as well. It is a simplistic approach, common in high school civics classes and, unfortunately, in many university political science courses. Yet it should be apparent that such an approach deals with only one dimension of power.

The Progressive Reform Era: Getting "Politics" Out of Government

Fortunately, historical events and theoretical developments outside their discipline have conspired to enlighten some political scientists in this century.

The labor movement in America offered a different analysis of power, insisting that government (particularly city government) was a tool of the owners of great industrial enterprises. Extensive use of police and national guard units to protect private industries and contain labor unrest made this point brutally clear. Yet although the labor movement fueled public debate and undoubtedly altered the way we think about politics, it ultimately had little influence on political scientists who were generally allied, personally and professionally, with those whose self-preservation depended in part on proliferation of the notion that the state stands above and apart from the owners of finance and industry.

The Progressive reform movement, rather than the labor movement, was the focus for politically involved academics for the first three decades of this century. As we will see in chapter 4, one of them wrote San Jose's 1916 city charter and became its first city manager. As reformers, these academics were prescribing governmental structures that they thought would destroy the political bosses and their machines.

The big-city machine governments were themselves evidence that power operated outside governments, manipulating them to the advantage of those who held power. Political scientists took a dim view of this, partly because their class was denied many of the benefits of machine politics—they had no use for patronage, since they ran no brothels or utility companies and didn't need a bucket of coal or shoes for the kids—and partly because machine politics wasn't legitimate. It wasn't the way democracy was supposed to work.

So, understandably, political scientists were active reformers throughout the nation, with elaborate plans for new ways of governing their communities. Their prescriptions included: nonpartisan, at-large, isolated elections; competitive bidding; civil service hiring; and the city-manager form of government. To many reformers, the goal was to remove politics from government, to make it more efficient and professional. Decisions were to be made by technically skilled experts on the basis of research rather than by corrupt politicians on the basis of favoritism. Decisions would be technical rather than political: there was "no Democratic or Republican way to pave a street." The reformers were, at least in part, acting as the agents of business interests, imposing capitalist values on local government, enhancing the influence of business over community politics, and diminishing the power of the working class.

Beneath their confident prescriptions for change, the reformers implicitly recognized that power could exist outside of government. But that power, as manifested by the political machines, was evil and had to be purged. They hoped, through structural reform, to accomplish that end. But the Progressives learned, to their chagrin, that changing the structure of government does not necessarily change the distribution of power in a community.

In some cases, the new structures worked as intended. In such cases, power had already shifted sufficiently for new interests to defeat old ones: Middle- and upper-class reformers had become numerous enough and sufficiently organized to defeat the old boss system. The reformers' first victory was the new structure. Their long-range success was making that structure operate to their own advantage, thus entrenching their power.

But as reformers learned in many cities, structural change did not eliminate opposition. Many bosses and machines learned to manipulate reformist structures. (It happened in our case-study city, San Jose, as we will see, when a new machine arose *after* reform.) Throughout the country, political scientists were learning about power outside government the hard way, through practical experience.

Systems Theory and Behavioralism

A few decades later—just after World War II—the development of *systems theory* gave further impetus to political scientists to examine power in a broader sense. Borrowed from the biological sciences and the concept of ecology, systems theory was based on the idea of a political system as an organism; its many parts were interdependent and existed within a larger environment. Governmental structure was only one part of the system, acted upon and in turn acting upon the society in which it functioned. Systems theory opened the door for the inclusion of virtually anything that affected political decisions, taking political scientists considerably beyond esoteric debates about checks and balances.

At about the same time, *behavioralism* also made an impact on political science. The study of how and why people behave the way they do, behavioralism took political science closer to the study of power outside government. Under the influence of both behavioralism and systems theory, political scientists were becoming more quantitative and empirical, beginning to live up to the word "science" in the discipline's name.

SOCIOLOGY AND THE STUDY OF POWER

These forces were not enough, however, to focus the attention of political scientists on power outside government. The most immediate impetus to do this came from another discipline, sociology. Perhaps because their subject has always been society in general rather than government in particular, sociologists seem to have been more willing from the start to search for power wherever it might be. In any case, it was the sociologists who first discovered the community as a unit of analysis—as a "fruit fly"—taking it as a microcosm of society and studying it in detail in order to understand society as a whole. Their findings challenged much of what political scientists believed about power, ultimately drawing them into the systematic study of power in communities.

The Stratification Theory of Power

The first of the classic studies of community power was the work of sociologists Robert and Helen Lynd.[4] For their fieldwork they chose Muncie, Indiana, which they called Middletown (until the 1960s, researchers tactfully, or coyly, gave their subjects pseudonyms), and they studied that city twice in the 1920s and again in the 1930s. Their methods were not particularly sophisticated. They read, interviewed, observed, delved into the public records, and wrote up what they thought was happening. Their books are social science classics, not only because they broke new ground in the study of society, but also because they sketched such a vivid portrait of a community—as it existed in the 1920s, and as it had changed in the 1930s.

Power was one aspect of what they described. Like a lot of sociologists, the Lynds felt that economic institutions and the class structure were dominant forces in society. They were adherents of what came to be called *stratification theory,* the idea that societies are stratified into layers or classes and that these strata are distinguished by certain characteristics such as wealth, prestige, and power. This notion held that if these resources were distributed equally, there would be no strata, no classes. But they are not distributed equally, and the variation in their distribution is what determines class structure: Some classes have more money, more status, more influence, and so on, than others.

The Lynds found this reflected in the power structure of Middletown. Businessmen dominated the political life of the community, with the wealthiest family at the top of a pyramidal power structure. The upper-class had a virtual monopoly on prestige and money and, with these, ruled the community. Political officeholders were viewed as men of "meager calibre, [who] the inner business group ignore[d] economically and socially and use[d] politically, a necessary evil" because the "operators of the economic institutions [did] not want to bother with the political institutions; on the other hand, they [did] not want too much interference" in their business.[5] The masses were apathetic, disunified, and, through socialization by the schools, churches, and media, accepting of business values and leadership. The elite maintained its power through "the pervasiveness of the long fingers of capitalist ownership" and "the thick blubber of custom that envelop[ed] the city's life."[6]

The Lynds' studies proved to be seminal. Other sociologists soon did similar studies of other communities and came up with similar findings. As with the Lynds, their methodology was essentially in-depth journalism, and their findings were subjective, depending heavily on the questions they chose to ask and their interpretation of the answers. Further, none of the studies focused exclusively on power. They were general studies of the social life of particular communities, with power and politics merely one chapter of the larger story.

The Elite Theory of Power

The single most influential work ever published on power was the book *Community Power Structure.*[7] It first appeared in 1953, and social scientists have been both criticizing it and imitating it ever since. The book reported on a study of power in Atlanta, Georgia, done by sociologist Floyd Hunter.

Unlike most academics, Hunter came to the study of power practically rather than theoretically. As part of his job with the United Service

Organizations (USO) in the 1940s, he had organized boards in various communities to raise and spend money. As he went into each community, he needed to find the people who could get things done. Sometimes they were elected officials, sometimes they were bankers or industrialists. But whoever they were, he had to find them quickly. In effect, he had to do a slapdash power study in each community in order to establish the USO. It's the sort of thing any good organizer or journalist or corporate executive would do upon entering a new community.

The practical-minded Hunter saw the need for a precise and reliable power-study method that others could use. But as he researched the literature, he began to realize that academics hadn't studied power as a singular phenomenon yet. Before he began his work in 1950, which would focus on Atlanta as its model, he determined to make power the exclusive focus of his study and to develop a precise methodology that could easily be replicated by other researchers. This clear and relatively simple methodology was described explicitly in his book. Thus the method could be criticized (and it was), but at least his readers knew exactly what that method was. The potential for replication was vastly enhanced. The Lynds had repeated their study of Middletown, but their methods depended on the same researchers returning to the same community. Hunter had developed an approach that others could use, in Atlanta or elsewhere.

Hunter's method was based on his personal need to observe and talk to real people. To do so, he first had to identify them, which meant observing the scene and talking with others. Using his common sense, for no examples were readily available, Hunter developed what came to be called the *reputational technique*. Basically, the reputational technique consists of the researcher asking people who they think has power, why they have it, and how they use it. Connections are then mapped to define the community's power structure.

But Hunter's method was more systematic than that. In Atlanta, he began by collecting lists of community leaders and activists from local newspapers and organizational membership lists. He came up with 175 names, too many for him to interview. He needed help in culling the list and focusing on who had relatively more or less power. He hit on the idea of having a panel of judges do the weeding out for him. Judges were selected on the basis of their positions in the community and their presumed knowledge about power and politics. They were then given the original list of 175 names and carefully interviewed. These interviews produced a second list which named the 40 most influential people in Atlanta. These 40 Hunter interviewed personally. Hunter asked each a number of questions. The most important one was, "If a project were before the community that required decision by a group of leaders—leaders that nearly everyone would accept—which ten on this list of forty would you chose?" Based on the answers, Hunter developed his description of the power structure of Atlanta.

The power structure he discovered has since been labeled "elitist." Its geometric form was pyramidal. At the top was a small group of businessmen, an elite upper class. Dominating the city's economy through a web of interlocking directorships, they also lived in the same posh neighborhoods, belonged to the same exclusive clubs, and frequently saw each other socially.

Only four of Hunter's forty influentials were public officials; the rest were mostly bankers, manufacturers, and other business leaders. The elites rarely held office and were not visible to the general public. Their power operated informally. Elected officials were subordinate to these leaders, doing their bidding but not fraternizing with them. The power of the elite was broad in scope and stable over time, exercised in the interests of the elite itself and affiliated with a national elite.

Like the Lynds and a generation of sociologists before him, Hunter saw the community he studied in terms of its class structure, with an upper class dominating and the political apparatus subservient to them. The main differences between Hunter's study and those that preceded it were Hunter's exclusive focus on power and his more systematic method.

Shortly after the publication of *Community Power Structure*, C. Wright Mills' *The Power Elite* (1956) made similar arguments, but about the *national* power structure, which Mills said was dominated by the bureaucracy, the military, and economic elites.[8] Other community power studies using the reputational method reached similar conclusions.

The Reaction to Elitism

Not surprisingly, political scientists reacted negatively to the findings of the sociologists. Their response was based partly on professional rivalry, partly on ideological disagreement, and partly on scientific criticism.

Professionally, political scientists didn't like having sociologists tell them how things worked in the political realm, which was supposed to be their turf. Robert Dahl, a political scientist and a leading critic of elitism, complained that the Lynds and Hunter "left very little room for the politician . . . [who] was regarded merely as an agent."[9] Some political scientists were annoyed that the subjects of their study were, according to the sociologists, on a secondary level of the power structure. Had they been spending their time studying mere pawns?

But the reaction of some political scientists was also ideological. Generally more conservative then their sociological colleagues, to them the analyses of Hunter and Mills seemed radical, even Marxist. The sociologists implied that genuine democracy was being subverted by the economic structure, while the political scientists believed in capitalism and its government. This was democracy in their view, not only as an ideal but as a reality. They simply didn't think things worked as Hunter and Mills said they did.

The political scientists made their attack, however, not on ideological grounds but as a criticism of the methods of Hunter and Mills. Dahl accused them of pandering to popular beliefs by offering a "simple, compelling, dramatic" theory "that 'they' run things," without adequately proving the theory.[10]

Specific criticisms of Hunter's reputational method began with questions about how well and thoroughly he had applied it. Were his initial lists sufficiently inclusive, or did they miss some individuals and institutions? Didn't the imposition of artificial numbers (40, 10) force respondents to pad what might have properly been a shorter list or to omit names from what should have been a longer list? Because the technique relied on interviews, the construction and phrasing of the questions were crucial. Were they neutrally phrased, or were they slanted to elicit a certain sort of response? Hunter seemed to be asking his respondents the question, "Who runs this town?," and some wondered if this didn't bias the survey unless there was clearly an opportunity for them to answer, "No one." Selection of interviewees was also crucial: Were they reliable? Did they really know who had power, and were they willing to tell a researcher the truth about what they knew? Were they operating with the same understanding of power as the researcher? Such questions about the interviews were particularly pertinent to a methodology that reached conclusions about power, not from first-hand observation, but from indirect information derived from talking to people. The researcher was heavily dependent on their truthfulness and accuracy.

Many critics of the reputational method objected that Hunter had subjectively narrowed his sample; then, when he asked these people who had power, they naturally told him that they themselves did. One typical critique held that Hunter "allowed his sample of community leaders to designate the issues which they thought were of major concern to the community. He then discovered that these leaders held a central place in the decision-making processes centering on the issues they had described."[11] But issues that were unimportant or unfamiliar to them might have been precisely those about which others have power. Perhaps, the critics said, the method was little more than a self-fulfilling prophecy. Based as it was on stratification theory, the critics thought Hunter "assumed the existence of a power elite and then [found] one."[12]

Some of these criticisms are constructive, but all can be corrected by careful selection of respondents, proper phrasing of interview questions, and research into issues and power connections that goes beyond the interview schedule itself. Hunter, in fact, made some of these adjustments himself. His technique was considerably more sophisticated than merely asking interviewees to name the "Top 10" in Atlanta's power structure. Unfortunately, some of his antagonists oversimplify his methods to suit their own ideology.

The method need not be a self-fulfilling prophecy. Virtually all of these criticisms can be overcome by careful research design. In assembling the primary list of community leaders (Hunter's 175), the researcher must simply seek to be as inclusive as possible. In choosing the judges who shorten and refine that list of candidates, the researcher must exercise extreme care to select a balanced cross-section of knowledgeable persons. The subjective judgment of the researcher can be treacherous at this point, but it can be checked by appropriate consultation. In the interviews that follow, questions must be carefully phrased so as to preclude predictable answers. If all this is done well, the variety of respondents and their viewpoints will automatically provide a check on each other.

Mapping connections among reputed elite institutions, known as *sociometric network analysis,* can flesh out data from interviews. By checking membership in prestigious community organizations and on boards of directors, a researcher can discern the ways the powerful work together. These connections extend to churches, neighborhoods, country clubs, and other social institutions. Research on selected issues that emerge from the interviews should also supplement network analysis. Further probing of public policy issues, such as a local redevelopment scheme or a municipal bond election, takes the researcher beyond an individual's reputation to the actual exercise of power.

In the view of the political scientists, the gap between opinion and action was the most serious failure of the reputational technique. Hunter, they said, based his study on opinions about who had power— on reputation rather than the substantive exercise of power. Thus, the reputational method was not an empirical test of power. Such a test, the critics insisted, required research on the outcome of actual decisions, which would reveal who controlled them. If it turned out that a small group usually won, you'd have a power elite. If not, they argued, you'd have something else.

While there was some merit in this criticism, it oversimplified

Hunter's work. Hunter did, in fact, study the history of some specific issues to see how certain individuals performed and did map the sources of power of Atlanta's elite and their connections with one another. And although he did ultimately rely far more on reputation than on the substantive exercise of power, it was because he viewed power as too complex and subtle to be readily measured or observed. Furthermore, reputation—itself a sort of power, a resource—is the best indicator of the more subtle manifestations of power. And it is doubtful that community leaders don't know who has real power.

Critics also charged that Hunter's descriptions of actual issues and outcomes were insufficient, resulting in an "inflation of power," especially of business elites.[13] Hunter, they said, "failed to specify the scope of power of different leaders . . . implying they were powerful across all issues."[14] And, they said, he mistakenly labeled as a "ruling elite" a group of individuals who simply had more influence than others.[15] In short, the critics were not persuaded.

Traditional political scientists were not the only critics of the reputational method. Although they seemed to be allied with Hunter and Mills in the 1950s, Marxists and other leftist theorists have come to see community-power research as excessively individualistic and insufficiently structural.[16] These critics believe that most students of community power focus too much on personalities and too little on institutions and structures. They tend to see individuals as powerful when in fact the power is in an economic and social institution and in the class it speaks for. Further, this personalistic tendency obscures the nature of class power, for to Marxist analysts, it is not a specific number of powerful individuals who rule but a class that dominates, using the state as its vehicle.

Admittedly, there is a tendency in community-power studies to focus on individuals. But this criticism is more of interpretation than of method. To address it, researchers must go beyond listing the names of those in power to specify *why* they have power (they command major institutions) and *to whose advantage* they use it (their own class).

The Pluralist Theory of Power

Robert Dahl and his fellow political scientists at Yale led the onslaught on elitist theory and the reputational method. They did not, however, merely criticize; they developed their own alternative theory, which came to be known as *pluralism*, and their own alternative method, which came to be known as the *decisional technique*. They argued that nothing could be assumed about the distribution of power in a community; it should instead be studied by examining specific decisions on specific issues. In this way, with concrete evidence in hand, conclusions could be reached about who had power.

The researchers were immediately confronted by the need to make a subjective judgment—which issues should they study? Dahl argued that it was best to study controversial issues, cases of disagreement. To prove that an elite ruled, it would be necessary to prove that their preferences consistently prevailed. Distrusting the opinions elicited by the reputational method, the Yale researchers wanted to look at actual behaviors.

Their method required the selection of "key issues" through newspaper coverage, observation, and interviews. Once the issues were selected, researchers delved into the decision-making process by traditional techniques: interviews, observation, documentary evidence, and news reports. In New Haven, the city they studied in 1958, the research was supplemented by participant observation: One of the researchers was a member of the mayor's staff.

Robert Dahl reported the results in his book, *Who Governs* (1961). The three issues selected were political nominations, urban renewal, and education. Dahl concluded that there was *no* power elite in New Haven. Rather, power was widely spread. Economic leaders were only one active group among many, and they were not particularly active at that. They also found that power varied over time and from issue to issue. No single group dominated in all issue areas. In fact, different groups and individuals were active in different issue areas. The only common figures were the mayor and the appropriate bureaucracy for each issue, precisely the people who should be active according to democratic principles. Dahl recognized that some individuals and groups had more power than others and that business leaders had great potential power. But he argued that much power was unused.

In other words, Dahl found that power was being exercised democratically in New Haven. Officials elected or employed by the public dominated the process. Democracy was at work, though partly because so many people—both the elite and the masses—did not exercise all of the power available to them. Elite theory was repudiated, or so it seemed.

Subsequent research, such as Frederick Wirt's study of San Francisco,[17] used similar techniques and reached similar conclusions: Variation appeared mainly in the degree of mayoral power, whether the mayor dominated the process as a "broker" among competing groups (as in New Haven) or failed to do so (as in San Francisco). This latter, "brokerless" form has been called *hyperpluralism*, for it is characterized by "many competing groups but very little power centralized in anyone's hands."[18]

Thus the political scientists produced a theory about power, a method for studying it, and a set of findings that differed substantially from those of the sociologists. Where elitists saw power as centralized, pluralists saw it as diffuse. Where elitists believed power was based on class structure, pluralists believed it was based on the formal political structure. Where elitists studied power through opinion, pluralists studied it through overt behavior.

The Reaction to Pluralism

The reaction to pluralist theory was almost predictable. Critics questioned the decisional method's reliance on behavior and the pluralist assumption that power was directly applied and observable, arguing that power was infinitely complex and subtle and not necessarily susceptible to observation or documentary evidence. The decisional technique might overlook socialization or anticipated responses, yet surely such subtle mechanisms are characteristic of the exercise of power, particularly by economic elites.

The economic elites in Dahl's study of New Haven were seldom active in issues such as education or political nominations and in other areas, such as urban renewal, were only active as rubber stamps. But could such decisions have been made without anticipating the reaction of the elites? Would a shrewd politician choose a candidate who was sure to be opposed by economic leaders? Would an urban planner propose redevelopment schemes that would hurt major downtown business interests, even if these interests did not assert themselves in the decision-making process? In other words, perhaps they did not assert themselves because they had no need to. This would signify enormous, unmeasured power. And perhaps they asserted themselves in ways not apparent to Dahl's observers.

G. William Domhoff, a leading elitist researcher, replicated Dahl's study of urban renewal in New Haven and concluded that Dahl was wrong. Using Dahl's data as well as minutes of the Chamber of Commerce and in-house memos of key economic and governmental elites that were not available to Dahl at the time, Domhoff found that major economic interests in New Haven were *instrumental* in the instigation of urban renewal and that the politicians merely implemented their wishes. Because he studied specific decisions during one period of time, Domhoff insisted that Dahl's work was narrow and time-bound, failing to delve into the roots of the urban renewal program and to discern the elite's state and national connections.[19]

Being time-bound was inherent in the decisional technique with its insistence on examining only concrete decisions and overt behavior. Through the study of specific events, the pluralists hoped to attain the goal of objectivity, but events have roots that may not be apparent when they occur. In the end, the objectivity of the pluralists was subverted because they rejected elements of the exercise of power that were difficult to measure. These subtleties were better measured by the reputational technique precisely because they were not concrete and so slipped through the decisional net.

Some critics of pluralism have also argued that the focus on key issues was itself wrong. There were "no objective criteria" for selecting issues, so the subjective bias of the researcher could creep in to distort the findings.[20] Besides, since most issues weren't controversial, the selection of such issues meant focusing on the atypical. Most decisions were made quietly, unknown to the public and unreported by the press. Perhaps controversial issues were restricted to those on which the elite was divided, or perhaps they were issues about which the elite did not care or were self-assured. By studying only controversial issues, pluralists might have been biasing their sample against the active participation of the elites. Pluralists tended to dismiss this criticism; one pointedly asked, "What sort of elite asserts itself in relatively trivial matters, but is inactive or ineffective in the most significant areas of community policy-making?"[21] Researching several issue areas in the same study, the pluralists insisted, provided a check and ensured accurate findings.

But supporters of elitist theory drew another distinction, between public and private decision making, and they answered that the pluralists focused only on the public ones. Thomas Dye, a political scientist and a critic of pluralism, posed the argument this way:

> There is ample evidence that many of the most important decisions in a community are private decisions. . . . How can the pluralist legitimately exclude these kinds of decisions from his analysis? He cannot claim that such decisions are not made. His only recourse is to distinguish between public and private decisions and to claim that his interest is in public decisions, i.e. visible decisions. In other words, his only recourse is to narrow the scope of political science to public decision making. By arbitrarily limiting his subject matter, he can escape the responsibility for dealing with private decisions—that is, decisions that are not highly visible.[22]

In addition to overlooking private decisions, critics also claimed that pluralism also overlooked "nondecisions"—that is, decisions that result "in suppression or thwarting of latent or manifest challenge to the values or interests" of those in power.[23] Nondecisions are difficult to study because they are "nonevents"; they are never actively fought over, yet they have real repercussions. Here, controversy that constitutes a challenge to the dominant powers in a community is avoided or suppressed—abetted by the mechanisms of socialization, anticipated response, and sometimes direct but informal veto by the dominant group. In light of the silent power of nondecisions, rather than asking, "Who rules?," proponents of this concept felt it might be better to ask, "What persons or groups in the community are especially disfavored under the existing distribution of benefits and privileges?" Then, as one analyst has put it, "if grievances are there, the investigator's next step is to determine why and by what means some or all of the potential demands for change have been denied an airing."[24]

Matthew Crenson's *The Unpolitics of Air Pollution* is an example of an attempt to study nondecisions. Crenson tried to ascertain why some cities gave more attention to air pollution than others. Using a mixture of case (decisional) and survey methods, he found great subtlety in the way power is exercised by industry. For example, Crenson argued that the United States Steel Corporation dominated the decision-making process in Gary, Indiana, although the corporation was itself passive. Without active participation in decision making, its interests were well-represented because decision makers consistently anticipated the response of U.S. Steel to their actions, fearing the corporation would cut production or leave Gary if restrictions were too severe. Simply put, the attitude was, "What hurts U.S. Steel hurts Gary"; so air pollution controls were modified to suit the industry. The pluralists were wrong, Crenson said; the influence of industry *was* tranferable from one issue area to another, if only because "issues do not rise and fall independent of each other . . . the prominence of one subordinates others."[25] Nor was the study of actions, as advocated by the pluralists, adequate.

> Actions, by themselves, are probably misleading guides to political analysis: alone, they fully reveal neither the impenetrability of local politics nor the location of political power. . . . There is a disjunction between industry's political actions and its political influence, and the mere perception of industrial power, unsupported by industrial actions, is sufficient to affect the survival prospects of the pollution issue."[26]

Issues can also be suppressed by control of information and control of the media. Newspapers, for example, are usually owned by members of the elite and have immense power to suppress issues by ignoring them or slanting or trivializing their coverage, thus robbing the issue of legitimacy. This view emphasizes that the ultimate suppressant is socialization and the *mobilization of bias*—the establishment of a set of values that systematically serve one group at the expense of others.

Is it not the most supreme and insidious exercise of power to prevent people, to whatever degree, from having grievances by shaping their perceptions, cognitions and preferences in such a way that they accept their role in the existing order of things, either because they can see or imagine no alternative to it, or because they value it as divinely ordained and beneficial? To assume that the absence of grievance equals genuine consensus is simply to rule out the possibility of false or manipulated consensus by definitional fiat."[27]

These criticisms of the pluralist theory were based on the tendency of the pluralists to overlook the dominance of business values in American communities. Using the decisional method, researchers may look in vain for visible interference by businessmen, simply because they need not act. Their fundamental values—what's good for business is good for Gary, for San Jose, for Middletown—are shared by public officeholders, voiding the necessity of "direct business intervention" in the political process.[28] Business elites have their economic clout to use if need be, but they also have considerable prestige. Note the respect with which they are addressed by political leaders and the way they are sought after for support and approval. If their active intervention becomes necessary, they have additional resources. They are knowledgeable and articulate and have the ability to employ professional assistance. Further, economic leaders are the most powerful over time because they are the most stable, while politicians come and go. Although businessmen may rarely use all this power to initiate policy, always waiting in the wings is their ultimate power of veto. Used sparingly, this power too may slip past the decisional technique.

Needless to say, pluralists vigorously have defended their method from these charges. Some have called the elitist criticisms manifestations of the continued self-deception and ideological bias of the elitists. Dahl dismissed criticisms that his methods lacked subtlety as being based on "quasi-metaphysical theory made up of what might be called an infinite regress of explanations."[29] To Dahl, the critics were saying that if the overt rulers weren't members of the economic elite, then researchers had to dig deeper to find the covert economic rulers, the true elite. But how, wondered Dahl, could researchers study things that couldn't be studied: unconscious actions, anticipated responses, the mobilization of bias, and, most outrageous of all, nondecisions? This fallacy of "infinite regress" was founded, the pluralists thought, on

a presupposition about elite power which was allegedly self-validating and impossible to prove. . . . related to the sociological view of power as something necessarily structured and persistent. If it is so persistent, it will not be found in the possession of men who come and go relatively rapidly in associational affairs. Rather, it will attach to individuals who have solid institutional power and who do not quickly pass from the scene.[30]

The pluralists insisted that the exercise of power be empirically proven and that theories of power that couldn't be proven be discarded as unscientific. The pluralists saw elite theory, with its insistence that power was subtle and operated behind the scenes, as merely a faith for true believers. Elite theory, Dahl charged, could "be cast in a form that makes it virtually impossible to disprove."[31] The pluralists insisted on concrete proof, and claimed they had it. The elitists scoffed and said the pluralists had been duped by the politicians. And each lamented the other's ideological bias.

TOWARD SYNTHESIS

By the mid-1960s, the two schools of thought appeared to be at a stalemate. Elitists, still predominantly sociologists but now with some allies in political science, defended their theory and methods. Pluralists, still predominantly political scientists, did likewise.

Both contributed substantially to our understanding of power. The elitists gave us insights on power as it existed outside the formal decision-making structures of government. They alerted us to the subtle exercise of power through informal consultation, anticipation, socialization, and the mobilization of bias. They succeeded in identifying latent and less visible holders of power, taking the study of power well beyond the traditional preoccupation with positions of formal authority. Perhaps more importantly, they were the first to attempt power's exclusive and systematic study. Only after Hunter's work did other academics concentrate on power and begin to develop explicit methods for studying it.

On the other hand, the pluralists shifted the focus somewhat from reputation to behavior, insisting on the need to study specific actions. This insistence stimulated both adherents and antagonists of elite theory to be more explicit about how actual decisions were made. The pluralists also alerted us to the possibility of power varying over time (stratification theorists said the upper class would always dominate) and by issue. Their discussion of *inertia,* or unused resources—power held but not applied—helped explain why the upper class was sometimes not visibly active as well as why the general public can sometimes lose in a system that is ostensibly democratic. They also advanced our understanding of the role of bureaucracy in the decision-making process, though it was left unclear precisely *who* controlled the bureaucrats.

But there remained what seemed to be an irreconcilable gap between the specific behaviors observed by the pluralists and the broad
but vague power described by the elitists. Which was correct? For a
time, it seemed that the answer depended more on which general theory you preferred than on the persuasiveness of the evidence.

This problem was exacerbated by the fact that all the evidence was
based on case studies, a useful but sometimes limited research technique. A *case study* is an in-depth examination of a single example of a
phenomenon. Power was studied community by community. From
each case, researchers strove to generalize about power to the universe
of communities. The effort to generalize is apparent in the researchers'
choice of titles for their works: The Lynds called their book *Middletown*,
not "Uniquetown"; Hunter titled his *Community Power Structure*, not
"Atlanta's Power Structure"; and Dahl wrote *Who Governs*, not "Who
Governs New Haven." But even if we accept the reliability of each
researcher's methods, are we willing to accept that all communities
function like Middletown or Atlanta or New Haven? Would a biologist
generalize from a single fruit fly to the species?

Replication of the reputational and decisional methods in literally
hundreds of community power studies has not resolved the dispute.
There is still the concern that different methods produce different
results, as G. William Domhoff eloquently illustrated in his reexamina-
tion of redevelopment decisions in New Haven.[32]

One way to resolve the dispute was to combine the methods, accepting the strengths of each. Such mixing of methods has been the trend
since the 1960s. One political scientist who used both decisional and
reputational techniques to study two communities found the methods
to be "mutually supportive," that is, in a sense testing one another's
validity:

> In effect, two discrete decision-making systems were found. One of these
> is essentially "political," in the narrow sense of the term (including com-
> munity organizations and elected officials). The second decision-making
> system is essentially economic, comprising leaders whose power resources
> rest on high formal positions in industry, finance and business, and supe-
> rior class status, and who draw essentially upon "private" local resources
> to carry out their programs. . . . Economic leaders tend to dominate es-
> sentially "private" types of decisions that entail the use of nongovern-
> mental resources. Political leaders generally control what we have called
> "public" issues. . . . There is some evidence that such issues are not very
> salient for economic leaders.[33]

Another researcher used a combination of methods to study four cities.
Delbert Miller found that each method revealed slightly different lists of

influentials. Reputational techniques discovered the concealed leaders, who Miller concluded were the top tier; decisional techniques produced symbolic leaders, whom he considered to be on a lower tier. But he found substantial overlap in the names on the lists provided by the two methods (58 percent in Seattle).[34] A review of studies using both methods found the range of overlap was from 39 to 93 percent, providing further evidence that the two methods probe slightly different dimensions of power and that a single method inevitably obscures one dimension.[35]

At about the same time (the mid-1960s), other analysts of community power studies were disputing whether the two methods really differed all that much. Both relied on interviews, documentary evidence, newspapers, archives, personal contact, and subjective impressions. The chief differences were the weighting of the sources, the elitist focus on the general in contrast to the pluralist focus on the specific, and, most important of all, the interpretation of the data.

So research on community power advanced to the extent that the strengths and weaknesses of both methods were growing ever more apparent and were being offset increasingly by the combining of the two. To generalize—and generalization is the business of academics, though they prefer to call it theory building—it was necessary to compare. But how do you compare when methods differ and their reliability is in dispute? Some researchers, like Presthus and Miller, began studying more than one city.[36] We might say that their generalizations were based on several "fruit flies" rather than one. An advance, surely, but still a small sample out of a population of thousands. How could social scientists study enough communities to get a valid sample for generalization?

The Community Power Continuum

The simple fact is, it can't be done. At some point, a leap of faith becomes necessary. How? By accepting the idea that all communities may *not* have identical power structures, that power *may* vary from community to community. Perhaps Hunter's Atlanta really was elitist, and Dahl's New Haven, really pluralist. And perhaps we will discover that our model city, San Jose, is somewhere in between. One might conceive of a continuum, then, which at one end is a typical pluralist power structure and at the other is a typical elitist power structure. Communities might be placed at any point on the continuum—at either end, in the middle, or slightly closer to one pole than the other—depending on the shape of each one's particular power structure. Various social scientists have generated such continua or typologies or categories of power structures. At one extreme is always the elitist model (also called pyramidal or monolithic) and at the other is something approximating the pluralist model (also called amorphous or polylithic). In between are types representing varying degrees of pluralism. A *factional structure*, for example, would be characterized by two major conflicting groups, perhaps organized labor versus industry or an old, landowning elite versus a new, manufacturing elite. Another type might be a *coalitional structure*, such as the one Frederick Wirt described in San Francisco, where various well-organized groups form coalitions on specific issues with no stable factions emerging.[37]

Some social scientists believe that the power of bureaucracy has grown so great that it constitutes a third alternative to the elitist and pluralist theories. They argue that through civil service job protection, public employee unions, bureaucratic expertise, and the exclusive power of day-to-day implementation of policy, bureaucracies have attained a power independent from both economic leaders and elected officials and should be considered a potentially dominant force in community power structures. Unfortunately, this hypothesis has yet to be tested by systematic, empirical study. Nevertheless, political scientists Robert Lineberry and Ira Sharkansky have formulated a triangular model of community power with economic elites at one point, political leaders at another, and bureaucratic administrators at a third.[38] Cities, they suggest, gravitate towards one of the points in the triangle, depending on their historical condition.

The concept of a continuum, whether linear or triangular, is at least theoretically useful because it enables us to generalize broadly about power and communities and to include many theories and findings. It should be cautioned, however, that while such a generalization may have a certain elegant appeal, it also can be simplistic.

Pure elite theorists, of course, would be loathe to accept the continuum model in either form, especially since it tends to support pluralist assertions that power varies in structure, over time, and between communities. We know that elitists base their analysis on stratification theory. As long as there is a class structure, it will be reflected in the distribution of power, with the upper class always dominating, though other classes may occasionally gain concessions, for they too have some power. What accounts for major variations in power structures over time or from community to community, however, is who (what people) comprise or represent the upper class. Depending on historical conditions and the local economy, these may be bank managers or developers or corporate executives, but they will still be the dominant class. What they want from community politics and how they go about getting it may also vary, as may the amount of power other classes attain; but the upper class, whoever it is composed of, will rule.

Still, most social scientists have accepted the theoretical utility of continua and typologies for the development of generalizations about community power structure, which take us beyond the description of single communities and include the intellectually appealing idea of variation in power over time and among communities.

EXPLAINING VARIATION IN COMMUNITY POWER STRUCTURE: AN INVENTORY OF CRITERIA

If we do accept that power varies from community to community and/ or over time, we still are left, as were social scientists, with one chronic question: Why is one community relatively pluralistic while another is relatively elitist? As risky as our answer must be, based as it is on many community power studies done in wildly varying ways by many social scientists, a measure of common sense and some educated guesswork can take us some distance in generalizing.

The best and most succinct inventories of such generalizations are those compiled by sociologist Terry Clark and political scientists Robert Lineberry and Ira Sharkansky.[39] The inventory which follows is based on their work. Remember, these are generalizations, pointing to tendencies, not absolutes or universal truths.

Size

To begin with, *size* seems to be a major factor in determining where a city will lie on the elitist-pluralist continuum. Larger cities are more likely to have pluralistic power structures, not due so much to size *per se* but because largeness is associated with increased potential for competition and conflict among varied groups. Smaller cities are less diverse and more easily dominated by a single major economic force, such as the family that ruled Middletown. As cities grow, they diversify; elites can't command all the community's organizations; competition and pluralism increase. We might hypothesize, then, that the power structures we will find in San Jose and other rapidly expanding Sunbelt cities will have become more pluralistic with growth.

Diversity

The second major factor, *diversity*, is related to size; they increase together. As a city diversifies, the potential sources of both competition and cooperation increase in number. The class structure grows more complex, the ethnic composition of the city becomes more elaborate, and special-interest groups emerge. The number of voluntary organizations increases, furthering pluralism because many of the organizations may challenge the dominant elite. San Jose is a case in point: With a proliferation of ethnic and neighborhood groups in the 1970s, there came a challenge to the city's growth policies and electoral system. Thus as the *number of community organizations* increases, we might expect the power structure to become more pluralistic.

Economic Diversity

Economic factors constitute a third major category. In general, as *economic diversification* increases, communities grow more pluralistic. The economic structure of a community is reflected in its power structure; if the economic structure diversifies, so must the power structure. If the community is dominated by a single industry, its power structure will reflect this domination and tend to elitism. If a community is economically diversified, its power structure will reflect the diversification and tend to pluralism. (As we will see, San Jose's economic power structure has diversified over the past three decades and competition among the economic elites has increased.)

Industrialization. Furthermore, according to sociologist Clark, "the more rapid the expansion of a particular sector within a community, the greater the involvement of members of that sector in community decision making, and the more community decisions are oriented toward the values and interests of that sector."[40] Expanding industrial sectors particularly need governmental assistance, for zoning, capital improvements, utilities, and so on. To get it, they are most likely to intervene in local government, perhaps challenging previously dominant interests, perhaps cooperating with them. *Industrialization* broadens "the economic base of a community beyond commercial and service-oriented enterprises and will introduce another potential center of power in the economic system."[41]

Unionization. Similarly, as communities industrialize, workers organize, and *unionization* may become the basis for challenges to the ruling elite: The stronger and more prolific the labor unions are, the more pluralistic is the power structure. But, as San Jose and many other cities indicate, industrialization is not necessarily associated with unionization. In fact, the absence of unions has been a major attraction of Sunbelt cities to industry. Unionization of these industries may come, but it has yet to have major impact. Perhaps it never will. Edward Hayes, a political scientist who did a power study of Oakland, California, has observed that "rarely in the literature of community power do any researchers find that organized labor assumes the leading role in politics."[42] This may be because the major political interests and activities of unions are at the state and federal level, sources of most labor legislation. Public employee unions are an obvious exception, but they generally confine their activity to their own wages and working conditions. Lineberry and Sharkansky, however, suggest that municipal workers' unions are a component of the bureaucratic machines that now run city halls.

Absentee Ownership. Yet another example of how political interest may focus on levels beyond the community is *absentee ownership*, but in this case the interests are corporate. If many members of a community's economic elite concentrate their political activity elsewhere, this may contribute to the shaping of a more pluralistic community power structure by opening it up to those who would otherwise be excluded. Thus, as Clark has noted, "the greater the number of absentee-owned and managed enterprises in a community, the more decentralized the decision-making structure."[43] Frederick Wirt has called the executives of absentee-owned corporations "birds of passage," whose lives and careers are not connected to a community but to a corporation and/or a career. They will advance by moving on, not staying in the community. Thus, stability, a major source of power for old elites, is reduced with new elites. Their political involvement will be confined more to those issues of direct and specific concern to their corporation, such as getting necessary zoning approvals, or to the gleaning of goodwill by participating in charitable organizations or contributing committee time or technical aid to city governments. These involvements are not trivial. Obtaining favorable zoning decisions may force a local government to violate popular and carefully developed land-use policies (as has occurred in San Jose). Participation in charities or local government committees are important ways of shaping a community. Still, the executives of these industries are likely to stay out of many other local issues, or to confine their political activity to support for the Chamber of Commerce or other locally based organizations.

Home-owned industries, on the other hand, are led by locals. They have stakes in their community that go well beyond zonings and goodwill. They are part of the community. They want their business to expand, which means the community must expand. They want a good place to live for themselves and their heirs. And they won't be transferred to Phoenix or Berlin next year. Their involvement in city politics will thus be greater.

On the other hand, organizations with higher ties such as branch plants of national corporations may find themselves with extra power in a community—by virtue of their substantial resources of money, expertise, and perhaps credibility—if they choose to use it.[44] Somehow, a spokesperson for a major corporation is more intimidating than some "local" a council member has known for years.

Mobility of Industry.   Furthermore, *mobility of industry* is a factor. Major organizations often need only threaten to locate elsewhere to strike fear into the hearts of local decision makers, who treasure their industrial tax base above all else. The threat to relocate is particularly potent if an industry is relatively mobile, lacking a major capital investment in a particular community. Some electronics companies have made good on such threats; steel manufacturers generally do not. Because of this, immobile industries tend to participate more in local politics.[45]

Structure of Government

Another set of community characteristics that indicates a city's location on the community power continuum is the *structure of government.* Cities with a "reformed," council-manager form of government and nonpartisan, isolated, at-large elections are generally thought to be more elitist, while cities with an "unreformed," mayor-council form of government with partisan, concurrent, district elections are thought to be more pluralistic.[46] As one urban observer has put it: "Political structures are not value free, they are policies themselves. . . . electoral structures are not neutral. Either directly or indirectly, they tend to shape the outcome of public decisions."[47]

Reform structures of government isolate decision makers from the public. The chief executive is appointed, rather than elected. Voter turnout in council elections is low, particularly among Democrats and the working class. The advantages of the reform structures accrue to Republicans and the wealthy because they have the organizational resources and the media influence to take advantage of them. Nonpartisan elections, for example, take away the cues provided by party labels and deactivate party organizations. Without these, many voters lose interest; others must get their information elsewhere. This information can come from the campaigns or from the media. But campaigns cost money and this gives an advantage to those who have it to give, such as developers in typical Sunbelt cities where campaigning for a city council seat can cost in the six-figure area. Alternatively, voters can get their information from the media; but the media, which are economic institutions first and foremost, tend to be allied with dominant economic interests.

The city manager form of government also suits elites well. Professional managers are trained to accept business values and many willingly operate as the agents of the elite. Some may even be brought into the elite. Even if they remain outside it, they are not directly accountable to the electorate, as a mayor is.

A pluralistic power structure is more likely where the old style municipal structures are operative: an elected, strong mayor with partisan, concurrent, and district council elections. Such structures provide more public accountability. As one theorist puts it, "The leaders of the dominant economic institutions ordinarily wield power, but they are forced to take others into account when popular democratic rules allow the lower levels of the community an opportunity to place their representatives in public office."[48]

If this is true, cities of the Sunbelt should lean towards an elitist power structure, since the vast majority use reform structures of government. For example, a survey of fifty-nine large Western cities, most of which are in the Sunbelt, found 81 percent with a city-manager form of government, 95 percent using nonpartisan elections, and 75 percent selecting council members at large. A more inclusive sampling found nonpartisan elections in effect in 84 percent of Southern, border, and Western cities.[49]

It's important to remember, however, that governmental structures do not appear out of thin air. At some time, somebody decides whether a city should be governed by a manager or a mayor and how city council members should be elected. When those decision are made, choices about power, access, and accountability also are made. Government structure is itself a *policy* that reflects power in a community. The winners in the struggle define the structure of government, and because the structure is frozen for a time, they entrench their own power. As we will see, the business leaders of San Jose defined its governmental structure in 1916, a system which, with a few revisions, is still operative today. Among many other significant repercussions, the structure they imposed effectively denied direct working class or minority representation on the San Jose city council for most of this century.

Competition. Another community characteristic associated with the shape of its power structure as well as its electoral structure is *competition*. Democratic—and pluralistic—systems require choices, and real choices imply competition, which may come from within the elite or may be between elites and nonelites. Competition is probably not a purely independent variable: it more likely reflects than creates a pluralistic power structure. Still, competition indicates a relatively pluralistic distribution of power.

Political Culture

The final and most ephemeral community characteristic thought to be related to the shape of the power structure is *political culture*. The shared values, traditions, myths, and accepted behaviors of a community constitute its political culture. Here we enter the realm of socialization, the inculcation of ideas that affect our behavior rather than the behavior itself. Included among these are such notions as "You can't fight City Hall," or "The X family runs this town," or "What's good for business is good for our community." The values of the community affect who are acceptable as leaders and who the leaders listen to and care about, as well as whether or not the public is active or passive in community decision-making.

It has been said that power is related to whatever is highly valued in a community. For example, members of professions which have high prestige in a locale have more power than those in positions of low esteem. In most American communities, the people with the most prestige, and so the most power, are successful businessmen. A study of Seattle, Washington, and Bristol, England, found business leaders far more dominant in the American city at least in part because they were held in far higher esteem there than in the English city.[50] Most Americans still believe that the best interests of business are synonymous with the best interests of the community, a further indication of the prestige and power of business leaders. And businessmen, too, perceive themselves as important people, as leaders, and behave accordingly. Politicians and the public react to them with respect.

Another element of a community's political culture that can affect power structure is the orientation of its leaders. Those with a strong local orientation will frequently intervene in local politics, while those with a more cosmopolitan orientation—with interests and ambitions outside the locality—may take less of an interest in local affairs. Thus we can anticipate that where cosmopolitans proliferate, there should be more room in community politics for nonelites.

A final element of political culture involves the value a community places on public participation. In some, the tradition of active involvement is strong and respected; in others, it is weak, and assertive interest groups are greeted with amazement and disdain. Communities which place a high value on public involvement should have, or be moving toward, "unreformed" government structures, a plethora of community organizations, and a variety of formal means of citizen participation (commissions, for example). Obviously, such communities would tend toward a pluralistic power structure.

How does political culture shape and change itself in an actual community? Let's briefly look at the situation in San Jose. There, political culture seems a mixture of these values. Businessmen were held in high esteem through most of the city's history, but especially in the 1950s and 1960s when growth was called "progress" and considered to be for the good of all. The 1970s saw a serious challenge to these values at the same time that the city's economy came to be dominated by managers of absentee-owned corporations, who tend to hold cosmopolitan rather than localist values. Business leaders still are highly respected, but today they are manufacturers and financial managers rather than developers. Because their orientation is more cosmopolitan than that of developers, they may permit a more pluralistic local power structure. Recent electoral changes in San Jose also indicate a cultural acceptance of the values of public participation and governmental accountability. A shift from isolated to concurrent elections, which quadrupled voter turnout and substantially increased the participation of lower-income neighborhoods, was virtually unopposed. Its quiet acceptance was based partly on the desirability of public participation and partly on economy: Consolidated elections cost less. The change from at-large to district council elections also succeeded largely on its appeal to the values of participation, responsiveness, and accountability. Many of the city's ostensible elite seemed loathe to argue against such time-honored values as citizen participation and sat out the campaign. Thus, although the cultural traditions of San Jose seem accepting of business values and leadership, there is also a cosmopolitan tendency and a strong commitment to democratic values which should be associated with a relatively pluralistic power structure.

Summary

We can summarize these generalizations about community characteristics and community power structures by applying them to San Jose (see Table 2.1). The cumulative effect of these characteristics seems to indicate movement in the direction of a more pluralistic power structure, or at least a power structure in transition from relative elitism to relative pluralism. While virtually every change broadens participation, nearly every one is related to growth, which may be the single strongest summarizing factor in altering a city's power structure. The irony is that although it is usually old-guard elites that force growth on a community, as they bring growth they sow the seeds of their own destruc-

TABLE 2.1
COMMUNITY CHARACTERISTICS AS APPLIED TO SAN JOSE

Characteristic	San Jose	Power Structure Trend
Size	rapid growth	more pluralistic
Diversity	increasing	more pluralistic
Number of community organizations	increasing	more pluralistic
Economic Diversity	increasing	more pluralistic
Industrialization	increasing	more pluralistic
Unionization	weak	no change
Absentee ownership	substantial and increasing	more pluralistic
Mobility of industry	substantial	still unclear
Structure of government	predominantly reform, but with concurrent and district elections	elitist but increasingly pluralistic
Competition	increasing	more pluralistic
Political Culture	business values prominent; high value placed on participation	still unclear

tion. And what happens when growth stops? Presumably, the community power structure freezes, or if the decline of the community is
sufficient to produce changes in any of the characteristics listed, the
trend reverses itself.

Such reversals do not yet affect Sunbelt cities. Like San Jose, all are
growing communities, and any trends we may project for San Jose are
likely to be operating in many other Sunbelt cities. In fact, the same
inventory of characteristics could be completed for any city. It will help
a researcher to understand the city's structure of power in a general
way, and perhaps predict what a formal power study would find. But
remember, these are tendencies—not absolutes. The hypotheses that
the inventory generates must be tested by empirical study. We will
carry out such a test of the hypotheses generated by our review of San
Jose's community characteristics in the following chapters.

THE DECLINE OF ELITES?

The foregoing generalizations about community characteristics suggest
two trends: Most changes bring a decline in the power of the elite, and
most are brought about by forces from outside the community.

The Lynds concluded long ago that "the major impetus" for change came from "events outside the control of [the] immediate local culture."[51] The Depression and the New Deal left their mark on Middletown's politics, as did the arrival of an absentee-owned corporation (General Motors) and national labor unions. Peter Bachrach and Morton S. Baratz, authors of a more recent study, agree:

> More or less permanent shifts in the mobilization of bias, and the value-allocation that flows from it, are brought about primarily because the previously disfavored persons and groups have gained additional resources of power and authority, usually from movements or institutions outside the polity in question.[52]

Considering these and other factors, Lineberry and Sharkansky declared that "power structures have fallen on hard times."[53] While a shift in power may have occurred, no social system is without a power structure of some kind. Elitist or pluralist, the distribution of power constitutes a structure. What Lineberry and Sharkansky meant was that the power of economic elites had declined. Among the community characteristics we inventoried in the previous section, virtually all changes in them have been in the direction of this decline, but there are also other challenges to the domination of the economic elites.

The federal government and its courts extended voting rights to minorities, desegregated schools, mandated district elections, and encouraged the political organization of the poor and minorities through President Johnson's historic War on Poverty program and other social programs, thus encouraging competition for the elites. States have regulated and limited the fiscal and land-use power of cities. Regional governments have gained authority in transportation and environmental decisions.

More overt challenges to the power of the economic elite have come from bureaucrats and community organizations. The increasing autonomy of bureaucracies weakens elite control, while the organization of minority and neighborhood groups has challenged elite policies in such areas as growth, government structure, and police practices. Both constitute competition for the economic elites.

Finally, the economic arrangements of many cities—particularly those of the Sunbelt—have been radically altered in recent years with the rise of the national corporate economy and the dominance of absentee-owned economic institutions in most communities.

These changes may redistribute and lessen the power of economic elites, but a power structure remains, if only in a new shape. Some people and institutions will still have more power than others, and stratification theory insists they will still be whoever occupies the upper class.

It is significant that so many of the changes are the result of decisions made outside the community. Cities seem to be left with residual powers, the ability to make only those decisions other forces don't care about.[54] Corporations move plants and workers around (and outside) the country at will, caring little about the effect such movement has on communities. States constrict the ability of cities to tax, borrow, spend, and control land use. The federal government dictates changes in police practices, education, and structure of government, and it gives and then withdraws financial aid. It also deeply affects growth through its housing and transportation policies, and employment through its defense spending.

The decline in the autonomy of communities may decrease the power of local elites or cause them to shift their focus to wider arenas. To probe such an expanding elite network, sociologist Delbert Miller extended the unit of analysis of his 1975 power study from "community" defined as a city to "community" defined as a region. Using a modified reputational technique to study the Boston-Washington megalopolis, he discerned an "embryonic" regional power structure with "high consensus about key leaders."[55] Wirt also recognized the importance of regional politics in his study of San Francisco.[56] It's not surprising that economic elites would shift their focus to whole regions, since their businesses are now regional. It follows that they have also been in the forefront of the movement toward regional government.[57]

A method for tracking such *national* connections of local elites has been developed and is known as *network analysis*. Through the study of membership lists and business connections, a network of contacts and interlocking directorates can be revealed, giving substance to the opinions that emerge from a reputational study and subtlety to the outcomes described by a decisional study. G. William Domhoff, the researcher who challenged earlier pluralist studies of New Haven, has used network analysis to show that local decisions are not made as independently as earlier studies implied. His reanalysis of New Haven's urban renewal decisions found an economic elite to be influential in the shaping of that program. They used their national connections to bring urban renewal to New Haven, but once it was established, they left its implementation to the mayor and his staff.[58]

Miller and Domhoff suggest that the arena for elite participation has shifted from the strictly local community to higher levels: the region, the state, the nation. Elite influence at these levels allows them to rule local communities through broad policy, leaving active participation at the local level to the less influential. In a sense this opens up local politics to nonelites. But how much is left to decide? What sort of victory is it when blacks elect a mayor in Atlanta, or when a minority/

labor/neighborhood coalition changes the way council members are elected in San Jose, if there is little left for their representatives to oversee?

CARRYING ON THE RESEARCH

Thus we arrive at an increasingly sophisticated understanding of the complexities of power. From highly subjective studies, social scientists have advanced to more systematic methods and finally to classifying patterns of power and, through comparison, to explaining variations in power structures. Unfortunately, they have all but abandoned the study of individual cities in the process. While this may be appropriate for the advancement of theory, it denies the practical application of their findings as well as popular understanding. People deserve to know who runs their communities. That is why researchers should continue doing case studies.

We understand the theoretical limitations of such studies; they won't take us much further than we've already come. But they will be useful in that they test the generalizations developed thus far and further our understanding of variation in power structures among communities and over time. Ideally, we will one day have studies of particular communities at different points in time—similar to the work of the Lynds in Middletown in the 1920s and 1930s. It was, after all, the proliferation of case studies in the 1950s and 1960s that brought us where we are today. "There will always be room for future studies of local power structures," Domhoff has written. "Changing conditions bring new leaders, new institutions, and new methods of rule to the forefront."[59] Does power, for example, work the same way in the increasingly populous communities of the Sunbelt as it does in the declining cities of the Frostbelt?

So case studies must still be done. But they should not be done in ignorance of the work of the past. Each study should build on those that preceded it. The purpose of this chapter has been to put contemporary studies in the context of earlier work. Contemporary researchers must understand the strengths and weaknesses of what has been done before. They must understand the danger of ideologically biasing their methods. They must be familiar with criticisms of past studies in order to anticipate and cope with criticisms of their own. By being theoretically informed, they can proceed, making intelligent choices about their methods and putting their findings in a larger context.

As the next chapter explains in detail, we have chosen to use the reputational technique for our study of San Jose. It has the advantage of easy application and replication, making it particularly useful to researchers who are not theoretical academicians. It also reveals the dimension of power that is least obvious. We already know who is mayor and who holds other positions of authority in the community. What we do not know is who, if anyone, holds power behind the scenes or who, if anyone, among the obvious power holders dominates the others. The reputational technique is particularly good at uncovering these subtleties, at unveiling the less visible, less "legitimate" leaders.

Bearing in mind the methodological and theoretical background of the complex phenomenon of power absorbed in this chapter, we can now proceed to the study at hand. For we must continue to study power in specific communities. We can't be intimidated by its many complexities. To do so would be to accept ignorance and to surrender power to those who now have it.

Notes

[1]Robert A. Dahl, "The Concept of Power," *Behavioral Science*, 2 (July, 1957), p. 202.

[2]Terry N. Clark, *Community Structure, Power and Decision Making* (Scranton, Penn.: Chandler, 1968), p. 4.

[3]C. Bonjean, and M. Grimes, "Community Power: Issues and Findings," in J. Lopresto, *Social Stratification: A Reader* (New York: Harper & Row, 1974), p. 382.

[4]Robert S. Lynd, and Helen Merrell Lynd, *Middletown* New York: Harcourt Brace and World, 1929; *Middletown in Transition*, New York: Harcourt Brace Jovanovich, Inc., 1937. Other key studies by sociologists include W. Lloyd Warner, *The Social Life of a Modern Community*, (New Haven: Yale University Press, 1941); and Arthur J. Vidich and Joseph Bensman, *Small Town in Mass Society* (Princeton: Princeton University Press, 1953).

[5]Lynd, *Middletown*, pp. 89, 329, 321.

[6]Lynd, *Middletown*, p. 490.

[7]Floyd Hunter, *Community Power Structure* (Chapel Hill: University of North Carolina Press, 1953).

[8]C. Wright Mills, *The Power Elite* (New York: Oxford University Press, 1956).

[9]Robert Dahl, *Who Governs* (New Haven: Yale University Press, 1961).

[10]Robert Dahl, "A Critique of the Ruling Elite Model," in Willis D. Hawley and Frederick M. Wirt, eds., *The Search for Community Power*, 2nd ed. (Englewood Cliffs, N.J.: 1974), p. 210.

[11]Ernest A. T. Barth, and Stuart D. Johnson, "Community Power and a Typology of Social Issues," in Hawley and Wirt, p. 267.

[12]Edward Keynes, and David M. Ricci, eds., *Political Power, Community and Democracy* (Chicago: Rand McNally, 1970), p. 157.

[13]Frederick M. Wirt, *Power in the City* (Berkeley: University of California Press, 1974), p. 364.

[14]Terry N. Clark, *Community Power and Policy Outputs* (Beverly Hills: Sage, 1973).

[15] Dahl, "A Critique of the Ruling Elite Model," p. 213.

[16]See Manuel Castells, *The Urban Question* (Cambridge: MIT, 1977); G. William Domhoff,

Who Really Rules? (Santa Monica: Goodyear, 1978); or Peter Saunders, *Urban Politics* (New York: Penguin, 1980).

[17] See Wirt.

[18] Robert Lineberry, and Ira Sharkansky, *Urban Politics and Public Policy*, 2nd ed. (New York: Harper & Row, 1978), p. 177.

[19] See Domhoff.

[20] Peter Bachrach, and Morton S. Baratz, *Power and Poverty* (New York: Oxford University Press, 1970).

[21] Nelson Polsby, *Community Power and Political Theory* (New Haven: Yale University Press, 1963), p. 114.

[22] Thomas R. Dye, "Community Power Studies," in James A. Robinson, ed., *Political Science Annual*, vol. 2 (New York: Bobbs Merrill, 1970), p. 57.

[23] Bachrach and Baratz, p. 44.

[24] Bachrach and Baratz, p. 49.

[25] Matthew A. Crenson, *The Un-Politics of Air Pollution, A Study of Nondecision Making in the Cities* (Baltimore: Johns Hopkins, 1971), pp. 161, 170.

[26] Crenson, p. 131.

[27] Steven Lukes, *Power, A Radical View* (London: Macmillan, 1975), p. 24.

[28] Edward C. Hayes, *Power Structure and Urban Policy: Who Rules in Oakland* (New York: McGraw-Hill, 1972), p. 9.

[29] Dahl, "A Critique of the Ruling Elite Model," p. 210.

[30] David Ricci, *Community Power and Democratic Theory* (New York: Random House, 1971), p. 99.

[31] Dahl, "A Critique of the Ruling Elite Model," p. 210.

[32] See Domhoff.

[33] Robert Presthus, *Men at the Top* (New York: Oxford University Press, 1964).

[34] Delbert Miller, *International Community Power Structures* (Bloomington: Indiana University Press, 1970).

[35] Howard J. Ehrlich, "The Social Psychology of Reputations for Community Leadership," in Hawley and Wirt, p. 231.

[36] See Robert E. Agger, Daniel Goldrich, and Bert E. Swanson, *The Rulers and the Ruled* (Belmont: Duxbury Press, 1972).

[37] See Wirt.

[38] Lineberry and Sharkansky, p. 179.

[39] See Clark, *Community Structure, Power and Decision Making;* and Lineberry and Sharkansky, pp. 182–186.

[40] Clark, *Community Structure, Power and Decision Making*, p. 101.

[41] Lineberry and Sharkansky, p. 184.

[42] Hayes, p. 186.

[43] Clark, *Community Structure, Power and Decision Making*, p. 103.

[44] John Walton, "The Vertical Axis of Community Organization and the Structure of Power," in Hawley and Wirt, p. 366.

[45] Clark, *Community Structure, Power and Decision Making*, p. 103.

[46] Clark, *Community Structure, Power and Decision Making*, pp. 108–109; Bonjean and Grimes, p. 388; Willis D. Hawley, *Nonpartisan Elections and the Case for Party Politics* (New York: John Wiley, 1973), p. 98.

[47] Willis D. Hawley, "Election Systems, Community Power and Public Policy: The Partisan Bias of Nonpartisanship," in Hawley and Wirt.

[48] Peter Rossi, "Power and Community Structure," in Clark, *Community Structure, Power and Decision Making*, p. 137.

[49] Raymond Wolfinger, "Political Ethos and the Structures of City Governments," in

Clark, p. 178; and Willis D. Hawley, *Nonpartisan Elections and the Case for Party Politics* (New York: John Wiley, 1973), p. 17.

[50]Miller, p. 40.

[51]Lynd, *Middletown in Transition*, p. 3.

[52]Bachrach and Baratz, p. 106.

[53]Lineberry and Sharkansky, p. 186.

[54]See Wirt; Domhoff.

[55]Delbert Miller, *Leadership and Power in the Bos-Wash Megalopolis* (New York: John Wiley, 1975).

[56]See Wirt.

[57]Committee for Economic Development, *Reshaping Government in Metropolitan Areas* (New York: Committee for Economic Development, 1970); and Pacific Research Center, "Regionalism and the Bay Area" (Mountain View, Calif.: Pacific Research Center, 1972).

[58]See Domhoff.

[59]Domhoff, p. 174.

3

A Primer in Power Structure Study

ADVANTAGES OF THE REPUTATIONAL METHOD

"Take me to your leader," the visitor from space says as he steps from the flying saucer that has just landed on your front lawn. What do you do? To whom will you guide him? Your spouse, minister, mayor, governor, president, police chief, political science professor, real estate broker? The possibilities are endless. So you think to yourself, "What he really wants to know is, Who runs the show around here?" Good question. Who *does* run the show around here?

The problems confronting researchers who have decided to study community power are not unlike those facing the hapless folks with the space traveler on their front lawn. Suddenly, we find *ourselves* feeling like strangers in a strange land, unsure of our next move.

Happily, as we saw in chapter 2, others have marked the path. Today, we are a long way down that path from the simplistic observations of traditional political science's "positional" approach to power. And of all the methods available, the *reputational technique* best suits our needs overall, as indicated in the previous chapter. To summarize briefly, there are strong reasons for preferring this straightforward approach. In particular, research has proved the reputational method to be an effective means of discovering those people, especially business and industrial leaders, who are crucial to the anointing and financing of candidates, whose exercise of power might otherwise go undetected by the casual observer or even by the experienced researcher.

Pinpointing Who Really Does "Run the Show"

To cite our case study city, San Jose, as an example of the reputational method's effectiveness, other methods likely would have overlooked the broad scope of influence of Frank Fiscalini, superintendent of the East Side Union High School District in that city.[1] Although not a man of great personal wealth or of exceptionally high public office, a 1979 study by the *San Jose Mercury News* found leaders in San Jose repeatedly saying that political or economic initiatives in fast-growing East San Jose were virtually impossible without Fiscalini's blessing, or at least his benign neglect. He also served as a connection between the large Italian community of San Jose and the growing Hispanic population, whose children mainly attended schools in Fiscalini's district.

Similarly, in studying Indianapolis, Indiana, no other method would likely have identified the influence of attorney Harry T. Ice.[2] His power was generally invisible. Few people outside the highest levels of government and business knew who he is or what he did. But during a study of that city in 1977 by the *Indianapolis Star,* respondent after respondent said in confidential interviews: "You have to check with Harry Ice if you want to get anything done with public money." And it turned out that in the opinion of the influential themselves, Ice's standing as the only bond counsel in Indiana gave him inordinate influence. If anyone there wanted to finance a bond issue, he would almost surely need Ice's approval. This constituted a form of veto power beyond even that of the governor.

Before thoroughly explaining how a reputational study of power is done, a few points about the practical advantages of this method are in order. First, and perhaps most important to many students, reporters, community researchers, and academics, is its cost.

This technique is inexpensive in terms of facilities and materials, but it does require about three months' full-time work. For those who have grants, this means that a living wage should be budgeted. Journalists may have to wedge power structure interviews between routine assignments, stretching out the time needed to complete the study. Students and community researchers are accustomed to labor-intensive, low-income work anyway.

For an absolutely stripped-down survey, a file-card box and note cards, plus photocopying expenses, are all that is really required. For easier and more reliable tabulation of results, a small amount of keypunch and computer time also can be useful. For those with access and funds, records may be stored by computer. With some relatively simple programming, results may be tabulated and displayed with ease. Even this is well within the means of a medium-sized newspaper or a moderate research grant.

A second advantage to the method described here is that it can easily be repeated, perhaps at five- or ten-year intervals, to track changes in the community power structure. By using the same method in follow-up studies, researchers are assured of meaningful comparisons. Particularly informative would be follow-up studies in Sunbelt cities where it is not yet clear whether grassroots forces have secured a place in the power structure or whether the industrial, financial, and commercial interests that generally dominate in the East and Midwest already have consolidated their power.

The object of a power structure analysis is to identify the most influential people in a community—those who by reason of their wealth, position, charisma, heritage, or abilities establish local policies, define the political and economic agendas, institute and set in motion major projects, and otherwise lead or rule. Their power may be transitory or enduring. What is important is to discover whose thoughts and actions carry the most weight.

Although the theoretical debate over the definition of power and power structures may have meaning for us as researchers, we need not embroil actual survey respondents in such speculations. All of us have an intuitive grasp of power, and our respondents will too. When using the method outlined here, it is preferable *not* to provide respondents with a definition of power. To do so would force them to measure their experience and observations by a theorum which may or may not have practical significance. Allowing respondents instead to apply their own perceptions leads precisely to the information our method seeks—the names of those persons in the community considered the most powerful. Experience has shown that most respondents will approach the subject from a basic notion of power as "the ability to get things done," a simple but practical measure. But for those respondents who hold different conceptions of power and influence, leaving fluidity in the definition allows them the opportunity to offer insights that otherwise might be overlooked.

CHOOSING OR DEFINING THE COMMUNITY TO BE STUDIED

In beginning a reputational survey, we must first determine what unit of study, or community, we wish to research. Since most of us will find that our most immediate need is to know who wields influence in our hometowns, this is a logical starting place. For those who have never attempted such a project, a city is amply ambitious. It also can serve as a building block for later studies of the county or region. The 1977 study of Indianapolis referred to in this book was in effect a regional project, since the city and the county have consolidated government and serve as the economic, cultural, and social center of central Indiana. Still, the basic question asked was, "Who has influence in Indianapolis?" and not, "Who has influence in central Indiana?"

Why Study San Jose?

This question of regional focus is an important one, especially in explaining why we chose to study San Jose, California, in particular. It would have been possible to study Santa Clara County or the entire Bay Area instead, of which San Jose is a part, but because no systematic study of San Jose ever had been attempted, the *San Jose Mercury News* decided in 1979 to study its own city. One question that arose before making the decision was this: Since San Jose is in many ways a satellite of San Francisco, its more economically and culturally potent neighbor, would the major interests in San Francisco overshadow those in San Jose? Could, for instance, A. W. Clausen, then-chairman of the board of the Bank of America, exercise greater power in San Jose than the mayor?

Obviously, this was a question that could not be answered until the study was completed, making sure to include in the list of suspected influentials some of those thought to exercise power in San Francisco and other surrounding communities. (In fact, one such person emerged among San Jose's ten most powerful—David Packard, chairman of the board of the Hewlett Packard Company of Palo Alto. Packard is a resident of Los Altos Hills, a residential town nearby, and his firm is located twenty miles north of San Jose, yet he was found to have inordinate influence in the city.)

When the *Mercury News* study began, it was not altogether clear whether San Jose would have a power structure of its own. But social scientists with whom the researchers consulted predicted that it would. They noted that studies had shown that even Oakland, immediately across the San Francisco Bay from the region's leading city, had its own power structure. A prestudy interview with one of the highest-ranking officials in the Bank of America supported the prediction that major firms with satellite interests defer to their local representatives on questions affecting the branch-office town.

If similar studies of San Francisco and Oakland were done, they, together with the San Jose study, could form the foundation of a regional study of the Bay Area. Even without these such a study could be done, but it would be an enormously complex endeavor, requiring a considerably greater investment of time and resources than the study of a single city.

OVERVIEW OF THE METHOD

A reputational power study of this kind proceeds in two rounds, each of which is broken into several steps. Before we begin to steep ourselves in detail, however, here in basic terms is how the method works.

We begin with a list of several hundred names—our *base list*—of suspected leaders in the community. We identify about 15 people—*informants*—who know about power in the community and ask them to winnow our list down to about 30 names, keeping in mind that they may add names if they see fit. Informants also respond to questions designed to narrow the field even further. The results of this first round are assigned point values, which when added yield the top 20 to 40 leaders, depending on where the natural break occurs. We then interview this group of 20 to 40 and ask them to identify the 10 or 12 most influential people. The precise number is unimportant, although some political scientists have suggested that asking for any number requires respondents to artificially select a predetermined group. We needn't fear this criticism. The purpose of our study is not to determine whether there is a group that has total control of the community. Our aim is to determine which people have the greatest *relative* power.

Establishing a Base List of the Influential

To meet our first goal of compiling the base list of names, we begin by pulling together membership lists of the significant organizations in our community. At this stage of the investigation, our goal is to cull the lists of virtually any organization we believe plays some role in the community, being as *inclusive* as possible. A good starting place is the world of business, finance, and industry. There are myriad publications available from which we can begin gleaning names. Among the most information-packed reference works are: the *Million Dollar Directory,* (which lists major firms by city), *Standard and Poor's Register of Corporations, Executives and Directors, Dun and Bradstreet's Reference Book of Corporate Managers, The Fortune Double 500 Directory, Who Owns Whom in America—A Directory of Intercorporate Ownership,* local chamber of commerce directories, state banking directories, and other business directories that can be found in almost any library. The leading officers and directors of local companies provide a start for our files, which should be organized, for easy handling, in alphabetical order by individual, with all of their affiliations noted.

Another valuable directory that can be easily searched is *Who's Who*, as well as its many spin-offs, such as the *Who's Whos* in *American Law, Government, Religion, Finance and Industry*, and *American Women*. Local bar associations generally publish directories, and lawyers may also be found in the *Martindale-Hubbell Law Directory*. *The Foundation Directory* offers major foundations, their directors and donors, and for virtually every community some local history books have been compiled in which famous family names can be found.

Other sources include lists of public officeholders and appointed officials, political parties, political clubs, lobbyist organizations, churches, grassroots groups, labor unions, minority groups, and charitable organizations such as the United Way, Boy Scouts, YMCA, and so on. Trade organizations such as the chamber of commerce, local booster club, small business association, real estate board, and manufacturing or industrial associations also are important.

We should also obtain lists of the directors of important civic organizations such as the League of Women Voters, opera guild, theater board, symphony association, hospital boards, Rotary Club, Junior Achievement board, universities, and zoological societies. Private country clubs and social clubs also have phone directories from which memberships can be determined. Some of these may be more difficult to obtain than others. One approach is simply to ask the club administrator for a copy. If this fails, we can try to find a member who is sympathetic to the study we are performing who will lend us his or her copy. Directors of these organizations may not be significant in our community, but tracking memberships is an essential part of determining if there is a network of leaders. Because club lists are so large and diffuse these should be used as cross-checks after other lists—business, legal, governmental, and so on—have been searched to determine who socializes with whom.

After thoroughly researching organizations, there may still be individuals who, although not active or leaders of groups or businesses, still have played important roles in local events. We can find many of these names in local histories and newspaper files. We should try to identify the people who surfaced in the unfolding of public issues, those who led skirmishes or founded important movements, philanthropic projects, or businesses. Who were the key leaders behind the local stadium drive, the renewal of downtown, the reform of government, crucial sewer or water bond issues, and so on? Who ran campaigns, raised money, or gave large donations? If our state or city has campaign-disclosure laws which require listings of all campaign contributors, these should be on file with the city or county clerk or the registrar of voters. As well as those who made direct contributions, we should make note of those who loaned any large sums to candidates.

Because members of minority groups historically have been disfranchised in urban politics, they inadvertantly can get left out of our study; thus it is especially important to identify these individuals. Although in most studies they seldom surface among the most powerful in the community, the scientific approach does not rely on such assumptions, and ensuring their representation on our early list is a guard against bias. The same is true for women. By including as many women and minorities as are logically appropriate in the early stages, we lessen the likelihood of inadequately reflecting their presence in the power structure.

If we have colleagues familiar with the community, we should ask them for suggested names. Since the first stage is a broad sweep, it's a good idea to gather suggestions from people whose opinions we respect.

This initial list, numbering generally about 200 names in a medium-sized community, should then be alphabetized so that we can easily find individuals. By now we will have established a file in which each card or computer record contains a name with associations, memberships, and affiliations. This alone is a valuable tool for later work.

Selecting Initial Informants

The next step involves selecting a panel of informants who can intelligently pare the initial list down to a reasonable and workable number. This is the most critical stage in the process because it is, as critics argue, a point at which our personal views could skew the results. But the liabilities are no greater than those afflicting other power structure methods, and since we are aware of potential problems, we can control any bias.

The people we will select must be knowledgeable about power and influence in the community. Many researchers simply begin by asking a few they know to be influential to name the most powerful people in the community. The method used here is different from this rather simple approach, and for a good reason. We start by selecting informants whom we suspect are not exceptionally influential themselves, but are people *close to the exercise of power*—people who have to know about power in order to do their job or simply because of who they are, near the locus of power but not at its center; we are starting with those who will not be tempted to name themselves or their cronies. These sophisticated observers of the power game often provide some of the clearest insights into the character, strengths, and weaknesses of those who are truly at the center. These insights can later be used when interviewing influentials themselves to pry loose more information, color, and background on life in the inner power circle.

Our panel of informants must be broad-based. Key city or county bureaucrats, charity fundraisers, chamber of commerce insiders, minority community leaders, socialites, grassroots organizers, bankers, news media executives, educators, labor leaders, political advisers and aides, religious leaders, elected officials—all of these should be considered. Of course, women must be amply represented on the panel of informants.

In the studies of Indianapolis and San Jose, about 15 initial informants were used, covering a spectrum of views on power and influence in the community. Each was interviewed alone and promised anonymity in order to elicit candid observations. In San Jose, confidential informants included a successful home builder, a Mexican-American program director, a labor leader, a planning official, a long-time local banker, a commercial real estate broker, an important behind-the-scenes political adviser, a city councilman's administrative aide, a superior court judge, a member of the county board of supervisors, a university official, a former newspaper executive, a neighborhood leader, a retired businessman, a staff member of a charitable organization, and a wealthy business executive.

Discussions with knowledgeable observers of the local community can help in choosing informants. Which labor leader will have the greatest insight? Which old-timer seems to have the longest view? College professors, journalists, and others with local knowledge can help at this stage. We should pick a group which offers a wide range of views and backgrounds.

Preparing a Questionnaire

After selecting a panel of informants, we will devise a uniform set of questions to ask them. Local conditions might dictate specific questions not included in the sample questionnaire that follows. Nor is the wording inviolate.

First, the list of suspected influentials is placed in alphabetical order on one or two sheets of paper. These are not stapled together because respondents will want to lay them side by side to scan the list. They also will want to mark them up, so we'll need plenty of copies. The questionnaire begins with the task of ranking:

1. Place in rank order, 1 through 30, those individuals who in your opinion are the most influential in the city—influential from the point of view of the ability to lead others.

If there are people not listed who you feel should be included in the ranking, please add their names.

This is a difficult assignment for the informants. Some will agonize over very minor differences, for example, who should be ranked 7 and who ranked 8. It simplifies matters if we explain that, while the list should be as close to rank order as feasible, what really matters is to which of three broad ranges an individual is assigned—that is, 1 to 10, 11 to 20, or 21 to 30. Although there is no need to explain why to the informant, we do this because, in weighting the responses later, we will assign three points to those in the top 10, two points to those in the middle 10, and one point to those in the bottom 10.

Here the typical respondent will probably hesitate and ask, "Influential at what? Some people have total power in one area but none in another." Explain that we are asking them to judge overall influence, social, economic, and political power, across the board. This, after all, is what our study hopes to determine.

From the ranking we'll move on to three other questions designed to flesh out and refine our first answer:

2. If a project were before the community that required decision by a group of leaders, which 10 could "put it over"?

3. Name the 10 people most effective at initiating projects.

4. Name the 10 people most effective at stopping projects.

Expect that some respondents will want to know, "What kind of projects?" We'll explain that a project, too, may be political, social, economic, or cultural. Others will have questions about initiating and stopping projects. And while the former has a positive connotation and the latter sounds negative, this need not be the case. Sometimes people are quite effective at setting in motion projects which might have been better left undone; others may be effective at putting an end to projects that would harm the community. Later, we'll want to ask them exactly what projects they had in mind for each of those listed in response to these questions.

Seeking Subtleties of Power

Questions 5 through 8 are aimed at distinguishing subtle differences respondents may have about power, influence, and their exercise in the community. These responses also lead to interesting discussions, providing valuable information for later use.

5. Name the person who *has* the most power in (name of city).
6. Name the person who *exercises* the most power in (city).
7. Name the most influential person in (city).
8. Name the top leader in (city).

To illustrate, in Indianapolis Eli Lilly, then the chairman of the Eli Lilly & Company pharmaceutical firm, was found to be the person who *had* the most power. But Mayor William Hudnut was named the person who *exercised* the most. Discussions with respondents made clear the distinction: Lilly had vast resources at his disposal which, if he so chose, could accomplish virtually any civic project. Once, for instance, Lilly was approached with a list of half a dozen project ideas that would require considerable private-sector investment. Lilly scanned the list and, pointing his finger at the page, said, "I'll take this one." And just that easily, $4.5 million was committed to rebuild City Market, now a central attraction in downtown Indianapolis.

Mayor Hudnut, on the other hand, who held the mayoral office at the time of the study, was chief executive officer of both the city and county. He exercised daily the economic, political, and social power of the entire city. Because, as respondents pointed out, anyone who held that office would be chosen the person who *exercised* the greatest power, they selected Hudnut.

Results were quite different in San Jose. There the mayor hardly has more real power than that of other city council members: Most important community projects there are generated by people outside of government. In San Jose, a leader from the private sector—P. Anthony Ridder, publisher of the *San Jose Mercury News*—was named both the person who *had* the most power and the person who *exercised* the most power. Ridder's pivotal position in the power structure was vouched for by informant after informant. For example, one local attorney explained it this way:

> I understand there have been changes over there [from the old management], but it's [still] the only newspaper in town and you've got to overcome it. Every politician is worried about it. You've got to deal with the newspaper. You don't ever want to be sandbagged—to get into a project and then find out the newspaper is against you.

At the same time, James Alloway, who had been city manager of San Jose just a few months when the city's power structure was studied, was named among the top 40 most influential people in the community. His position, like the position held by the mayor, was itself influential. Alloway was later dismissed when it became apparent he was unable to manage San Jose's bureaucracy. But no one in San Jose could force Tony Ridder out of the *Mercury News*.

Completion of the questionnaire plus time for an interview generally takes about 45 minutes to an hour for each. Answers are then scored by a point system, with responses to questions that call for naming single-most-influential people weighted slightly over responses that identify groups.

As valuable as the questionnaire is, its effectiveness is limited without a discussion afterwards with the informant about his or her answers. From this interview we can greatly expand our picture of the community power structure built up from the questionnaire answers—sometimes with surprising results.

In San Jose, for instance, it appeared after gathering data for the initial list that James Miscoll, then the regional vice-president of the Bank of America, would surely wind up among the top two or three most influential persons. The Bank of America is headquartered in San Francisco, but because California has statewide banking (branches of the same bank are allowed throughout the state), the regional vice president in San Jose is the approximate equal of the leading banker in most other cities where statewide banking is not permitted.

Miscoll was in charge of about 40 percent of the banking business in Santa Clara County. In addition, Miscoll, whose bank is the cornerstone of the largest office complex in the county, also was a member of an impressive array of civic boards.

But during interviews with the first round of informants, including a banker and others in key business positions, it became apparent that Miscoll was considered a "corporate nomad." Although as an executive his immediate economic position was significant, he was still not a long-term member of the inner circle of business and industrial leaders. As one informant put it: "He's only passing through."

No respondent could name an issue or project in which Miscoll had provided pivotal leadership, although subsequent interviews found that simply because of his position with the largest bank in the region he was accorded considerable influence—enough to place him among the top 20, but not enough to make the top 10.

It also became evident from the early informant interviews that Joseph B. Ridder, the former publisher of the *San Jose Mercury News*, no longer carried the big stick he once had brandished with such authority. Said one respondent, "I can recall going out there [in the old days] to the newspaper and it was like going to see the king. He'd have congressmen backed up for two hours because he was running late. If he got behind something in the community, he could make it go."

These are just two examples of the substance and color that informants can offer beyond their simple answers to the power structure questionnaire. Therefore, allow an hour for each interview, moving through the questionnaire quickly and discussing answers thoroughly.

Tallying Responses

Now, after completing our first round of interviews with our informants, we have two forms of material: our completed questionnaires and the notes we've taken during discussions. Our next task is to score the questionnaires. We'll do this by assigning points to those persons our informants have named.

First, we have the list of 30 names given in response to the initial question. Those in positions 1 through 10 each are given three points for being in the top third, those in positions 11 through 20 receive two points, and those in positions 21 through 30 receive one point.

Second, we have questions 2, 3, and 4, which ask which 10 people can best put projects over, initiate projects, or stop projects. Each person listed will be given three points each time he or she is named.

Finally, we have questions 5, 6, 7, and 8, which ask the informant to name one person who: (5) has the most power, (6) exercises the most power, (7) is most influential, and (8) is the top leader. The person named in each case will be given five points.

Let's look at a sample completed questionnaire from the San Jose study to see how this stage of the process can be easily scored. (See p. 66.)

Why did the informant, a man in this case, rate James Alloway, the city manager, so highly? "I don't really know the man," he explained in the postquestionnaire interview. "He seems an intelligent person. I have to assume he'll use his position, and the city manager is the final answer to all kinds of things. You have to deal with him. All the council members say, 'I'd better check with the city manager.' I can't think of any major project—the Center for the Performing Arts, Park Center Plaza, Convention Center, freeways, Spartan Stadium, who gets to build what where—that doesn't boil right down to that city manager's job."

This kind of information, obviously, is valuable material on which to build. The informant's view may not be shared by most of the influential leaders themselves. That too will tell us something about the structure of power in the community.

Sample Questionnaire with Scoring

1. Rank ordering (placed in relative thirds):

1. Alloway	11. Boccardo	21. Beritzhoff	
2. DiNapoli	12. James	22. Bloom	
3. Goldeen	13. Ruth	23. Jinks	
4. McEnery	14. George	24. Levitt	
5. Mineta	15. Gilliland	25. Lima	
6. Packard	16. Hayes	26. Mitchell	
7. Ridder	17. Lund	27. Moss	
8. Swenson	18. Miscoll	28. Ruffo	
9. Wolff	19. Poche	29. Weinhardt	
10. Burke	20. Raisch	30. Morgan	

3 points each (col 1)   *2 points each* (col 2)   *1 point each* (col 3)

2. The people who can put a project over:

Alloway	Goldeen
Hayes	James
Packard	Swenson
Ruth	Miscoll
Wolff	Ridder

3 points each

3. Who can initiate projects:

Wolff	Bloom
Swenson	Lund
Lima	George
McEnery	Hosfeldt
Mineta	Morgan

3 points each

4. Who can stop projects:

Hooker	Packard
Goldeen	Lund
Ruth	Moss
Mineta	Miscoll
Ruffo	Beritzhoff

3 points each

5. Has the most power: Packard

6. Exercises the most power: Alloway

7. Most influential: Alloway

8. Top leader: Mineta

5 points each

From this one respondent, then, Alloway received 16 points; Mineta and Packard, 14 points each; Goldeen, Swenson and Wolff, 9 points; Lund, Miscoll, and Ruth, 8 points; Ridder, 6 points; and so on.

After completing the first round of interviews, we add up scores, based on the simple system outlined above, and determine what cluster of people we want to consider for the second interview round. Generally there is a clear-cut group of people scoring higher than the others. In both Indianapolis and San Jose, there was a drop-off of points after the highest-ranked 32 names. But specific numbers are very flexible here; there is no reason why 20 or 40 would not suffice. Our goal at this juncture is not to state unequivocally who is and who is not influential in the community. Rather, we are seeking a cluster of people at the top who will be the best-qualified panel for the next round of interviews, in which we will *then* attempt to distinguish the 10 or so most powerful persons in the community from other important leaders.

Starting the Second Round

For journalists, the prospect of calling 30 of the most influential people in the community and asking them for an hour of their time to participate in a study of power is less intimidating than one might think. Reporters are used to this sort of thing since they interview politicians, businessmen, and community leaders routinely. But other researchers may shrink at the notion of imposing themselves on such salient personalities. Gathering the courage to ask some of these people may well loom as a fearsome task. It needn't be one. By and large, community leaders are intrigued by power structure studies, especially because their insights into power and influence are being sought. Most are flattered to be asked and curious to find out what the project is all about.

How will we first approach these people? We'll simply call them on the phone and explain to them that we are doing a study of power and influence in the community. We'll tell them that their names have been selected from among approximately 200 others by a panel of informed judges, and that we would like to interview them confidentially about the exercise of power in the community. We'll explain that we'll need about an hour and ask them to name a time for our appointment.

For this round of interviews we will alter the questionnaire to narrow respondents' choices. The same basic questions may be used, but fewer names will be asked for in response to each question.

Alphabetize the list of second-round respondents on one sheet and prepare the rest of the questionnaire. Before, we asked for the 30 most influential individuals' names; this time the question should read:

1. Place in rank order, 1 through 10, those individuals who in your opinion are the most influential in the city—influential from the point of view of the ability to lead others.

If there are people not listed who you feel should be included in the ranking, please add their names.

This time we will want our respondents to be as precise as they can, ranking each person accurately from 1 to 10. Although we need not explain it, we will later assign points to each person named based on the ranking he or she is given. Name 1 will receive ten points, name 2 will receive nine points, and so on. Once again, it is important to emphasize that respondents are not bound by the list of names we have supplied. They also should be told before they begin that they should not name themselves. This eliminates two problems—humility in some and hubris in others.

We continue on in the same manner with questions 1 through 6, although note that they ask for fewer names, or even for a single name.

2. If a project were before the community that required decision by a group of leaders, which 4 could "put it over"?

3. Name the 4 people most effective at initiating projects.

4. Name the 4 people most effective at stopping projects.

5. Name the person who *has* the most power in (city).

6. Name the person who *exercises* the most power in (city).

Before asking the final two questions from the first-round questionnaire, this is a good place to insert questions that, if left until the end, might not receive as many responses.

7. Who is the most underrated leader in (city)?

8. Who is the most overrated leader in (city)?

9. Who is the most trusted leader in (city)?

10. Who is the least trusted leader in (city)?

Finally, repeat from the first-round questionnaire the last two crucial questions.

11. Name the most influential person in (city).

12. Name the top leader in (city).

In both first- and second-round interviews, it simplifies work for the respondent if we provide a pencil to change answers as necessary. Also it helps to give the list of names to the respondent as a work sheet and then provide one page of questions at a time. All papers should be retrieved at the end of the session both to protect the respondent's answers and to minimize discussions among respondents about the study before we have a chance to interview them all.

This time scoring, in addition to the points assigned for the rank ordering, is as follows:

Questions 2, 3, and 4—five points.
Questions 5 and 6—10 points.
Questions 7, 8, 9, and 10—zero points.
Questions 11 and 12—10 points.

Drawing Out Additional Information

The discussion of interview answers is just as important as the questionnaire itself. The kinds of detail that provide insights into the interconnections among individuals and the methods by which major decisions are made can only be gathered from conversations with those who have first-hand experience. These dialogues with the insiders are what add color and meaning to the study of power in a community. In San Jose, for instance, they made it possible to research background on an important and controversial project, the construction of the San Jose Center for the Performing Arts.

San Jose has always suffered from a feeling of inferiority. Living in the shadow of San Francisco, leaders of its southern neighbor have for years wanted to build their own cultural center. But despite the many millionaires in the area, few have invested money and time in San Jose's cultural affairs. In short, as one politician reported, "San Jose's millionaires are cheap."

Starting in the late 1950s, a series of behind-the-scenes maneuvers took place when a group of influential San Jose citizens tried to make their dream of a San Jose cultural center a reality—but at the taxpayers' expense. At first the approach was fairly direct; two bond issues were proposed—in 1961 and 1964—that would have allocated approximately $6 million for the building of a community theater. But despite aggressive campaigns coupled with effusive, orchestrated "news" coverage from the local newspaper, the bonds failed, and the movers and shakers were forced to seek another route. A bond financing scheme, known as a "lease-back" arrangement, was authorized by a city council vote, thus bypassing public approval. *After* the council vote, a local state legislator pushed legislation through the state government making this kind of bond financing permissible for a theater. And even though a rogue councilwoman started a last minute rebellion against the council plan, the performing arts center bond issue managed to narrowly squeak by to victory, due to low voter turnout in a timely off-year election. The future looked rosy for San Jose's cultural competition with San Francisco.

But during the planning stage cost estimates began to rise rapidly, by several million dollars, and construction bids began to arrive even before bond buyers could be secured for the project. Building needed to begin immediately if costs were to be kept from rising to an impossible figure. It was then that a handful of influential businessmen held a pivotal emergency meeting. At that single session, after making a few strategic phone calls, these influentials were able to reassure the city fathers: $100,000 would be available that very day to get construction underway. When the city's power structure was studied more than a decade later, those who had participated in building the theater were found to be among the most influential people in the city.

The dates, the names, the votes involved in the decision to build the cultural center are a matter of public record; all could be gathered from newspaper clippings and local histories. But they do not tell the whole story. Only through careful follow-up interviews of our questionnaire respondents can we elicit the kind of inside detail needed to understand the complete workings of a community's power structure.

Encouraging Candor

Respondents may be reluctant at first to offer candid views of their peers. They should be reminded that their names will not be linked to their comments. Learn to take notes quickly. Respondents, many of whom will be major business and civic powers in our community, will not commit their candid comments to tape, especially if the person with the tape recorder is a stranger.

Sometimes a respondent will balk at virtually every question, finding it increasingly uncomfortable to share the inside views we are asking him or her to reveal. This won't happen often, but when it does we should be persistent but not belligerent. After all, we'll have more than enough interviews to provide the background we are after, and the respondent could, if he or she is well-connected, make things difficult for us with just a phone call or two. Usually, however, once a respondent has participated in the study he or she becomes a part of our team, helping us separate good information from bad. Once a respected businessman or important politician has told us something as candid as who he or she thinks is the least trusted leader in our community, we've been told in effect that we are trusted not to reveal that view.

How candid will respondents be? Brutally so. One informant from the top 10 in San Jose, for instance, had this to say about James Boccardo, a millionaire attorney and bank founder:

> He's probably got the most money and yet he's contributed the least to the community. We had a list of people to complete the Ridder Lounge at the Center for the Performing Arts—people who could afford $50,000 to $75,000. Boccardo wouldn't do it unless it was named for him.

Or, as another respondent said of Mayor Janet Gray Hayes:

> If I wanted some frosting on the cake I'd call Janet Gray because of her position. She's politicking all the time and ostensibly she exercises power— she'll make you think she can accomplish anything. But she isn't actually the one who says, "Here's what we're going to do." She *appears* to exercise the most power in San Jose. *Anybody* in that position would. I don't care who it is. It could be an idiot.

While it is important for the sake of objectivity that we not ask leading questions or impart a point of view in giving directions, we can relax during the discussion of respondents' answers. It is time to employ the time-honored if slightly devious skill of parlaying a small bit of information into a complete understanding of an event.

Because information from our case study survey of San Jose was provided confidentially, it is difficult to discuss how certain anecdotal material was gathered; but an example of how *emerging*, fragmental information, which could not have shown up in research, was used to elicit a detailed picture of an important power shift in that city is instructive.

In an early first-round interview during the San Jose study, one informant casually mentioned that a new businessmen's organization, the Santa Clara County Manufacturing Group, had recently formed, started by a top U.S. manufacturer, David Packard, who made his home in the region. These leaders of the county's most vital industrial and financial firms felt compelled to organize because, to them, the Greater San Jose Chamber of Commerce was simply too provincial for the needs of large manufacturers. This was information that, if true, reflected a decline in the relative influence of the chamber and a corresponding rise in the perceived power of the manufacturing group.

In subsequent interviews, when discussions of either the president of the chamber, Ron James, or of Packard came up, this notion was used as a sounding board. Respondents were asked if they had heard that idea or if they believed it was true. A surprising number not only expressed the same view, but then launched into attacks on the chamber for having become so parochial as to have permitted a rival group to have usurped its position as the leading voice of business.

There were other views as well. But in general, a new picture of James and the chamber emerged. To have questioned James's power in the community at one time would have been unthinkable. Now James and the chamber board were seen by many leading businessmen as ineffectual, small-time operators. At a time when they should have been expanding their organization, they were instead protecting it from outside takeover and maintaining an overly narrow focus. Meanwhile, major local industries were sending their chief executive officers to meetings called by the manufacturing group to discuss and become involved in the major issues affecting the county—jobs, housing, transportation, and energy.

It was apparent that the balance of industrial and business power had shifted from San Jose to the county and that the relative influence of the San Jose Chamber of Commerce had likewise declined. James was still judged to be one of the ten most influential persons in San Jose. But his peers had begun to question his effectiveness. Besides the color it adds and the insight it provides in areas that could not otherwise be researched, anecdotal material is important for another reason: It responds to one of the critiques of the reputational method—that the technique focuses too much on individuals and not enough on institutions.

Few members of any power elite enjoy their status simply because of who they are. Rather, they gain power through their institutional roles, though personality may enable some to use these roles to greater advantage then others. It is crucial then, when using the method described here, for the researcher to discuss with respondents the question of institutional versus personal power. Is the mayor a key leader because he or she has a wide political base and great charismatic skills? Or is it the position that lends the mayor his or her power? Would *anyone* elected mayor automatically be considered one of the most powerful people in the community? What about the city manager? The newspaper editor? The leading banker?

Mapping Institutional Interlocks

Another way to further refine our analysis of the power structure is to trace the interconnections among key institutions in the community through their boards of directors and key officeholders. This is an approach we have already encountered in chapter 2: that is, *sociometric* or *network analysis*. Simply detailing membership on boards of leading organizations can itself be revealing.

One measure of the rapid rise of the manufacturing group in San Jose became apparent in follow-up investigations into interlocking boards of directors. Although little more than a year old when the study was done, the manufacturing group already had on its board of directors two of San Jose's ten most powerful men—Packard and Halsey Burke, president of Burke Manufacturing, a rubber and floor-coverings firm—plus the city's two leading bankers—Miscoll and McKenzie Moss, president of Bank of the West, which was, until 1980, San Jose's largest home-grown financial institution. Tony Ridder, the newspaper publisher, later joined the board.

While not a part of the research method *per se*, network analysis is an essential element in the study of power. Each community is different, and each has its own constellation of interlocking institutions; so network analysis is an effective way of capturing and understanding these patterns.

Figure 3.1
INTERLOCKING SAN JOSE INSTITUTIONS, 1979

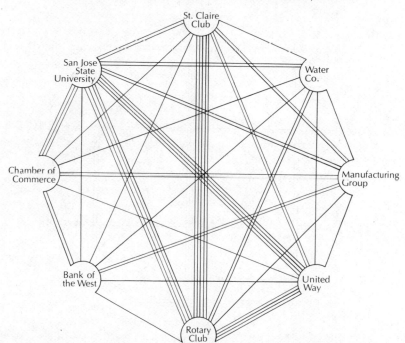

For example, the institutional network found in San Jose is quite different from that which was found in Indianapolis. Most large industries and banks in San Jose are branch operations run by corporate nomads—they tend to be "outsiders." So it is the locally controlled *civic organizations* which tend to form an interlocking network of institutional power there.

Examining those power centers, as identified by respondents during the course of the study, yielded the pattern shown in Figure 1.1.

Each line on the diagram represents one individual from the study's top 40 leaders who was either on the board of directors of a major San Jose institution or a member of one of the two leading clubs. Note especially that only *two* of the interlock points are private companies (the bank and water company).

Indianapolis, on the other hand, illustrates a significant difference between San Jose and other large cities where large corporations are headquartered. In Indianapolis, major banks and corporations have their Indiana headquarters, and the men (almost exclusively) who run those firms have deep roots in the city. Figure 3.2 shows interlocks

Figure 3.2
INTERLOCKING INDIANAPOLIS INSTITUTIONS, 1976

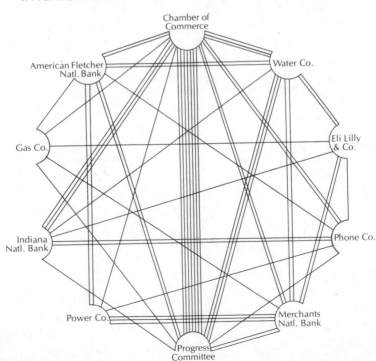

among institutions enjoying considerably more economic power than the San Jose institutions wield.

Here the diagram includes only two institutions which are *not* public corporations (the local progress committee and chamber of commerce). Other points on the diagram are the state's three largest banks, four major utility companies, and one of its largest locally owned corporations. Once again, each line represents one individual from the study's top 32 leaders who was a director or top officer of the institutions plotted.

Even without the civic organizations, there was, in Indianapolis, an impressive network of interlocks among the salient economic institutions (see Figure 3.3).

Another way to display the interlocks among institutions is a simple institution-by-institution matrix, with the number of officers or directors common to more than one numbered in the intersecting boxes. Table 3.1 shows, for instance, that the Merchants National Bank was the most-connected institution of all, with eight interlocks with the water com-

Figure 3.3
KEY INTERLOCKING INDIANAPOLIS CORPORATIONS, 1976

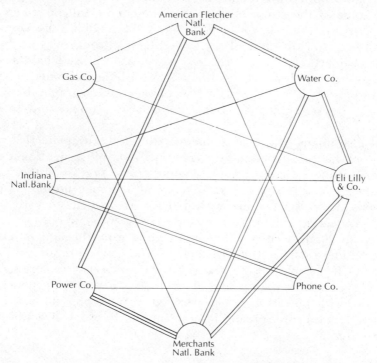

Table 3.1
MATRIX SHOWING KEY INDIANAPOLIS CORPORATIONS BY INTERLOCKING INDIVIDUALS, 1976

	AFNB	WATER	LILLY	PHONE	MNB	POWER	INB	GAS	TOTAL
AFNB		2		1		2		1	6
WATER	2		2		2		1		7
LILLY	2			1	2		1	1	7
PHONE	1		1			1	2		5
MNB	2		2			3		1	8
POWER	2			1	3				6
INB		1	1	2					4
GAS	1		1		1				3
TOTAL	6	7	7	5	8	6	4	3	41

pany, power company, and the city's leading industrial firm. The table also shows that eight companies have forty-one interlocks from individuals named in the city's top 32 power structure.

In some cities, even this kind of grid may not suffice to display the myriad interconnections among corporations. In Detroit, for instance, where some of the nation's largest and most powerful companies are headquartered, the *Detroit News* found it useful to publish the names of the full board of directors of the city's "Big Six" companies—General Motors, K-Mart, Chrysler, Ford, Detroit Edison, and National Bank of Detroit—showing, for each, the interlocks to these and other national corporations such as American Telephone & Telegraph, Bank of America, Chase Manhattan Bank, Proctor & Gamble, and several others.

The institutions that form the network of local power elites will vary from community to community, some involving more significant economic institutions than others depending on the *function* of the city in question, its relative status in its region, and the concentration of corporations. But each community will have its own network through which local elites maintain contact and exercise influence.

In many Sunbelt cities where industries are not headquartered or where businesses are not publicly held, a power structure study is likely to find, as it did in San Jose, that civic organizations are more significant interconnectors than corporations. In Frostbelt cities or those Sunbelt cities with powerful, publicly traded corporations, the interlocks among them will offer greater insights into the network of power linking institutions.

Notes

[1]Philip J. Trounstine, "Indy's Movers and Shakers," *Indianapolis Star,* Indianapolis, November 28–December 7, 1976.

[2]Philip J. Trounstine, "Power in San Jose: Who Has It, Who Wields It," *San Jose Mercury News,* San Jose, August 12–21, 1979.

4

Flashback:
A Short Political History
of San Jose

Power structures, political systems, and social problems have deep roots. Studying them at a given moment in time is useful, but to fully understand them, it is essential to know where they come from. With a little background, it is possible to view contemporary power structures in perspective, noting changes over time and emerging trends.

Each city has a unique history, with its own turning points; each has been affected in its own way by individuals, institutions, and the current of events. Yet cities have enough in common that telling the story of just one can contribute to an understanding of the others.

To a large extent, San Jose and other cities of the Sunbelt have functioned as "growth machines."[1] Their histories have been based on increasing intensity of land use and their politics dominated by the beneficiaries of that increasing intensity, subject to occasional challenges from grassroot movements. As these cities grew, they passed through three distinct phases, which political economist David Gordon has defined as commercial, industrial, and corporate.[2] In *commercial* cities, the economy is based on trade and ruled by merchants, who also attain great political influence. In the *industrial* phase, manufacturing takes center stage and factory owners dominate the political process. The most contemporary stage is the *corporate*, reflecting the expanding role of a relatively small number of large corporations in the national and local political economies. Although Gordon largely views Sunbelt cities as products of the corporate phase, an understanding of their

78

Table 4.1
CITY OF
SAN JOSE AND COUNTY OF SANTA
CLARA, POPULATION, 1777–1980

Year	San Jose	Santa Clara County
1777	66	
1820	240	
1830	540	
1840	750	
1852	2,500	6,764
1860	3,430	11,912
1870	9,089	26,246
1880	12,567	35,039
1890	18,060	48,005
1900	21,500	50,216
1910	28,946	83,539
1920	39,642	100,676
1930	57,651	145,118
1940	68,457	174,949
1950	95,280	290,547
1960	204,196	658,700
1970	445,779	1,064,714
1980	625,763	1,265,200

Sources: U.S. Census, San Jose Chamber of Commerce.

economic evolution through all three phases of growth can take us a long way towards understanding their political development.

San Jose's story is similar to those of many other cities of the Sunbelt. While some locations in the region, such as Los Angeles and Atlanta, have been major urban areas for well over a century, most of the Sunbelt cities grew rapidly, gaining big city status only in recent decades. Table 4.1 details just how swiftly San Jose grew to be the seventeenth largest city in the country in 1980.

To understand the phenomenal growth of San Jose and cities like it, and to set the stage for the 1979 power study, a little history is in order.

THE FIRST HUNDRED YEARS: AN AGRICULTURAL CITY

Cities have reasons for being where they are. Most are situated on a great harbor, a navigable river, or an important crossroads. Others are located near a natural resource like coal or oil. Sunbelt cities often trace their roots to such resource extraction, or to agriculture. Indeed, although San Jose has become a crossroads, the principal reason for its existence until recently was the fertile agricultural land of the Santa Clara Valley.

The city was founded in 1777, part of the Spanish colonization of the Pacific Coast. Located in a verdant valley, with abundant water, a mild climate, and a small population of nonaggressive natives, San Jose was a perfect site for agricultural development. Within a few years, the small band of Spanish settlers were raising cattle, sheep, and corn to supply the Spanish military bases and missions in the area.

Fifty years later, settlers from the United States began arriving. Seeing a greater potential for commercial expansion through affiliation with the United States, they broke with Mexico in 1846, and in 1850 California attained statehood. Yankees took over leadership of the town and San Jose became, briefly, the state capital. The County of Santa Clara and the City of San Jose were given legal status through state charters, and the city adopted a mayor-council form of government.

Perhaps even more significant for the growth of San Jose was the discovery of gold in California. Most of the men in the city, including the mayor and the jailer with ten prisoners, left to seek their fortunes in the gold fields. Some returned to establish businesses and ranches in San Jose, using their gold as capital. But the city also benefitted indirectly from the gold rush. It was located on one of three major routes to the mines, and providing supplies to the miners considerably expanded the market for the valley's agricultural products.

During the following decades, the town developed rapidly as the commercial center of the Santa Clara Valley. New businesses, homes, churches, and schools were built. A support system for future expansion was developed, as the city established police and fire departments, a public library, and a sewer system. A teachers' college that later became San Jose State University was founded, and the first newspaper was published.

Technological advances brought more rapid change and growth. The railroad and the telegraph came to town, linking San Jose more directly to the rest of the world. Private companies brought gas, electricity, telephones, water, and streetcars to the growing town.

Farmers shifted to more intense use of the land, planting orchards and growing vegetables. Fruit drying and canning, combined with rail transport, gave the valley farmers access to a world market. The town became a center for food processing, with canneries as a major seasonal employer. Even now, in parts of San Jose you can tell the season by the smell of stewing tomatoes; it's like driving through someone's kitchen.

By 1880, the town was dominated, like so many others in that era, by a political machine. The new utility companies, streetcar operators, and canneries were intimately associated with the machine. Each needed government to maximize its profits. Utility companies and streetcar lines needed franchises—or monopolies on service areas—granted by local government. Canneries needed a system for disposing of their massive effluent, preferably subsidized by the taxpayers. Inevitably, these companies became involved in community politics.

And then there was the greatest power of all, the railroads. San Jose, like the rest of California, was almost totally dependent on the railroads to transport its products. Combined with their extensive landholdings, the railroads gained enormous power and used it. Southern Pacific, after a period of absorbing smaller railroads, came to dominate both the city of San Jose and the state of California.

Their machine, known as "the gas house gang" because of its utility connection, was Republican but depended on working class voters, seduced by jobs or lesser favors. Friendly merchants were rewarded with city contracts. But the main job of the machine was to protect the interests of the railroad—the Southern Pacific—and utility companies. That meant maintaining the prevailing distribution of the spoils rather than enhancing the community.

1880–1940: EMERGENCE OF A COMMERCIAL CITY

With an expanding market and transportation network, San Jose began to move into the commercial phase of its development. By 1890, San Jose had grown to 18,060. The town was becoming a city. As in other growing cities throughout the Sunbelt, a new, urban class was emerging in San Jose. Merchants and professionals were growing in number and organizing socially through the formation of a country club, a yacht club, and a women's club. And although San Jose's economy still centered on agriculture, this new class was interested in more intense economic development to expand the market for their department stores, newspapers, instruction companies, and legal services. It was only a matter of time before the commercial classes organized politically to oppose the machine, which they viewed as corrupt, amateurish, and inefficient. Perhaps even worse, it served big business and the working class but not the merchant and professional classes.

They felt the machine was doing too little to foster economic development. The city had not adapted rapidly enough to new technology, particularly the automobile. Streets weren't being paved and lighted, and storm drains, sewers, and other improvements weren't being built quickly or well enough under the machine. San Jose—and its merchants—were missing out on the growth other cities were enjoying, and the machine was to blame. As one historian has said, in order to get things moving again:

. . . governments had, first of all, to find new sources of revenue to build the unprecedentedly expensive new facilities. The tax rate for individual taxpayers could be—and was—raised. But a far more palatable course was to increase the overall tax *base*, which could be accomplished merely by annexing outlying populated areas to the central community, or, with more difficulty, by attracting new residents and new business to town. Another means of finding new funds was to demand an end to the inefficient spending of existing city governments.[3]

The political machine was the obstacle to such growth, and a group of businessmen, orchardists, doctors, lawyers, and judges began a reform movement in San Jose that was bent on ending the machine's existence. In 1896 they succeeded in revising the city charter to weaken the powers of the mayor and strengthen the independent commissions that were in charge of schools, police, fire, and other city departments. The machine was still strong enough to win the next election, however, and it wasn't until 1902 that the reformers elected their own mayor. Their success seems to have been due to their growing numbers, their acquisition of two of the city's three newspapers, and an accommodation with the Southern Pacific Railroad.[4]

The Reformers

The reform administration cleaned up City Hall and paved and lighted the streets. Business boomed. Real estate prices rose rapidly. The city grew from 21,400 in 1900 to 27,868 in 1904. The leader of the reform movement was elected to Congress, and it seemed that the reformers had the town sewn up.

After their victories, the reformers returned to their businesses, uninterested in the jobs and favors machine supporters had expected when their side won. But those jobs and favors proved better at holding an organization together than the ideals of the reformers. The machine remained popular with policemen, firefighters, and school teachers. Nor were liquor and gambling interests pleased with the reformers. In 1906, the local attorney for the Southern Pacific pulled these elements together to recapture City Hall.

The reformers were out of power for a decade, but they spent those years building a movement for more substantial changes in the structure of city government. Winning elections, they could see, wasn't enough. They had to modify the system to purge forever the politicians and replace them with efficient administrators who would govern on a businesslike basis—and who would serve *their* businesses.

The Good Government League, the New Charter Club, and the

Women's Civic Study League, all made up of middle- and upper-class business and professional men and their wives, worked for a decade to accomplish these ends. They became part of the state and national Progressive Movement, which was mentioned in chapter 2. Nationally known muckrakers passed through San Jose, speaking to frenzied middle-class audiences. They attacked the bosses, the railroad, the utilities, the monopolies, and the immigrants. They studied innovative governmental structures designed to lessen the influence of their enemies while bringing good government and enhancing their own power.

In 1914 the reformers regained control of City Hall, and the following year a committee of freeholders, dominated by members of the Chamber of Commerce and the Merchants' Association, was elected to rewrite the city charter. They called in an expert, Professor Thomas Reed of the University of California, to write their new charter, which won voter approval that same year. The reform newspapers campaigned hard for the charter revision, and the only opposition came from labor leaders, who argued that working people had been left out of the process and would have less accountable government under the new guidelines.

The reform charter was based on Professor Reed's concept of replacing "amateurs in the art of administration" with professional city managers:

> The administrator has no concern with "policy," except to offer such suggestions and advice as his experience warrants. The administrator's relation to the people is the same that is borne by the general manager of a corporation to its stockholders. [Therefore the administrator] should be appointed, not elected, and should be removed as far as possible from the immediate effects of public opinion.[5]

Thus the office of mayor was abolished, and a manager appointed by the city council became the chief executive. The manager was meant to be a neutral professional, implementing council policy, making suggestions, and responsible for the budget and for hiring and firing other city employees. The city council was expanded from five to seven, all to be elected at large, thus reducing the parochial influences of wards. They were given minimal pay because they were meant to serve only part time, leaving local government to the professionals under the leadership of the manager.

By 1915, San Jose also had primary elections for city council, recall of elected officials by petition and election, and the initiative and referendum to allow the voters to make or review laws. All were a part of the reformers' efforts to lessen the machine's stranglehold on the city. As a result of a 1911 amendment to the California constitution intended to weaken the Southern Pacific machine's control on state politics, all local elections were nonpartisan, meaning that candidates were not party nominees and party labels were not allowed on the ballot. Thus, by 1916, San Jose's governmental structure was almost purely reformist, consisting of: (1) a city manager; (2) at-large, nonpartisan, council elections; and (3) the recall, referendum, and initiative. There was no longer even a titular mayor. The council chose a president by seniority rotation, but his powers were confined to presiding over council meetings.

The effect of all these reforms was to solidify the influence of the business class and to lessen that of the general populace. Administrative powers were in the hands of a supposedly neutral, professional manager, expected to govern in a businesslike manner and accountable to the voters only indirectly through the city council. The council itself was elected at large; no longer were individual council members responsible to any section of the city.

In combination with nonpartisan elections, the at-large system gave electoral advantages to the well-known and affluent members of the business class who could secure newspaper support and raise the money necessary for a campaign. Without a party label to establish legitimacy or a party organization to supply workers, ethnic and working-class candidates had difficulty getting elected. The system as a whole was a businessman's model government, insulated from the voters and emphasizing professional management. Even today, the city's public information brochure compares city government to a corporation: the voters are the stockholders, the council is the board of directors, and the person in charge is the manager.

Such a reform structure is typical of Sunbelt cities. A substantial majority use the council-manager form of government and at-large elections, and 94 percent of western cities and 78 percent of southern and border-state cities use nonpartisan elections.[6] The adoption of these structures in the Sunbelt reflects the dominance of business elites at the turn of the century. They seized local government and molded it in their image. They attempted the same in Frostbelt cities, but with considerably less success because the machines there were stronger, thanks to their alliance with the large ethnic-immigrant population. In the North and West, instead of structural reform businessmen had to reach an accommodation with the machines.

But what was happening in San Jose was typical of events in many Sunbelt cities. Business interests were forging a city government that could hasten the growth they wanted and needed. San Jose was going to be a city that did more than pack prunes and stew tomatoes.

The reformers won the 1916 election, the first under the new charter, and made Professor Thomas Reed their first city manager.

Reed introduced competitive bidding for city contracts, awarding them to the lowest qualified bidder rather than giving them to supporters in the style of the machine. He also introduced a civil service system for hiring, promoting, and firing municipal employees on the basis of merit, not loyalty to the machine.

But Reed's ideals soon foundered on the rocks of political reality. As Reed and many other reformers learned, changing the structure of government didn't necessarily consolidate their control. The reformers had won, but the machine was still around, active in county politics and leading the resistance to Reed's tight budgets, competitive bidding, and civil service system. Again it retained control of the police and fire departments, and also the schools, through the carefully cultivated loyalty of the workers in them. Reed lasted two years, then left San Jose with his ideals profoundly shaken. By 1920, the Southern Pacific machine reclaimed control of the city council.

Clarence Goodwin, the young city engineer, was then appointed city manager. For twenty-four years—one of the longest tenures in the profession of city management—he held the post, and unlike his predecessors, Goodwin had great political acumen and was able to adapt to the shifting political winds. Many years later a magazine writer described him as "the perfect public servant of an agricultural metropolis: a firm Methodist, a public prohibitionist and, in the words of one of his admirers, 'economical to the point of parsimony.' "[7] He performed an admirable political juggling act, too. On the one hand, he accepted "the theory that he [was] an employee of the council."[8] His image suited the reformers, and he gave them enough efficiency to keep them happy. At the same time, he accommodated the demands of the machine when it was in power.

The Bigley Machine

In the late 1920s, in what must have come as a great shock to the reformers, a new machine became a power in city politics. Charlie Bigley, a beer distributor and ambulance operator, became the boss and controlled a majority on the city council through the 1930s. Bigley never consolidated a base as substantial as the old machine's, but with gifts of shoes and clothing, he maintained support among low income voters, and through his control of the police and fire departments he kept liquor and gambling interests loyal. Needless to say, his influence came in handy for his own ambulance company. Both police and fire-fighters campaigned in uniform for machine candidates, and Bigley's control over hiring in both departments was his strongest base.

Ray Blackmore, who was later chief of police for twenty-five years, illustrates Bigley's powers of patronage with the story of his hiring: A naive lad, Blackmore approached the city manager for work as a policeman but was told there were no positions. Blackmore wandered across the street to Bigley's office, told his story, and was asked if he could play baseball. He replied he could and was sent back across the street where a position had suddenly opened; Bigley needed players for the police baseball team.[9] Thus was San Jose's reform government made to adapt to the power of the machine through the cooperation of City Manager Goodwin.

1940–1979: EMERGENCE OF AN INDUSTRIAL CITY

Agricultural and commercial cities can grow only to a certain point, after which further expansion will depend upon the development of a solid industrial base. All across the Sunbelt—in Houston and San Antonio, in Phoenix and in our case city, San Jose—local business leaders knew this, and after World War II they set about industrializing their communities with all the vigor they could muster. Happily for their cause, these local leaders were aided and abetted by national forces and the federal government, ultimately causing the growth machine to shift into high gear.

I. The Internal Forces

By 1940, San Jose had become a thriving commercial city of 68,457 people. The pleasant downtown shopping district, with classic movie palaces and busy department stores, attracted people from farms throughout the valley. The city's principal function, however, was still as an agricultural center; canneries were the major employer.

As in many other Sunbelt cities, the new generation of business leaders coming of age were not content for their city to remain a modest commercial center. They were concerned that, with half the city's work force employed in canneries, San Jose "feasted in the summer and starved in the winter."[10] They began boosting growth, persuading the city and county governments to spend money to recruit industry, inviting Boeing to locate in San Jose (although, as it turned out, this offer wasn't accepted), and celebrating when, in 1943, IBM built its first West Coast plant in the city. They lobbied for freeways, a municipal airport, and a Naval air base.

As an earlier generation had at the turn of the century, they felt government wasn't doing enough to bring about the growth they wanted. It was corrupt and inefficient, and change was in order. They criticized City Manager Goodwin and the chiefs of the police and fire departments but could not get enough votes on the city council to fire them. To circumvent the council, they introduced a charter amendment requiring a vote of confidence for the city manager. Putting the manager before the voters violated the ideal of the city manager as an apolitical administrator, but they weren't worrying about ideals—they just wanted to get rid of him. Nevertheless, Goodwin survived his first vote of confidence.

The Progress Committee.   To rid themselves of Goodwin and Boss Bigley permanently, the business boosters formed their own political organization in 1944. In naming it the Progress Committee, they expressed their hope for the future and looked back to an earlier generation of reformers. The one hundred members of the committee, proudly listed in the local press which supported their cause, were almost all merchants, attorneys, industrialists, and major property owners.[11] They were members of the Chamber of Commerce and the Merchants Association, mostly young and aggressive. They wanted "to build . . . a new metropolis, in the place of sleepy San Jose."[12] They wanted growth and economic progress for the city and themselves. They wanted to take advantage of the boom they knew was ahead.

But to do that, they had to overcome the resistance of large landowners and labor unions who were against new taxes "to do things the voters actually needed" and seemed to support the "veto-power politics" of the machine.[13] The Progress Committee produced a slate of candidates for the 1944 city council election. With the newspapers' endorsements, they swept to easy victory and soon began cleaning house. Although City Manager Goodwin had won his vote of confidence in the same election, the new council ended his 24-year tenure as manager and also fired the police chief and the fire chief, charging them with "bossism," "mismanagement," and "political interference."[14]

Once they controlled City Hall, the interests represented by the Progress Committee held it for thirty years, although the committee itself soon ceased to function formally. "We were all boomers then," said one community leader, and the new expansionist consensus rolled forward with enough momentum to elect the candidates of the business interests without much effort.

Having purged the city administration, they set out to promote industrial development. Subsidized by the city and county governments, the Chamber of Commerce spent $60,000 on a national advertising campaign in 1944. As a result of the campaign, or more likely because San Jose was the right place at the right time, industrial development followed. The Food Machinery and Chemical Corporation (FMC), a local manufacturer of equipment for farms and canneries, had shifted to building armaments during World War II and expanded following the war. IBM made San Jose its Pacific headquarters. General Electric, Pittsburgh Steel, Owens-Corning, and Kaiser all built plants in or near San Jose.

Despite these apparent successes, the boomers soon faced dissent within their ranks. In 1946, one of their leaders denounced the Progress Committee as "reactionaries" and charged that they had acquiesced to a "land grab" by FMC, selling the corporation municipally owned land at well below its market value.[15] A court agreed, much to the embarrassment of the Progress Committee and the company. Others split with the majority on the issue of water, arguing for municipal rather than private ownership. But the newspapers and the Progress Committee soon put the dissenters in their place by labeling them socialists, an effective charge in the heyday of anticommunism.

Industrial recruitment proceeded, and the water stayed in private hands, but other public investments were necessary to bring the growth the Progress Committee wanted. "Company's coming, we must be ready," urged the newspaper.[16] The boomers agreed that the city needed streets, storm drains, an improved sewer system, an airport, a new city hall, and even a deep water port. But to build these needed facilities, they needed voter approval of general obligation bonds, so the city could borrow money for long periods of time, at low interest. The bonds were paid for by property taxes, and that's where the voters balked. Election after election, they were unswayed by the fervor of their leaders and the newspapers. Although waste from the canneries made sewage a special problem in San Jose, the voters obstinately refused to vote for sewage treatment bonds; perhaps they were unwilling to subsidize the canners. By 1948, the problem was so bad that the state even declared San Jose in violation of pollution regulations. Nor were voters much more enthusiastic about other growth bonds. The Progress Committee did manage to get approval for airport expansion, although that was mostly done with federal funds. They also finally won authorization to move the site of City Hall, a decision that symbolized their ambitions for San Jose. The new City Hall was to be built outside the central business district and adjacent to new county offices; the ultimate goal was the consolidation of the two.

The Progress Committee and the newspapers had attempted to repeal the charter vote-of-confidence provision for the city manager on grounds that it politicized what was supposed to be an apolitical position and made it difficult to recruit professionals. After Goodwin's firing in 1944, the city council had replaced him with a nationally known professional manager; he resigned in 1950, however, partly in protest over the vote of confidence. But the voters, who evidently liked having this power, rejected the repeal.

The boosters needed a multifaceted manager, someone who could cope with the referendum, who shared their vision, and who could get voter approval for their bond measures. They pushed for and ensured the hiring of Anthony P. "Dutch" Hamann, whose professional background consisted only of being business manager for the nearby University of Santa Clara and a representative for an oil company. Hamann's connection with the university was useful, however, because it was the alma mater of most of the Catholic business leaders of the city, including Mayor Albert J. Ruffo. And although Hamann had no training or experience in city management, he was a skilled politician and a public relations expert—in short, a salesman. That was what the Progress Committee wanted and needed. Hamann was like them: he knew how to get along and he wasn't an unbending professional. As one leader later put it, "as a city manager, Dutch was the best salesman we ever had."[17]

Hamann added a needed component to the progrowth coalition which was riding high in 1950. Two years later, another shot in the arm came when the Hayes family sold the morning *Mercury* and evening *News* to the Ridder group of newspapers. The elder Hayeses, who had acquired the newspapers during the Progressive era, had died, and the succeeding generation had lost interest in San Jose. The newpapers had not been as vigorous in boosting San Jose as they might have been. Joseph B. Ridder, the new publisher of the newspapers, promised an end to anemic leadership, declaring, "We hope to make the *Mercury News* not only among the best newspapers on the Pacific Coast but a vital and constructive force in the development of San Jose and its territory."[18]

II. Outside Forces: Stimuli to Growth

With the local boosters of growth solidly united, the city boomed through the next three decades. In 1950, the population was 95,280 in a compact 17 square miles. Ten years later, San Jose had grown to 204,196 people and 64 square miles. In 1970, the city of 445,779 sprawled over 149 square miles, and in 1980, the population reached 625,763. The population of Santa Clara County grew proportionately.

It would be easy to give full credit—or blame—for what happened to boosters like the Progress Committee, to Dutch Hamann and Joe Ridder; for good or bad they deserve much of it. But local forces can't create growth all by themselves. There have to be reasons for people and industries to come to a city besides the fact that the welcome mat is out. Although the boosters did a lot to make San Jose grow, they were going with the flow of history.

Like other Sunbelt cities, San Jose offered a good climate, low taxes, plenty of land for low-rise, low-cost buildings, and an absence of unions. It was also near San Francisco, a financial center. But the key to the industrial development of San Jose and the Santa Clara Valley was the electronics industry, the roots of which can be traced to Stanford University. In the 1930s, encouraged by Professor Frederick Terman, young Stanford engineers began to establish their own companies in the area. In 1938, William Hewlett and David Packard took Terman's advice and formed Hewlett-Packard, now a major local employer. In 1946, financial, industrial, and university leaders to the north of San Jose established the Stanford Research Institute (SRI), which did industrial and defense research and later became an essential component of the industrial growth of the Santa Clara Valley. The federal government had already established similar facilities nearby at a naval air base and at the Ames Research Center.

Three stimulants to growth were already in place in the valley: friendly local government, plentiful land, and technological skill. Now the federal government added a fourth, money, through massive injections of defense and aerospace spending. The effects on the fledgling electronics industry were rapid: IBM and FMC expanded. New companies that soon would be household names, like Lockheed, Hewlett-Packard, Philco, General Electric, Sylvania, Fairchild, Memorex, National Semiconductor, and dozens of others, located in or near San Jose and expanded through the 1960s and 1970s. By 1979, two hundred thousand residents of the county were directly or indirectly employed in the electronics industry;[19] twenty of the largest manufacturing firms in the county were either defense-, aerospace-, or electronics-related; only five were not.[20] And Santa Clara County was the recipient of $2 billion annually in federal defense contracts, 3 percent of the national total.[21]

The jobs were there, then, for a nation eager to migrate to California, a movement that began in the 1930s and accelerated after the war. Millions of people were coming to California

> . . . in search of something . . . seen in a movie or heard on the radio . . . [a place where] the air smells of orange blossoms and it is a long way to the bleak and difficult East, a long way from the cold, a long way from the past. . . . For the war was over and the boom was on and the voice of the aerospace engineer would be heard in the land. "VETS NO DOWN! EXECUTIVE LIVING ON LOW FHA!"[22]

The job boom stimulated another growth sector. With thousands of new workers on their way, housing was needed. Local government gleefully provided the zoning, but federal policy also played an important part. Veterans Administration (VA) and Federal Housing Administration (FHA) mortgage insurance "made it possible for the average American to fulfill his dream of private suburban housing and made it profitable for developers to create the spreading housing tracts that began to characterize" San Jose and other Sunbelt cities.[23] The tax benefits of real estate ownership were an added stimulant: it was economically irrational *not* to own a home.

Federal and state aid also was essential for supplying the growing city and its industries with water and for subsidizing the construction of sewage treatment facilities and an airport. But the biggest direct assistance of both the federal and state government came in the form of highway construction. Three major freeways were built, running through and encircling San Jose and connecting it to San Francisco, Oakland, the Pacific Coast, and Southern California, as well as opening up new areas of Santa Clara County for development.

These external forces—federal defense spending, the location of industry, the migration of people, federal housing policy, and highway construction—contributed greatly to the growth of San Jose. The local supporters of growth, well aware of this, did all they could not only to promote San Jose but to support those state and federal programs that were useful to them and to make sure San Jose got its share. State and federal legislators from the Santa Clara Valley became cheerleaders for these programs, assisted by local economic and political leaders.

In sum, San Jose couldn't have become the city it is today without enormous outside forces working in its favor and at its urging. Growth was occurring throughout the Sunbelt: in California, in the San Francisco Bay Area, and in Santa Clara County. It would have happened without Dutch Hamann or Joe Ridder or the Progress Committee, though the pace might not have been so fast in San Jose in particular. But they were there, and their endeavors put San Jose in the forefront of growth in the South Bay. "They say San Jose is going to become another Los Angeles. Believe me," said Hamann, "I'm going to do everything in my power to make that come true."[24]

III. The Growth Machine at Work

While some of San Jose's growth was inevitable, much of it was consciously brought about by the very interests that benefitted most from it. These interests were in charge of the city virtually without challenge from 1944 to 1969. Their policy was growth. Their tool was city government.

Since World War II, they had been promoting industrial growth to diversify San Jose's economy and as a basis for overall growth. San Jose and other cities in the area were also eager to strengthen their property tax base with industrial development. So they waged advertising campaigns to recruit industry and catered to industry's every whim when it located in the city. Between 1950 and 1965, the Chamber of Commerce spent a million dollars plugging San Jose, subsidized by the city and county governments. Arriving industry found a cooperative local government eager to provide the zonings and capital improvements it needed. What industry wanted, it got. When IBM planned to expand south of the city, San Jose simply annexed the area for the corporation's convenience. Scenarios like this were repeated many times over as the city did everything it could to woo and accommodate industry.

As early as 1954, the *Mercury* was celebrating the benefits of such growth. Trumpeting progress, an article crowed that new industry provided a "year round [rather than seasonal] industrial payroll."[25] By 1956, new industrial wages equaled cannery wages. And while 101,666 acres of Santa Clara Valley land had been devoted to orchards in 1940, by 1973 only 25,511 acres were put to such uses.[26] What had once been the "Valley of Heart's Delight" was becoming "Silicon Valley."

But San Jose promoted more than industrial development. Indeed, much of the industrial expansion was outside of San Jose and might have occurred without much activity by the city at all, for the decisions to build plants were essentially private ones. San Jose was, in fact, more vigorous and successful at promoting growth in housing than in industry, perhaps because the profits were more immediate.

Former mayor George Starbird approvingly explained, "Dutch [Hamann] built a city organization that provided the right atmosphere for the developer and subdivider. The city employees were cooperative. The city council exuded friendship, and togetherness was a by-word."[27] Through aggressive annexation, ready provision of capital improvements, and other concessions to developers, San Jose retained its position as the dominant city of the growing Santa Clara Valley.

Dutch Hamann's Panzer Division.   The city approved 491 annexations between 1950 and 1960 and more than 900 in the next decade, adding 132 square miles to its domain.[28] The city did not accomplish this by awaiting humble petitions from landowners and residents eager for its services. Annexations were hustled, and sometimes even coerced. Instead of the planning department taking responsibility for annexation, the normal practice in most other cities, in San Jose the city manager was in charge, and his aides were known as "Dutch's Panzer Division." Among other things, they went door-to-door persuading farmers and residents to annex and offering lucrative concessions to landowners and developers. Growth came so fast that local mapmakers issued monthly packets of stickers to add to their master maps.[29] As Hamann explained:

> If you wanted to grow and be able to pay the bill, you had to annex surrounding areas to the city. To do that you couldn't sit on your hands. Pretty soon you would become like Bakersfield and St. Louis, an enclave circled by small incorporated cities or special service districts that would tie you up forever. If you got bottled up, your tax rate would put you out of the running for new industries.[30]

The city government wanted to give developers and landowners what they needed, but they also wanted to make strategic annexations that would maintain San Jose's dominance of the valley, "bottling up" other cities rather than being trapped by them. The city manager's "Panzer Division" was vigorously engaged in urban imperialism, at war with neighboring communities. San Jose developed a policy of "shoe-string" or strip annexation, adding a street or just one side of a street to reach a parcel of land the city wanted because of its strategic location or because some landowner had advantages to be gained. San Jose sought to capture key intersections where shopping centers would one day be built. San Jose also used strategic annexations to block the expansion of adjacent cities.

The rationale for the policy of leapfrog annexation was that it would insure one large city, which, according to Hamann, would be "better . . . than a lot of little ones" because "it gives you the opportunity to plan."[31] Though gaps were left by the leapfrogging, they would supposedly be filled in later as landowners prepared to develop and wanted city services. Thus, "by annexing and expanding services to territories several miles beyond its developed core, San Jose preordained the future annexation and development of most of the intervening lands."[32]

Beginning Opposition to Aggressive Annexation.   Defenses against San Jose's aggression were not entirely successful. Individual residents and property owners frequently alleged skullduggery and sued the city, delaying or blocking annexations. The city dealt with this resistance by ignoring it. Officials simply annexed around pockets of resistance, assuming that someday the surrounded areas would have no choice but to join the city. As San Jose's land grab continued, groups of residents in developed areas to the south and east attempted to incorporate as cities themselves in order to avoid being absorbed. Their efforts failed, but at least three other cities in Santa Clara County were incorporated for this reason. Existing cities like Santa Clara found themselves in constant annexation battles with San Jose, and although they sometimes won the battles, they lost the war because of San Jose's central strategic position.

Perhaps the most serious opposition to San Jose's annexations came from school districts. Until 1954, California cities and school districts were required by state law to have the same boundaries; when a city annexed territory, that territory joined the city's school district. Rural school districts adjacent to San Jose were seeing their tax bases and their schools annexed away from them. They responded with lawsuits that delayed and sometimes stopped annexations. Resistance from the schools ceased when San Jose's state legislators gained passage of a law separating school districts from municipal boundaries. But the children of San Jose today attend school in two dozen different districts, a factor that has contributed to the city's fragmented politics, lack of identity, and racial segregation.

San Jose's ambitions went beyond annexation where necessary. Two incorporated cities, Alviso and Milpitas, lay in the path of San Jose's drive to the northeast, where it sought access to the San Francisco Bay and more direct control of its own sewage treatment facilities. Agents of San Jose instigated campaigns within these small communities for consolidation with San Jose. Their efforts failed in Milpitas but ultimately succeeded in Alviso, giving San Jose what it wanted.

Flexible Land-Use Policies.   But annexation was not the only means by which San Jose facilitated growth, nor were city services and the prestige of being part of a big city all that persuaded landowners to annex. Another means of enticing them was San Jose's flexible land-use policy. By and large, the city let developers do what they wanted wherever they wanted to do it.

Most cities have general plans that set forth guidelines and policies for land use. Yet until 1960, when the state and federal governments began making general plans a prerequisite for certain grants-in-aid, San Jose had none. Although the city's population had more than doubled in the preceding decade, the plan San Jose produced in 1960 was not much more than a collection of the public works department's maps of streets, sewers, and storm drains. No policy goals were included. A 1966 general plan was an improvement, but just having a plan wasn't enough. If a plan is to be effective, a city must follow it; but San Jose was far more concerned with cooperating with developers than with good planning.

A general plan is a statement of goals; those goals are put into effect through specific zoning decisions which dictate what particular uses specific parcels of land may have. Thus, through zoning cities regulate land use and control the quality of development. But San Jose's use of these controls was, to say the least, lax. The city approved subdivisions on flood plains, hillsides, earthquake faultlines, and wetlands and in areas without water or sewer connections. Later, some of these subdivisions cost the taxpayers a lot of money, either in reparations or in building needed facilities. But at the moment of their approval, they satisfied the developers.

Such policies ensured that given a choice of what city to annex to, landowners would opt for San Jose. Whether in future land sales or in developing themselves, they could be sure to be rewarded with "lower lot sizes, less stringent construction requirements, unusually low rates on service extensions to the developments, and an almost 100 percent probability of favorable rezoning.[33] Milpitas, for example, required a 6,000 square foot minimum lot size for residential development; San Jose required 5,000 square feet. The city's research section produced a report showing that builders saved 50 percent on lot preparation costs in San Jose as compared to Milpitas.[34]

Much land was annexed without these enticements. For the developers of this land, there were other advantages. Through its vigorously anticipatory annexation policy, the city always had "plenty of land . . . ripe for development," so builders could do their work furthest from the center of the city, where land was cheapest and had the additional marketing advantage of "country living."[35]

Capital Improvements Through General Obligation Bonds. To facilitate the development of annexed areas as well as to entice others to annex, San Jose's boomers used capital improvements like roads and sewers. Such improvements cost a great deal of money. Federal grants paid for some: during those years, San Jose received federal money for highways, sewage treatment, libraries, parks, and its airport. But most of the money had to be extracted from local taxpayers through general obligation bonds.

Typically, in approving general obligation bonds, voters authorize their city government to borrow money, usually at relatively low interest rates over a long period of time. The money is spent for improvements—like a road or a library building—that will last a long time, so it seems reasonable to take a long time to pay for them. That payment is generated by an increase in the property tax, a commitment made by the voters when they approve the bonds.

But in San Jose, while the bill went to the taxpayers, the biggest benefits went to the developers. It was they who needed the capital improvements in order to build. For a time San Jose voters balked, but then, in bond elections in 1957, 1961, 1966, and 1969, the voters approved $134 million in general obligation bonds, most of which financed capital facilities in new areas. Dutch Hamann and the *Mercury News* were the principal propagandists for the bonds, but the campaigns were steered by a group of contractors, developers, businessmen, and public officials that came to be known as the Book (or Buck) of the Month Club.[36] They raised $57,000 for the 1966 bond campaign, with major contributions from construction companies, the San Jose Water Works, Pacific Telephone, Pacific Gas and Electric, the Real Estate Board, the Chamber of Commerce, packers, and canners.[37] With voter turnouts as low as 15 percent, their lavish campaigns and the strong support of the newspapers usually turned the trick.

Once voters approved bonds, they still had to be sold to investors. Here again, Hamann and the boosters met success. Former mayor George Starbird explained that "much of the growth of the city was due to the confidence of the investment interests in New York in San Jose bonds—Hamann, the real architect of this city, had a lot to do with that.[38] He organized promotional trips to the East, "telling our story" and "creating a favorable market." The bonds did better than some expected, and one informant had this theory why:

> On a strict basis of classification, San Jose voters were carrying a heavy load indeed and the bonds shouldn't [have sold] as well as they did, but with the glamor we painted into the picture . . . I guess everyone wanted to invest in California if they couldn't live there.[39]

Hamann and other city officials began to commute regularly to the East, "and the results were really fantastic," noted the same observer. "You don't build a city by staying in a vacuum," Hamann once declared. "You build, you sell. . . . And I was the gun for hire."

With the money now flowing in, much of it was used for capital improvements aimed specifically at accelerated growth. Improvements went where developers wanted to develop. Sewers, for example, were "planned" by putting pins in a map with each inquiry from a developer; when there were enough pins, a sewer line was built.[40] Often streets and sewer lines were constructed larger than necessary. The city argued that this was just good planning for anticipated future growth, but it also encouraged and to some extent subsidized that growth. The subsidy was produced by selectively exempting newly annexed areas from paying for municipal bonds that provided them with capital improvements. Only the taxpayers who resided in the city at the time the bonds were originally approved paid for them. Part of the bargaining process in the packaging of annexations, unacquired areas were often fatally tempted to annex with the promise of "free capital improvements."[41]

San Jose's Sewage Monopoly.   San Jose's greatest weapon in the annexation wars was its control of the sewer system. What water was to Los Angeles, sewage was to San Jose. In the 1880s, San Jose had built a drainage "outfall" to the San Francisco Bay large enough for a city of 250,000. The scale was partly needed for cannery effluent, although as early as the 1930s, San Jose was in trouble with the state for polluting the Bay. With the state threatening to cancel building permits, San Jose passed bonds for new treatment facilities in 1950. The city was cited again in 1967, 1979, and 1980, but despite the problems, San Jose had the largest sewage disposal system in the South Bay, and had it first.

San Jose used this sewage monopoly in its battles with adjacent cities and with recalcitrant landowners. In 1951, the city council banned outside links to the system; annexation was to be the price of sewage disposal. At one point, Hamann boasted, "We're in this fight to the finish, and if we have to use sewage disposal to bring [neighboring] Santa Clara to some point of reasoning, we'll do it."[42]

A Paradise for Developers.   The combination of aggressive annexation, lenient zoning, eagerly supplied capital improvements, and the sewage monopoly sped growth on its way. San Jose was a paradise for developers, who maintained good relations with the city council through the Book of the Month Club and generous campaign contributions. But the council and city administrators also benefited directly from growth. "Illegal activities" and "payoffs" were suspected although never proved.[43] But collusion was patently obvious. Builders, local merchants, and politicians were, after all, part of the same class; they thought alike and they met frequently. Exchanging information or making deals involving land speculation or development was easy, even natural. And with minimal conflict-of-interest laws, it was even legal. City Manager Hamann himself was involved in more than fifty property transactions during his tenure; some of his property later became sites for major intersections and shopping centers.

The most avid booster of all the projects and candidates of the growth machine was Joe Ridder's *Mercury News*, which clearly benefited from the growth it promoted: "We don't have newspapers," said the circulation manager, "we have catalogues."[44] For, as San Jose boomed in population, it was growing into one of the major retail markets in the country, a trend that would make the *Mercury News* one of the nation's most profitable newspaper combinations.

In addition to the local growth facilitating policies, the boomers successfully lobbied the state and federal governments to build freeways and water supply systems. And to enhance San Jose's image as a major city, its leaders promoted an expanded City Hall, a community theater, and a sports arena. But the voters resisted, unpersuaded that these projects were as essential as sewers and roads. Proposals for the new City Hall had to be submitted to the voters four times before winning approval. The financial manipulating necessary to win construction of the community theater has already been outlined in chapter 3. The sports arena never was approved.

Recognizing the Need for Urban Renewal.   Ironically, the boomers' vigorous annexation and pro-growth policies had in some ways hurt their own San Jose pocketbooks. Though retail sales for the region had sky-rocketed during the growth years, most of the increase was in suburban shopping centers, not downtown. Some of the shopping centers were not even in San Jose but in adjacent municipalities. By 1963, San Jose accounted for only 9.4 percent of the county's retail sales, down from 67 percent in 1920. The city administration had contributed to the decline of downtown by encouraging the growth of shopping centers, failing to solve downtown parking problems, and moving City Hall and hundreds of workers out of the area. By 1970, every downtown department store had closed or moved elsewhere.

So as early as 1956, even as they continued to peddle the freeways and shopping centers that helped create the problem, business leaders pushed for urban renewal. They established an urban renewal agency eligible for federal funds and empowered to condemn property. But by the time the new agency had acquired and cleared land for redevelopment, it was too late. No major department store or hotel has yet been built in downtown San Jose. Land has been vacant for years, removed from the tax rolls and demoralizing to view. Gradually, there has been some improvement. As the electronics business burgeoned, a number of banks built regional headquarters to oversee their investments. But although the new office buildings have brought many workers there, much of downtown San Jose remains a wasteland.

Keeping San Jose Autonomous.   Underscoring all the actions of the boosters of the 1950s and 1960s was the effort to make San Jose the dominant force in the South Bay and to retain San Jose's autonomy. It was, after all, the government the boosters controlled. They ran roughshod over smaller cities, with conflict continuing until San Jose's annexation policies had done their work and cut off expansion from their competition. They fought the "ranch house conservatism" of the county government, which attempted "to retain agricultural areas as buffers among the expanding towns."[45] San Jose also guarded its political autonomy and its physical and symbolic independence from the larger cities of San Francisco and Oakland to the north. In 1950, San Jose successfully resisted being included in the San Francisco-Oakland standard metropolitan statistical area by the census bureau. San Jose and Santa Clara County became and remain a separate metropolitan statistical area. More substantively, the city and county rejected participation in the Bay Area Rapid Transit District when invited to participate in 1957, a decision now regretted by many. A decade later, when the federal government mandated a regional council of governments, San Jose was a reluctant participant.

IV. The Challengers: Growth Versus "Liveability"

As the city grew, its nature and functions changed. The economy diversified. Construction and electronics displaced agriculture and canneries as the economic base of the community, introducing new interests to city politics. A subtle shift in power had occurred as early as the 1950s when developers and new industrialists became major political forces, edging out the orchardists and merchants who had been in ascendance for the first half of the century.

And as the city grew, newcomers came to outnumber old-timers. Eventually, as in many other Sunbelt cities, these new residents began to question the old leadership. The growth machine faced its first electoral challenge from the grassroots in 1962, a challenge that has been in progress ever since. The very people who had been brought to the city by growth began to question that ethic.

"The election of 1962," former Mayor George Starbird said, "cast a shadow that falls across our political scene even today."[46] Councilwoman Virginia Shaffer and two other new council members were elected on a vigorously anti-incumbent platform with the support of emerging homeowners organizations. Starbird incredulously observed that "City Hall audiences became unruly for the first time in history.... You could not seem to get the pulse of the voters—what they actually wanted."[47]

But the concerns of the insurgents were not really so difficult to understand. San Jose had grown so quickly that the city was unable to provide the services its affluent residents wanted and expected. The city sprawled across what had once been the Valley of Heart's Delight. But the new residents didn't care much about what had been there before them. What they did care about was their own immediate environment and, to a lesser extent, the loss of the remaining open space.

The dependence of the sprawling city on the automobile meant polluted air. The incapacity of the sewage treatment plant to keep up with the rate of growth meant polluted water. But the most important issue for the new residents was the inadequacy of basic city services: police and fire protection, libraries, parks, streets, and schools. The affluent aerospace engineers and electronics technicians that thronged to the valley expected good municipal services. But sprawl put a heavy strain on the ability of government to provide them.

The police and fire departments had to protect a huge and constantly expanding area. Leapfrog growth made it difficult for them even to know where their jurisdictions began and ended. There were stories of firefighters from two or three cities converging at the scene of a fire and watching buildings burn as they disputed whose responsibility it was. Schools couldn't keep up either, and by the 1970s, many were on double sessions, a development that affluent parents of the city abhorred. Open space disappeared and was not replaced by an adequate system of parks. Yet the taxpayers continued to carry a heavy burden for capital improvements. Bonded indebtedness had doubled between 1950 and 1970—twice as fast as in other large cities in California.[48] Residents paid the city's bills, but their money went for growth-inducing capital improvements, not for the services and facilities they wanted.

Councilwoman Shaffer and the homeowners—upset over the inadequate city services, the tax burden, and the city's emphasis on growth—took the offensive. Both past planning practices and new proposals came under their fire. They condemned shoddy developments—some built on hillsides subject to earthslides, others unconnected to the water system, and many that were simply badly constructed. They opposed a "new town" of 100,000 people on recently annexed land at the edge of the city. They accused city officials of involvement in land-use deals and the suppression of scandals, pointing their finger too at the district attorney and the *Mercury News* for ignoring corruption because of their own connections to the growth machine. The homeowners' criticisms were supplemented by occasional complaints from business leaders that City Hall was allowing too much housing construction and doing too little to promote industrial development.

The Growth Machine Retrenches. In 1962 Shaffer and her allies launched a recall of the council members who supported City Manager Hamann. Not surprisingly, the *Mercury News* and the old Progress Committee and Book of the Month Club rallied round Hamann and his council. Hamann later boasted that an industrialist friend had called up a councilman who was hassling him and said "no more [campaign] funds from FMC if you don't lay off." Hamann and his council supporters survived the recall, but their share of the vote was far below the once-typical landslide levels. Changes were brewing, but they chose to ignore them: immediately after the election they reaffirmed the city's aggressive annexation policy.

In a defensive move, leaders of the growth machine undertook a revision of the city charter. They proposed to eliminate the vote of confidence for the city manager, something they had disliked for a long time, although it had worked well enough for Hamann. They also proposed that the mayor be elected directly instead of being selected from among the council. This, they thought, would give the city a more visible and authoritative spokesperson. Still, the powers of the office were strictly limited to presiding over council meetings. They also considered discarding at-large city council elections and replacing them with district elections, which they hoped would make residents of unincorporated areas more willing to annex to the city.

Proposals for district elections came to nothing at the time, but the vote of confidence was eliminated; beginning with the 1967 election of businessman Ron James, San Jose has had a directly elected mayor. The campaign for the charter change brought the growth coalition together once again. The *Mercury News* was vigorously supportive, and the campaign was funded by FMC, the San Jose Water Works, Pacific Gas and Electric, Pacific Telephone, various homebuilders and realtors, and *Mercury News* publisher Joe Ridder.[49]

Low-Income and Minority Residents Speak Out.   Besides the challenges from relatively affluent homeowners, the growth machine faced accelerating demands from low-income and minority residents. The 1970 census reported that 22 percent of the city's population was Hispanic and 4 percent, black—minorities sufficiently large to have considerable potential power. But as a 1973 Rand Corporation study pointed out, the minority population had not prospered as much as the Anglo majority: "poor [largely Hispanic] neighborhoods [had] deteriorated relative to better-off neighborhoods, and segregation had increased."[50] The boom had not benefited them.

During the 1960s, the era of the civil rights movement and community action, it is not surprising that San Jose's minority population began demanding its share of the pie. Complaints focused on police brutality, housing discrimination, and inadequate services, but City Hall was largely unresponsive except to appoint the first minorities to the council since the end of Mexican rule. In 1967, Norman Mineta, a

Japanese businessman, was appointed to fill a vacancy on the council—
in part at least as a gesture to the minority community. Not until 1971
did a Chicano gain a seat on the council, again by appointment. The
appointments were a beginning, but still, no minority person had been
able to win election because the city's Anglo majority dominated at-
large council elections.

The federal government was more responsive to the minority community, however, providing aid the city refused and even enticing the
city into cooperation in order to obtain federal funds. A community
action agency was established in 1967 as part of the federal War on
Poverty. That same year, the city applied for and won federal urban
renewal funds for a program for the Hispanic barrio; the money was
used to induce the area to annex to the city. In 1969, San Jose began
receiving federal Model Cities funds, targeted to low-income neighborhoods and intended to spur model community development projects.

Although these programs were the center of much attention and
controversy in the late 1960s, their long range impact is difficult to
ascertain. Much of the energy of the minority community went into the
effort to control the programs, as opposed to forming significant electoral coalitions that actually could alter the balance of power, but by the
time program control was attained, the federal government was phas-
ing out its funding. The budget cuts and internal squabbling, as one
poverty program expert has put it, left "little energy and fewer resources for an attack on more substantial elements of the power
structure."[51] The model cities program in San Jose, as elsewhere, seems
to have been "used . . . to insulate city hall from minority demands, to
minimize opposition . . . and to divert minority discontent" from city
hall to agency leaders. The "dominant coalition" resisted efforts to
"redistribute power to minorities" and "moved decisively to eliminate
what it saw as a thorn in its side" when the opportunity arose.[52]

Although these programs did not bring about substantial change in
San Jose they did help define the issues and caused new leaders and
organizations to emerge. Chicanos and blacks continued to demand
fair representation, fair housing, and reforms in police practices, finally focusing on plans for a police review board and district council
elections to win their goals.

"Urban Development" Replaces Aggressive Annexation. Meanwhile, the
electoral strategy of the homeowners was meeting greater success, winning important victories against the boomers in 1969. A slate of three of
their candidates was elected, along with the city's first avowed environmentalist. Shortly thereafter, City Manager Hamann resigned. A new,
professional city manager was hired, and in 1970 the city's aggressive

annexation policy was abandoned and replaced with an urban development policy that emphasized improvements within the city's existing boundaries before further outreach. The new city manager also tightened the city's fiscal and planning functions, and the council made its first, hesitant uses of cost-benefit analysis in its review of new proposals. In a 1971 election another environmentalist, Janet Gray Hayes, went on the council. The tide was turning, or, as ex-mayor Starbird lamented, "the voices of the builders and the doers became lost in the many-voiced demands of the users. The veto was back."[53]

By 1971, San Jose had a mildly liberal city council and a city manager who expressed concerns for the minority community and the problems of growth. The police slaying of a black IBM worker that year resulted in weeks of angry protest. After a lengthy study of police practices, some modest reforms eventually followed. Concerns about growth produced more cautious reviews of proposals, but building went on. The council and manager were having difficulty grappling with the issue, and even the environmentalists were susceptible to the persuasive lobbying and pervasive campaign contributions of the developers, who adapted to the changed circumstances with more subtle methods.

The years 1973 and 1974, for many, marked the watershed confrontation between the old guard and the emerging new establishment. The new city manager resigned in 1972, largely for personal reasons, although he had been unable to master the entrenched bureaucracy he inherited from Hamann. In choosing his successor, the council was under heavy pressure from the old guard to pick a local man, the leading contender being former-mayor Ron James, then head of the Chamber of Commerce. But the council's four-vote liberal majority chose Ted Tedesco, a professional and an outsider, instead. On the day of their final decision, Mayor Mineta, their leader, was called to the offices of *Mercury News* publisher Joe Ridder for a harangue and a last minute effort to push former-mayor James. That the mayor went to the publisher's office is itself evidence of where power in San Jose lay at that point. But Mineta returned to City Hall and, with his three allies, hired Tedesco. They had defied the old guard, but they were also protecting their own power. Tedesco would be their man. James, with a political base of his own, would have been difficult to control.

The old guard suffered other defeats in the 1973 election. Dissatisfied with council efforts to control growth, a group of middle-class mothers put an initiative on the ballot prohibiting new residential zonings where the schools were overcrowded. Campaigning with minimal funds, opposed by the newspaper, and outspent 10 to 1 by the builders, they nevertheless won a narrow victory. By giving the impact of growth a definition that the parents of San Jose could understand, they made it an issue that could not be ignored. Two council candidates who endorsed their initiative were also elected, firming up the controlled-growth majority on the council. These victories were brought about by voters in new parts of the city. While the older sections of town were still accepting of growth, the new ones rejected it. New residents had long out-numbered old, but it had taken them years to settle in and express themselves politically.

A Final Showdown Between Old Guard and New?   The 1974 election brought what many political activists at the time felt would be the final showdown between the old guard and the new. With Mayor Norman Mineta running for Congress, Vice Mayor Janet Gray Hayes became a candidate to succeed him. Opposing her was Bart Collins, retired ex-chief of detectives, a pro-growth conservative and the candidate of the old guard, the developers, and the *Mercury News*, which pulled out all the stops to promote him. Hayes had the support of homeowner and neighborhood association activists, environmentalists, liberals, and the city's emerging feminist organizations. The minority community also rallied somewhat reluctantly to her support, appalled at the prospect of an ex-cop as mayor. Her slogan, "Let's make San Jose better before we make it bigger," put the desires of these groups in a nutshell. Each candidate spent more than $100,000 in San Jose's first hotly contested race for mayor, and Hayes narrowly won it.

Hayes's victory was partly due to a change in the date of municipal elections, indicating how procedural reforms can sometimes affect an urban power structure. Once separate from state and national elections, since 1974 San Jose municipal elections have been concurrent, primarily for reasons of economy. But the change in date also quadrupled voter turnout. While turnout had been a mere 16 percent in the 1973 run-off election, in 1974 it was more than 60 percent. In isolated elections, those most likely to vote are the relatively affluent and well-educated; they tend to be Republican and conservative, and election results reflect this propensity. But concurrent elections not only increase the size of the electorate, they also shift its composition, significantly increasing the proportion of voters who are newer to the community, working class, minority, and Democratic. Election results show the change. Undoubtedly, the liberal Hayes would not have beaten her conservative opponent in a traditional isolated election.

Although the tide had seemed to turn, some surprises were still in store in 1978. Up for re-election, Mayor Hayes faced serious challenges. Councilman Al Garza, who rallied the support of builders and developers as well as parts of the Hispanic community, forced Hayes into a run-off election. Meanwhile, a new block of four votes on the council (called the Fearsome Foursome or the Gang of Four) pushed for development, fired the city manager, and ran roughshod over the mayor and her remaining two allies on the council. But the Gang of Four collapsed when one resigned following his second episode of public drunkenness and another was defeated in the November election by an ally of the mayor's. And Garza himself was decisively beaten by Hayes. The new guard had had a scare, but they were back in command.

In that same election, a coalition of minority, feminist, labor, and neighborhood groups had succeeded in winning voter approval of district council elections, a victory that took a decade of effort. Labor, minority, and feminist organizations were convinced that the high cost of at-large compaigns would forever keep working people, women, and minorities off the council. District elections could improve their chances.

Crucial additional support came from neighborhood and homeowner groups. By 1978 there were 118 such groups in the city, a relatively high density for such an affluent community. Some of the neighborhoods they represented had never had a council member reside in their area; between 1950 and 1975, 78 percent of the council members had lived in just two neighborhoods.[54] For these neighborhoods, as for the Hispanic eastside, the issue was direct representation. They felt their needs had been ignored by council members, who didn't know they existed and who paid more attention to the developers and businessmen with the cash to fund their expensive campaigns.

Opposition to district elections came from some remnants of the old guard and from the *Mercury News,* which feared the parochialism districts might bring. The campaign against districting, which was paid for almost entirely by corporate developers, predicted that district elections would bring back boss politics. But the proponents of districting narrowly won the election, apparently hammering another nail into the coffin of the old guard.

The Impact of Grassroots Victories. These victories for the grassroots have done more than just change the personnel at City Hall; they have *reshaped* city policy. The era of aggressive annexation has ended and that of managed growth has begun. First growth was limited in areas where schools were overcrowded. Later, restrictions were set on development in areas of traffic congestion, where flooding is a problem, and on hillsides. A special tax was imposed on new construction in an effort to pay for capital improvements "as you grow" rather than financing them through general obligation bonds, which the voters were in no mood to approve. Neighborhoods got more sympathy from the city council and more attention from the planning and public works departments. Standards for design and construction of new developments improved. And development of the area where boomers had planned a "new town" of 100,000 was deferred to 1990. The 1976 general plan made these changes policy. In addition, the minority community won better representation through district elections and some improvement in police-community relations.

These victories were the result of hard work and the force of numbers, but they were also won because the old guard was exhausted and the interests it represented were changing. Many of the individuals who had been active during the boom years had retired or died. Many of the institutions they represented had changed. The native sons who had built FMC (once known as Food Machinery Corp.), for example, had died; the corporation had gone national, moving its headquarters to Chicago. Since the move, the local FMC managers have played no visible part in city politics other than once when they wanted to expand one of their local plants. Even the *Mercury News* changed. The Ridder newspapers merged with Knight Newspapers, Inc., and new, professional editors and managers took over. Joe Ridder was eased out as publisher in favor of his nephew Tony Ridder, a sophisticated and contemporary corporate man. News coverage became more balanced, and the editorial pages endorsed Hayes for mayor (and even Jerry Brown for governor) and called for balanced growth in San Jose. Similarly, the construction industry came to be dominated by large corporations, headquartered elsewhere and very sophisticated in their approach to the politics of growth. Meanwhile, the balance of employment had shifted to electronics manufacture, also corporate and often located outside the city. So instead of local merchants and builders, economic power was increasingly in the hands of corporations, usually absentee-owned and less interested in local politics than their predecessors had been.

Had the power structure of the city been altered? Had the dominance of business elites been replaced by a more numerically pluralistic elite with greater power in the hands of community groups and the voters? The electoral victories of the new forces suggested a major shift of power, but the local "revolution" may have been more superficial than real.

Big corporations still get what they want, although that is now usually confined to zonings or the like for plant expansion. And building continues to boom. During the "controlled-growth" 1970s, San Jose was, oddly enough, the fastest growing major city in the United States. The quality of the new construction was better and more rationally planned. The boom has slowed somewhat, but only relative to how much building there was: 9,516 dwelling units were built in 1970, but the number had only declined to 6,647 by 1977. Rather than being defeated, the developers, with an instinct for survival that would have impressed Darwin, adapted. Their techniques became more sophisticated. Instead of the buccaneer developers of the Book of the Month Club era, today San Jose has something called "the development community," made up of corporate developers represented by pin-stripe-suited lobbyists at City Hall. They inform, befriend, and cajole, and they generally get their way. They are rational and accommodating. If there are complaints about their plans, they change them. To improve the climate for persuasion, they make lavish campaign contributions to all major candidates, especially incumbents. Developers have always funded council campaigns, but with the cost of a campaign running $100,000 for a council seat and double that for mayor, candidates are even more dependent on them. Janet Gray Hayes, the slow-growth candidate, still received huge campaign contributions from the building industry in 1974 and 1978. By "spreading their bets" across the field of incumbents, builders are assured of access and, barring serious public opposition, they're still likely to get what they want. Even with district elections, the builders, under the banner of "Citizens for Housing and Economic Stability," still contribute heavily to council campaigns. There is no evidence yet that the new system has seriously diminished their influence.

Furthermore, the problems that aroused homeowners, environmentalists, Hispanics, and others have grown more severe. The minority community still lags behind economically. Police and fire protection are more overextended than ever. Other city services have been cut back, partly due to budget reductions brought on by California's "taxpayers' rebellion" in 1978 that enacted the tax-cutting Proposition 13. San Jose's sewage treatment plant is near or past capacity. A sewage spill in 1979 nearly destroyed marine life in the southern part of the San Francisco Bay; another in 1980 further aggravated conditions. Traffic congestion has grown worse, due to inadequate new construction and the city's past policies. Much housing, built in areas which were to be served by state freeways, has been "stranded" since those freeways were canceled. Exacerbating the problem is the failure of San Jose to attract employment in proportion to its population. Smaller cities north of San Jose have been more successful at concentrating industry there while employee housing is disproportionately concentrated in San Jose. Each morning streets and freeways are clogged by the massive commute to the north, which reverses itself in the evening. San Jose has attempted in recent years, without great success, to bring jobs and population into balance, but its efforts are too late for today's unhappy commuters. Because of the economic vitality of the county there is also, despite San

Jose's growth, a housing crisis. Demand is high and prices are higher. The problem is severe enough that there is a growing concern that the industries on which the community depends for employment will migrate to greener pastures in Arizona or, for that matter, abroad in Taiwan, leaving San Jose to face the same problems burdening the declining cities of the Frostbelt.

A CORPORATE CITY OF THE SUNBELT

San Jose in 1979 appeared to be a city in transition. Like many other Sunbelt cities, it had become a metropolis *suddenly*. The old political elite seemed to have crumbled as the new city emerged. Power seemed to be more widely distributed, but was it? Or had the old elite merely been replaced by a new, corporate elite?

These are the central questions in the study that follows, an attempt to dig below the surface of events described in this chapter. The answers are of interest to the people of San Jose, who need to know if they have gained control of their own community or if the struggle continues. But the answers are also of interest to those who live in other Sunbelt cities and to students of community politics in general. For San Jose is, in many ways, like other cities of the Sunbelt, the new urban America.

By 1979, San Jose had become the seventeenth largest city in the nation. Its 625,000-plus people were young, their median age of 27 reflecting the city's suburban lifestyle—families, kids, detached housing. They were also affluent and well-educated. Although some Sunbelt cities have large populations of retirees, most are otherwise similar to San Jose in demographic make-up.

Like San Jose, other Sunbelt cities also grew rapidly, a growth brought partly by local boosters but largely because of fortuitous location, good timing, and general liveability. Their good climate, cheap land and energy, and low taxes and cost of living made them magnets for both people and industry. These attractions were supplemented by federal highway and housing policies, but more significantly by federal defense and aerospace spending upon which many Sunbelt cities depend for their livelihoods. A further attraction for industry, much promoted by some Sunbelt cities, was the weakness of labor unions. For instance, in 1977 only one-sixth of San Jose's work force was unionized.

As we have learned, the burgeoning of the Sunbelt cities brought with it substantial change in their economic and political life. Industrial diversification redistributed economic power, with national rather than locally owned corporations gaining dominance. Like San Jose, many

Sunbelt cities became branch office towns, changing the political role of the economic elite which in some ways lost interest in local affairs. On the other hand, the new corporate leaders had greater power because of their national connections and the credibility of their threats to move if conditions did not suit them.

As growth accelerated, it became the central political issue in these communities. Initially it was put on the agenda by those who wished to foster growth. Later, it was kept there by the newcomers who wished to control it. For all the advantages of growth—a booming economy, jobs, housing—there were also problems. Like San Jose, other Sunbelt cities suffer air and water pollution, traffic congestion, expensive housing, and minority populations left behind by the boom.

These problems led to political conflict. San Jose was only one of many Sunbelt cities to witness an assertion of neighborhood, home-owner, environmental, and minority interests, challenging the boosters that dominated in the recent past. Managing growth has become a key issue. Many Sunbelt communities have also considered reforming their government structures, which, again like San Jose's, generally date from the Progressive Era and were designed for much smaller and less diverse cities. District elections have been revived not only in San Jose but in Albuquerque, Dallas, El Paso, Sacramento, and San Antonio, and debated in several other Sunbelt cities. With more conflictual politics, the office of mayor has received increasing attention and some-times increased authority.

As in San Jose, the old guard seems to have faded. A decade ago, journalists, activists, and many citizens could have easily named the powerful people in their Sunbelt cities. Today, they would be less certain. Change has brought new people and new economic forces. The new people and industries have struggled with the old in a period of transition. But that period is coming to an end. We must return to our basic questions: Have growth and change redistributed power? Has the old elite been replaced by a new one? If so, who are they? Our search for the present movers and shakers of San Jose should provide some clues about other Sunbelt cities as well.

Notes

[1]Harvey Molotch, "The City as a Growth Machine: Toward a Political Economy of Place," *American Journal of Sociology*, vol. 82, number 2, 1976.

[2]David M. Gordon, "Class Struggle and the Stages of American Urban Development," in David Perry and Alfred Watkins, eds., *The Rise of the Sunbelt Cities* (Beverly Hills: Sage, 1977).

[3]David Eakins, ed., *Businessmen and Municipal Reform* (San Jose: Sourisseau, 1976), p. 2.

[4]Eakins, p. 9.

[5]Eakins, p. 15.

[6]Willis D. Hawley, *Nonpartisan Election and the Case for Party Politics* (New York: John Wiley and Sons, 1973), p. 17.

[7]Richard Reinhardt, "Joe Ridder's San Jose," *San Francisco Magazine*, November 1965, p. 48.

[8]Robert Thorpe, "Council-Manager Government in San Jose," Master's Thesis, Stanford University, 1938, pp. 48, 57.

[9]Unless otherwise noted, the source of quotes and other material is interviews or public speeches.

[10]George Starbird, "The New Metropolis" (San Jose: Rosecrucian Press, 1972).

[11]*San Jose Mercury*, February 16, 1944.

[12]Starbird.

[13]Starbird.

[14]*San Jose Mercury*, March 28, May 19, and May 23, 1944.

[15]*San Jose Mercury*, April 1 and 9, 1950.

[16]*San Jose Mercury*, November 25, 1950.

[17]Reinhardt, p. 66.

[18]*San Jose Mercury*, July 1952.

[19]Pacific Studies Center, *Silicon Valley* (Mountain View: Pacific Studies Center, 1977), p. 28. See also Daniel J. Alesch and Robert A. Levine, *Growth in San Jose* (Santa Monica: Rand, 1973).

[20]*San Jose Mercury, Almanac*, 1981, p. 76.

[21]*San Jose Mercury*, October 19, 1980.

[22]Joan Didion, *Slouching Toward Bethlehem* (New York: Penguin, 1968), pp. 22, 30–31, 146.

[23]Alesch and Levine, p. 12.

[24]Reinhardt, p. 70.

[25]*San Jose Mercury*, January 31, 1954.

[26]Mitchell Mandich, "The Growth and Development of San Jose," Master's Thesis, San Jose State University, 1975, p. 97.

[27]Starbird.

[28]Mandich, p. 65.

[29]*New Yorker*, May 4, 1963, p. 150.

[30]Starbird.

[31]Reinhardt, p. 70.

[32]Stanford Environmental Law Society, *San Jose: Sprawling City* (Stanford: 1970), p. 64.

[33]Stanford, p. 23.

[34]Stanford, pp. 27–28.

[35]Stanford, pp. 23–24.

[36]*The Weekly Mayfair*, January 25, 1964.

[37]Mandich, pp. 197–198.

[38]*San Jose Mercury*, March 29, 1977.

[39]Starbird.

[40]Mandich, p. 116.

[41]Mandich, p. 68.

[42]*San Jose Mercury*, February 6, 1952.

[43]Mandich, pp. 158, 112.

[44]Reinhardt, p. 68.

[45]Reinhardt, p. 68.

[46]Starbird.

[47]Starbird.

[48]Stanford, p. 15.

[49]Jack Corr and Fred Keeley, "San Jose City Charter, A Bicentennial Proposal," 1976, p. 17.

[50]Alesch and Levine, pp. vii, 3, 4.

[51]Ralph K. Kramer, *Participation of the Poor* (Englewood Cliffs, N.J.: Prentice-Hall, Inc., 1969), p. 236.

[52]Rufus Browning, Dale Rogers Marshall, and David Tabb, "Implementation and Political Change: Sources of Local Variations in Federal Social Programs," *Policy Studies Journal*, vol. 8, special number 2, 1980, pp. 620–621.

[53]Starbird.

[54]Corr and Keeley, p. 21.

5

Power In a
Sunbelt
City

"The Sainte Claire Club used to be the center of power in the Santa Clara Valley," a long-time insider at the fusty men's club said wistfully in an interview. "But not any more. The valley has grown and the club hasn't grown with it."

This view, from one still deeply committed to the San Jose club where ranchers, bankers, lawyers, and businessmen once made private political deals, was only half true. The club, founded in 1888, had been an important gathering place through the years, and membership once was coveted dearly. As a center of power, however, it had been more a backdrop than a stage. Now, even as a backdrop, it has faded. Many newcomers, leaders in politics, business, finance, and industry, have no use for the club's overstuffed leather chairs, cut crystal, and pressed linen. The Sainte Claire Club, with the clan that once occupied it, has gone to seed.

As we saw in chapter 4, times have changed in San Jose. A woman has been elected mayor; the locally owned banks have been swallowed up by others and overshadowed by San Francisco financial empires; the ranching profession is in decline; the *San Jose Mercury News* no longer performs public relations for pet civic projects; and voters have put the brakes on unbridled growth. The days of political bosses, dictatorial city managers, crusading publishers, and king-makers have passed. The initiative and referendum have arrived. The grassroots have taken hold.

"The nature of San Jose is that it doesn't work with two dozen people calling the shots any more," said former City Manager Ted Tedesco, who, in his seven years in office, called more than his own share on the political firing line. Still, not all citizens are equal. Some have more power, more influence, more clout than others. Their views, their actions, and sometimes their money can make or break major civic projects. In San Jose, they are the movers and shakers—directing the local banks, the water company, business and manufacturing groups, philanthropies, universities, and, in many ways, City Hall itself.

In 1979, when the *San Jose Mercury News* studied the city's power structure, it found members of the influential elite in the best clubs and the richest neighborhoods. Several lived outside of San Jose but wielded influence in the city through their professional positions. Some of them were well-known, public personalities who thrived on media coverage. Others were virtually invisible; working behind the scenes, they quietly exerted their influence but seldom drew attention. As one high-powered businessman explained, "One of the great traits of having power and influence is never having to use it."

What follows are the results of the *Mercury News* study of power and influence in San Jose, an investigation based on the method described in chapter 3. Completion of the study took three months; when it was done, the editor and the publisher of the newspaper, who were discovered to be among the most powerful people in the city, reviewed, but did not censor, the material.

SAN JOSE'S TOP LEADERS

The *Mercury News* study identified forty persons in all who formed the top tiers of the power structure in San Jose. Ten leaders were at the peak of the influence pyramid. Although some of them were prominent public names in the community, others were barely known outside the confines of political, journalistic, social, and business circles. Another thirty persons made up second and third tiers of power. Some of these individuals had even greater influence on selected issues than members of the first tier. But in judging across-the-board economic, political, and social clout in San Jose, the influentials themselves returned again and again to the names in the first tier as their community's "Top 10"—and to one name in particular.

Listed below in *alphabetical order* are the ten persons the *Mercury News* study found to be the most influential. In the table that follows, the second and third tiers are shown. Tier 2 lists twelve individuals judged to have substantial but significantly less overall influence than those grouped in tier 1. Tier 3 lists eighteen leaders who were generally considered to have less, although still considerable, clout in San Jose. Again, all names are alphabetically ordered.

San Jose's "Top 10"

Halsey C. Burke, 56, San Jose. President and chairman of the board of Burke Industries, a rubber and floor-coverings firm with 600 employees and annual sales of $21 million.

Frank Fiscalini, 56, San Jose. Superintendent of schools, East Side Union High School District, with 1,475 employees, 21,500 students, and an annual budget of $45 million.

Glenn George, 48, San Jose. Chairman of the board of Joseph George Distributor, the largest liquor wholesaler in Santa Clara County, with 310 employees and $60 million in sales.

Janet Gray Hayes, 53, San Jose. Mayor of San Jose.

Ronald R. James, 51, San Jose. President and chief executive officer of the San Jose Chamber of Commerce with 2,150 members and a $1.2 million budget; former mayor of San Jose.

Larry Jinks, 50, Los Gatos.* At the time of the survey vice-president and editor of the *San Jose Mercury News*, two of three daily newspapers in Santa Clara County, with 240 editorial employees.

Norman Y. Mineta, 47, Washington. Democratic congressman, deputy whip at large of the House of Representatives, and a member of its Budget and Public Works committees; former mayor of San Jose.

David Packard, 66, Los Altos Hills.* Chairman of the board of the Hewlett-Packard Company, with $1.4 billion in sales and 41,000 employees worldwide. Also founder of the Santa Clara County Manufacturing Group and his own $17-million family foundation.

P. Anthony Ridder, 38, Saratoga.* President and publisher of the *San Jose Mercury News* with 1,400 employees, $88-million gross income in 1978—one of the most profitable newspapers in the United States.

Albert J. Ruffo, 71, San Jose. Former mayor of San Jose; at the time of the survey president of the Ruffo, Ferrari & McNeil law firm, specializing in corporation, tax, and real estate law with sixteen associate attorneys.

*These are wealthy, residential towns near San Jose.

A quick glance at the list of the top ten and at Table 5.1 leads to some interesting conclusions. Although San Jose often is touted as the

Table 5.1
SECONDARY TIERS OF THE SAN JOSE POWER PYRAMID[1]

Tier 2	Tier 3
James A. Alloway, city manager of San Jose	Sigmund E. Beritzhoff, banker
Alfred E. Alquist, Democratic state senator	Sanford A. Berliner, attorney
Frank S. Bernard, chairman, Bernard Food Industries, Inc.	Maxwell H. Bloom, stock broker
James F. Boccardo, attorney and chairman of Community Bank of San Jose	Terry Christensen, university professor[2]
Charles W. Davidson, civil engineer	J. Philip DiNapoli, attorney, banker, and packing-company executive
Rod Diridon, Santa Clara County supervisor	Don Goldeen, retail merchant
Don Edwards, Democratic U.S. congressman	Robert M. Hosfeldt, cable-television executive
Philip L. Hammer, attorney and chairman of San Jose Unified School Board	Mort Levine, retired newspaper publisher
Dan McCorquodale, Santa Clara County supervisor	Arthur K. Lund, attorney
James P. Miscoll, regional vice-president, Bank of America	Tom McEnery, San Jose city councilman
Leo W. Ruth, architectural engineer	James P. McLoughlin, labor leader
Clifford W. Swenson, president, Swenson construction company	McKenzie Moss, banker
	Larry Pegram, San Jose city councilman
	Conrad Rushing, superior court judge
	Jerry Smith, state senator
	Jose Villa, community program director
	Susanne Wilson, county supervisor
	Lewis N. Wolff, developer

[1]Government offices or private positions listed here were current at the time of the study; some have changed since then.

[2]Terry Christensen is in fact one of the authors of this book. He played no role in the *Mercury News* power structure study except for providing some background on San Jose politics and, before the study was begun, helping the researcher decide whether San Jose could and should be studied separate from Santa Clara County. He was named to the top forty primarily because he has been a leader in several successful political campaigns, including the charter-amendment drive that brought district elections to the city in November 1978—a few months before the power study was begun. He also is known as a member of the Central Labor Council and one of its political advisers; he is a leader in the Campus Community Association, a neighborhood group of downtown residents, and an unofficial leader in the San Jose Chapter of Campaign for Economic Democracy, the organization founded by Tom Hayden and Jane Fonda. We provide this detail because we recognize that some readers will suspect collusion where none exists.

"feminist capital of the nation" because it was the first major city to elect a woman mayor and because of the number of women in important government, legal, and educational posts, only two women were named in the top forty power structure of the city. And while Mexican-Americans were estimated to constitute nearly one-fourth of the population, only one Chicano was considered a serious power broker. In terms of the make-up of the top ten, only two held elective office. For the entire top forty, there were eleven elected officials, yet the majority, 23, were businessmen and professionals; three held appointed office, two were grassroots organizers, and one was a labor leader.

The low number of elected officials in the top ten came as no surprise to many of the influentials themselves, some of whom held politicians in contempt even while they bankrolled their campaigns and whispered advice in their ears. "The politicians are there to interpret what the community wants," said one businessman, who like others interviewed in the study agreed to offer his candid views only if promised confidentiality. "They're overrated in their ability to deliver," said another. "The city council has always been weak," said still another. "A couple of years ago you had nobody on the council who employed more than two people. The intelligent, successful people don't run for office. They're reduced to manipulating these people who have not been outside successes in other fields—housewives who get the political bug, for instance."

Perhaps one civic leader put it most succinctly when she said, "Mayors may come and mayors may go, but you're still going to have Al Ruffo and Tony Ridder exercising power and holding prestige in the community."

Even the officeholders themselves admitted that San Jose depends heavily on the private sector for leadership in public affairs. Said one elected leader: "A politician isn't going to get out there unless he's got the support. No one's going to get out there on a [controversial issue like] Spartan Stadium or a Center for the Performing Arts unless he knows he's got people behind him."

Nor was there satisfaction with the level of leadership from the business and professional ranks. "One of our biggest concerns is the transitory nature of the leaders of the top industries," said one long-time San Jose businessman. "In many instances, the corporations have to go to their home offices to carry through on major projects."

"The trouble with San Jose," said another businessman, "is that it isn't locally owned." Companies like General Electric, IBM, Pacific Telephone, FMC, and Bank of America—all with large facilities in San Jose that one might expect to wield considerable, long-lasting influence—were not represented in the city's top tier of leadership.

As noted in Chapter 3, the Bank of America's James Miscoll was viewed as a transient executive with limited local power. Despite his efforts to convince San Jose businessmen that he should be viewed as a bona fide local leader, Miscoll was perceived (correctly, as it turned out) as a man on the move upward and onward in the bank, and consequently, San Jose's leaders did not place him in the top tier of power. "He's a very intelligent, experienced guy," said one leading lawyer. "But he may be here and gone tomorrow. It happens to guys in those positions. He'll get promoted somewhere else and he won't be here long enough to be effective."

Miscoll himself found the appraisal disturbing. "The notion that I'd rather be in New York is a misconception," he said for the record. "I'm always amazed by that. I enjoy San Jose and I've poured my heart and soul into San Jose."

The reason for his concern: The Bank of America expects its executives to become involved. To be named in the top leadership of a community is a feather in one's corporate cap. Yet to be regarded as a nomad indicates to higher-ups that the executive in question lacks the ability to penetrate the highest local social, economic, and political circles.

Apparently, Miscoll passed muster with the bank. About a year after the *Mercury News* study, Miscoll was named executive vice-president of the bank's Asia Division, headquartered in Tokyo. He soon moved onward and upward, just as respondents had predicted.

A number of leaders felt that any occupant of the city-manager position had to be considered among the ten most powerful persons in the community. "The city manager has overwhelmingly superior control of information," said one. "He can define the questions to be asked, the opinions to be considered, and the development of information. And power is the ability to control and package information, to define the questions, the problems, the options, and the opportunities."

Virtually every respondent interviewed agreed that if Ted Tedesco still had been city manager, he would have been named in the top ten. Many would have put him first on the list. Tedesco's replacement, Jim Alloway, had been on the job just a few months when the *Mercury News* study was done. Businessmen, developers, and other civic leaders had not yet had time to judge how Alloway would handle the power inherent in his office. Their consensus was that although the position held great potential power, it did not necessarily assure the incumbent would be a mover and shaker.

"Alloway's going to be different from Tedesco," said one respondent. "He's less assertive." Said another, "The position isn't necessarily going to be that powerful unless the person who occupies it lives up to it."

"I don't think [Alloway] has had a chance to earn his spurs yet," said one top ten businessman. "I don't think he could lead anybody anywhere yet. If somebody said Jim Alloway thinks we ought to do this, 99 percent of the guys on this list would say, 'So what?' "

The cautious appraisal of the city manager by others in the community later proved to have been prophetic. In his first year, Alloway, who had pledged himself to act as the city council's supplicant, failed to earn the respect and confidence of the 4,000-person bureaucracy at City Hall. He also failed to establish the confidence of the city council, hiding information from them on significant issues, only to have the matters exposed in the newspaper, and displaying a lack of managerial sense that eventually cost him his job.

Nor were any residential developers named to the top ten—a finding that at first seemed bewildering, given San Jose's struggle during the past two decades over issues of growth and the consistent success with which builders have been able to expand the city's boundaries and population. "There are too many of them and their banner was really carried by the city government and the newspaper," one leader explained. "There's not one dominant builder and some of them are national corporations with local divisions."

The developers did have one leading candidate for the top ten— Charles W. Davidson, an Oklahoma-born civil engineer with close ties to Mayor Hayes and an uncanny ability to feed the city council just enough facts to make his proposals palatable. But other influentials saw his power as narrowly focused in land-use issues—matters of great concern in San Jose but not so crucial as to rate Davidson at the top; they placed Davidson in the second tier. "I see him strictly as a zoning and land-use guy," a business leader commented. "He's had plenty of political ability but I don't see him on the side of the community. Even his concept of land use and zoning pretty well focuses on his own interests as opposed to the broad community interests." Said another, "I've never been involved with him in any of the community crusades. He does have political influence, but I don't put him in the category of anyone who can be motivated for any other reason than making a buck."

Pro-development interests were well-represented in the top ten, but not directly by builders. Rather, people like Burke, George, James, and Ruffo were named. These were leaders who had encouraged growth and supported the politicians who had voted for expansion but who had been active on other major community issues too. Water and sewer-bond drives, downtown redevelopment, United Way campaigns, the symphony and art museum, various economic initiatives—such widespread concerns made them prime candidates for the power elite. Still, of San Jose's top forty leaders, four were professional developers, three were attorneys for builders, and three others were heavily invested in real estate and development projects.

At the same time, six people with roots in the controlled-growth movement of the past decade also were named to the top forty. In addition, Mayor Hayes had a national reputation as an advocate of managed growth. And while the *San Jose Mercury News* of the past had been a fervent cheerleader for progrowth interests, the *Mercury News* of 1979, run by top-ten members Ridder and Jinks, advocated caution and some controls on the pace at which the region was expanding.

As San Jose and the "Silicon Valley" have matured, the dynamics of growth versus controlled-growth have become more subtle. Those advocating rationally planned residential and industrial development are no longer on the fringes of local politics, no longer the outsiders beating on the doors behind which decision-makers cast the die. It has become necessary to manage growth in order to preserve the environmental attributes and economic base which originally made the area attractive to high-technology industries. Too much growth too fast has taxed the ability of citizens to pay for streets, parks, libraries, and sewers. Too much industrial development without adequate provisions for affordable housing in the northern part of the county already has begun to make hiring difficult in the electronics industry. Too much residential development without concurrent industrial expansion in the southern parts of the county has overburdened neighborhoods and created massive transportation problems.

In San Jose, managed growth has in fact become synonymous with corporate responsibility. As David Packard, the county's wealthiest and, according to some, most powerful businessman, explained, "San Jose and the South Bay have one overriding problem—how to manage growth in this area to provide an attractive environment for people to live in and an attractive environment for business and industry."

THE INTERLOCKING WEB

While membership in the Sainte Claire Club no longer is the standard by which social, political, and economic status are measured in San Jose, memberships—in clubs, on corporate boards, and on boards of civic organizations—still serve as measures of acceptance by the economic and social elite. In addition, the interlocking memberships of individuals who direct or belong to common institutions place them at the heart of a network that embraces San Jose's most influential institutions.

Table 5.2
INTERLOCKING CLUB MEMBERSHIP MATRIX FOR SAN JOSE, 1979

"Top 40" Influentials Belonging	Sainte Claire	S. J. Country Club	La Rinconada	Rotary	University Club
Beritzhoff	X			X	
Bloom		X		X	X
Boccardo		X		X	
Burke	X		X		
DiNapoli		X	X	X	X
Diridon		X			
Fiscalini		X			
George				X	
Goldeen	X			X	X
Hosfeldt				X	
James		X	X		
Jinks	X				
Lund	X				X
Mineta			X		
Miscoll			X		
Moss					
Packard	X	X			
Ridder	X	X	X	X	
Ruffo					X
Ruth		X			X
Swenson	X				

Club Membership

San Jose never had a social register. It was, like many newer Sunbelt cities, more informal and less structured in its social existence than the cities of the Northeast and Midwest. More than ever before, today it has become possible for newcomers, rebels, and outsiders to exert influence in the city. In 1979, only seven of the forty most influential people in San Jose belonged to the Sainte Claire Club, which cost $2,000 to join, $50-a-year dues, plus a $25-a-month luncheon minimum. A few others had quit, and at least one declined an offer to join. Still, the seven influentials who were members represented a notable portion of the elite business corps of San Jose. (See Table 5.2.) More popular and less exclusive was the San Jose Country Club, considered San Jose's "best" country club although it was basically just a golf and swimming facility. In 1979 it cost $7,500 to join, plus $90 monthly dues and a quarterly minimum for food and beverages. None of the top forty were members. More expensive still ($18,000 to join, plus $97 monthly and a food minimum) but easier to get into was La Rinconada Country Club in Los Gatos. At least six power survey influentials were members.

In most large cities, the Rotary Club is merely a hangout for middle-level managers. In smaller cities, however, it still can be an important business institution. In San Jose, only recently transformed from a farm town, Rotary, the oldest and best-established businessmen's service group, still was a significant organization. Luncheons often provided serious discussion of major city issues, and many of the city's top businessmen marked them sacrosanct on their appointment calendars. Members in 1979 included eleven of the top forty. Another luncheon gathering place was the University Club. Count seven more elites there in 1979. Neither club permitted women members.

Institution Membership

In most major cities there are a number of large banks, industries, and institutions that exchange directors routinely, forming a corporate network of considerable influence. In San Jose, there are few locally based, publicly held corporations at all. Bank of the West was one in 1979 (it was later bought out by a huge French bank), and San Jose Water Works was another old-line local firm with several of the top movers and shakers among their boards. (See Table 5.3.)

In the absence of powerful local corporations, civic organizations have become the loci of institutional clout. United Way, the favored

Table 5.3
INTERLOCKING MAJOR INSTITUTIONS MATRIX FOR SAN JOSE, 1979

"Top 40" Influentials Belonging	Bank of the West	San Jose Water Works	United Way	Advisory Board, San Jose State University	Advisory Board, San Jose State Business School	San Jose State Spartan Foundation	Spartan Stadium Expansion	University of Santa Clara	San Jose Chamber of Commerce	Chamber of Commerce Advisory Board	Metropolitan Associates Trust Fund	Santa Clara Manufacturing Group	Plaza Bank of Commerce	Hospital Boards
Beritzhoft							X			X				X
Bernard								X					X	
Bloom													X	
Burke	X	X	X	X			X			X		X	X	
DiNapoli			X		X									
Diridon														
Edwards								X						X
Fiscalini		X	X											
George			X		X	X	X	X		X				
Goldeen			X		X					X	X			
Hosfeldt				X		X	X		X					
James				X	X	X	X		X		X			
Lund								X			X			
Miscoll	X		X	X					X			X		
Moss	X								X			X		
Packard			X	X		X	X			X		X		
Ridder			X	X		X	X		X	X		X		
Ruffo								X	X	X				X
Ruth										X	X			
Swenson													X	
Wolff														

philanthropy of the power elite, included on its local board six individuals from San Jose's power structure.

The advisory board of San Jose State University was another meeting ground for the elite. Although Gail Fullerton, president of the university, was not among the city's top leaders, she had on her board six of the most powerful forty. Four more were on the San Jose State Business School Advisory Board. The university's Spartan Foundation booster club included five top leaders, and the campaign to expand the university's Spartan Stadium had involved eight in prominent roles in addition to David Packard, who loaned the drive $750,000 interest free.

The University of Santa Clara's Board of Regents, its graduate school of business advisory board, and its law school board of visitors drew on six members of the top forty.

The San Jose Chamber of Commerce was another common ground for several members of the power structure. James was president, and his board included Hosfeldt, Miscoll, Moss, and Ruth. Many other members of the top forty had in the past served as Chamber directors, and some, like Ridder, had been chairmen. In addition, five of the top forty were on the Chamber's thirteen-member advisory board. Also attached to the Chamber was the Metropolitan Associates Trust Fund, a $1.5-million slush fund for downtown improvement, chaired in 1979 by Goldeen, and including two other influentials on the board.

The Santa Clara County Manufacturing Group, formed in 1978 and representing the largest industrial and financial firms in the area, had grown increasingly influential. The group was established by board member David Packard, and with him on the board sat four more from our list. Another new power bloc formed in 1978, the Plaza Bank of Commerce. Among the founding fathers of the bank were four of the elite, including one developer who built Park Center Plaza, from which Plaza Bank leased its offices.

Hospital boards are another place where the influential are called to serve and guide. And in 1979 a number of the city's most influential citizens and their companies supplied the funding that sustained many of San Jose's civic and philanthropic activities as well. Although too numerous to detail here, one popular endeavor that serves as an example was the San Jose Symphony, which was based in the Center for the Performing Arts, the previously mentioned pet project of the economic, social, and political elite. In 1979, Ridder's *Mercury News* gave more than $10,000, the David and Lucile Packard Foundation gave $5,000, and Miscoll's Bank of America, Packard's Hewlett-Packard Corporation, Ruffo's law firm, and others each gave at least $1,000. Many other names from the top forty can also be found on the symphony's donor list.

Law offices, naturally, were important centers of elite membership. In the decades preceding World War II and for a time afterward, the law office that represented the Southern Pacific Railroad had the most political "juice" in the area, reputedly able to handpick judges. In 1979, the law firm with the strongest state-capital connections was Berliner, Cohen & Biagini (Berliner being among the top leaders). Berliner's partner had been special counsel to California's Governor Edmund G. Brown, Jr., from 1977 to 1978.

ACCESS AND INFLUENCE

Power and influence sometimes may be measured by *who* has access to *whom*. This is one of those subtle indicators of power that often escapes the study of community power. But it is important, because those with access can determine both how issues are framed before they are presented to the public and even which issues arise.

In San Jose, having the ear of the city manager, the city's most powerful bureaucrat, has long been a distinct form of influence. At the same time, a city manager can strengthen his or her own power base by maintaining access to key business leaders, financial officers, and professionals.

We saw in chapter 4 how, during the boom years of the 1950s, a collection of high-powered businessmen formed the Book of the Month Club, an unofficial kitchen cabinet that wrote the public agenda and pushed the passage of bond issues needed to finance capital improvements and make even more growth possible. But since the passing of the Book of the Month Club in the 1960s and the rise of the slow-growth movement in the 1970s, San Jose's business elite has had no such organization. This has been so partly because it didn't need one—the capital improvements were in place and City Hall was being run by people whom the businessmen could trust—and partly because the business elite itself was being transformed by economic changes.

Still, in the late 1970s, City Manager Ted Tedesco, who had staked a considerable portion of his reputation on his intention to revitalize downtown San Jose and to run City Hall with businesslike efficiency, understood the advantages inherent in having a steady alliance with the business elite. And the leading businessmen themselves, some of whom operated home-owned firms with deep interests in governmental policy, and others whose absentee corporations had intermittent but significant needs from city government, also understood the value of regular meetings with the top municipal officer.

In 1978, Tedesco and his close friend Halsey Burke put together a series of meetings that suggested the revival of the business-government

nexus that in many cities is routine. Had Tedesco not become the casu-
alty of a political coup by precisely the business interests he did *not*
include in this new alliance, he might have succeeded in creating the sort
of progress committee commonly found in Frostbelt cities in which permanent, semi-public groups of business elites often are thoroughly inte-
grated into key government activities. But even in the eleven months
that Tedesco's effort survived, the group considered some of the most
important issues facing the city.

"The purpose was for us to be able to relate some of our concerns to
him and to have him express his concerns," Burke explained during
the power study. They talked about redevelopment, a downtown hotel,
airport expansion, transportation, land use, housing, city spending,
and district elections. The settings were lunch at the Mediterranean
Room of the Hyatt Hotel or the board room of the city's largest construction company. And while they never actively conspired to keep
them secret, the meetings were unknown to members of the city council, including the mayor, nor did many others outside of the highest
levels of business know of them. The *San Jose Mercury News* publisher
attended the meetings and his editor, Larry Jinks, who knew of them,
never passed the word to his newsroom.

It is not possible to document every discussion the group held. And
after Tedesco was fired during the brief pro-growth power grab by the
city council's "Gang of Four," he threw away or shredded all of his
correspondence and memoranda from the meetings, although much of
it was on official city stationery. Meeting members maintained in interviews that no covert deals were struck away from the public eye.

Mercury News editor Jinks later explained that what he learned then
and afterward "led me to believe that fundamental community policy
was not being made at those meetings. I was satisfied that nothing
nefarious was going on. If you acknowledge that there are times when
the city manager has the right to meet with business leaders, it's hard to
know where to draw the line." Jinks said it was his assumption, based
on what he had been told by publisher Tony Ridder, "that they were
private meetings in which only one paid city official was present. We
[the newspaper] had no legal right to be there. I assume he [Ridder]
told me to keep me informed and not as a tip."

Perhaps no major decisions were made at the meetings. And as Jinks
pointed out, "there was nobody there who had a vote on anything." But
the meetings provided local business leaders the kind of regularly
scheduled government access that few citizens enjoy. As one of those
who attended explained, "What he [Tedesco] was really doing was giving the business and industrial community a chance to express their
views on the overall development of the city."

Members of the group included *half* of those who turned up among the ten most powerful persons in the city in the *Mercury News* power-structure study (Burke, George, James, Ridder, and Ruffo). Five others were among the top forty. The former city manager recalled: "It was a group of guys who have always been interested in the community, who said, 'I wonder if we can have Tedesco come in and tell us what's going on so we can get another perspective.' "

Some saw it differently. "It was almost back to the Book of the Month Club with all these guys sitting around talking about the city," said one of those who attended. "When [Tedesco] was working on the hotel project he asked them to talk with various members of the council about the merits of the project," recalled another. "Or he'd ask us to contact our state representatives when it came to a state problem like a highway or an off-ramp for downtown."

Tedesco briefed the group on political divisions within the city council and on the growing power of the pro-development faction. He kept them up to date on expansion of the San Jose Municipal Airport, and asked for their help in lobbying members of the adjacent Santa Clara City Council when it looked like they were about to permit houses to be built under the airport's take-off pattern. He asked them to see if Congressman Norm Mineta or Assemblyman Al Alquist could help the city obtain a freeway off-ramp for downtown. He asked their advice on whether the city should invest millions in low-sodium or high-sodium street lights. He detailed city plans for a downtown-hotel project and asked the businessmen to lobby the city council in support of it. (Attorney Al Ruffo, who represented the hotel developer, attended the meetings.) They talked about transportation, land use, and city spending.

One of the topics that came up was district elections. On April 14, 1978, the day after the city council received a report from the Charter Review Committee recommending that council members should be elected by geographic districts rather than at large, Tedesco sent a letter to his luncheon partners, urging them to speak out on the issue at a May 16 council meeting. The text read:

As a matter of interest, my personal view is that the establishment of districts would not be beneficial for our community. During 1974, I was chairman of a national committee, composed of academicians, public officials and others, dealing with a study of the role and organization of local government. This study encompassed over 2,000 communities. The conclusion reached during that analysis persuaded me that the establishment of districts or wards has been detrimental to the community, and, in fact, has resulted in bringing about less responsive government and more fractionization within the community. At the public hearing on May 16, I intend to present some of these views in the strongest context possible.

Notwithstanding my opinion on this matter, however, I believe it would be most important for community leaders to be aware of these developments and to participate in public dialogue and decisions on them.

This was, in effect, a call to arms, for Tedesco knew quite well that the business elite he was addressing were less than enthusiastic about changing the status quo. Corporate interests provided the bulk of campaign contributions needed to run $100,000 council campaigns in at-large elections, giving them more influence, and it seemed to him unlikely they would willingly surrender such leverage.

But Tedesco, who had recognized the shift in the distribution of power from the development-oriented homebuilding interests to the corporate and professional elite and had so artfully pulled the ascendant powers together in his luncheon group, overestimated the fervor with which these same men would oppose structural changes in the city government. Except for James and Ruffo, the former mayors who themselves had benefited from the at-large system, there was little interest in the group in challenging the grassroots forces that were pushing for district elections. Most members, if not all, of Tedesco's luncheon group, individually were opposed to districts. But the issue was not sufficiently antithetical to their interests to cause them to organize against the charter amendment.

The district elections discussions did have some impact, however. What one luncheon partner called the "march on the *Mercury News*" took place in November 1978 involving a group of business leaders. In part, the meeting with the publisher, editor, and editorial page editor was to complain about an "anti-business" bias that these businessmen believed was prevalent in the newspaper. It was also a lobbying session, designed to encourage the paper to editorially oppose district elections.

The meeting, which took place in the *Mercury News* board room, included Hosfeldt, James, Miscoll, Ruffo, Ruth, and Swenson from the top forty along with seven other businessmen representing construction companies and real estate and insurance firms—and it was something of a moment of truth for Ridder. Since he had become publisher and Jinks had come in as editor, they had tried to make clear to the business establishment that no longer could they count on the paper to report only the version of events that corresponded to the needs of business. Now, however, some of the most powerful businessmen in town were telling Ridder that the paper had gone too far and had turned its back on business and industry.

"Tony [Ridder] listened to the criticism," recalled one of the businessmen who was there. "But he was very strong on his reporters' ability to cover the story as they saw it." In short, publisher Ridder informed his peers that he would not, as his uncle had done, order reporters and editors to slant coverage of the news. He was, in effect, taking away from the business elite a tool that had been theirs for decades. This was not because his economic and class interests were in any way separable from those of the men who were complaining to him. Instead, it was his own reputation as a publisher and his status within the Knight-Ridder newspaper chain, the parent corporation of the *Mercury News,* that demanded he rule the paper in the enlightened style of modern journalism.

Newspaper ethics did not, however, demand neutrality from the publisher with regard to the opinions expressed on the editorial page and, at Ridder's urging, the *Mercury News* eventually did oppose district elections. Because of a sharp split among the newspaper's editorial board, however, the editorial itself was a mild rebuff of the charter amendment, not the kind of choleric, rancorous battle charge that characterized the paper in the "good old days."

Why was it so important to San Jose's businessmen to attempt to alter the newspaper's new direction? Because in San Jose, the newspaper seemed to wield inordinate influence. Tony Ridder, the publisher, was what sociologist Floyd Hunter calls a "star isolate"—a center of power that shines far brighter than all others. He could not necessarily win every issue or give orders to anyone all the time, but because he ran the newspaper, he was considered singularly influential in the community.

The business community's need to influence the newspaper was also a function of history and of the monopoly position the newspaper enjoyed in the San Jose area. That is, it was a reflection of the *lack* of power centers elsewhere in the city capable of standing up to or overcoming the *Mercury News* on a consistent basis. Weak political parties and nonpartisan elections, branch office business and industry, and the absence of competing media outlets all combined to lend greater power to the *Mercury News.*

LEADERS RANK THEIR PEERS

So far in this book we have approached the subject of understanding and investigating community power from two fairly distinct angles. We have explored the theories that have abounded about what power is, how one gets it, and how powerful individuals in a community affect both each other and those who, more like the rest of us, must do their best to wield their own marginal influence. As a tool to study power structures in specific communities, we looked in detail at the reputational method. At the same time, first interspersed in the chapters on power study theory and practice, and later concentrated in chapter 4's historical background, we have followed the growth and development of power in an actual city of the Sunbelt—San Jose, the principal case study for this book's approach to power studies.

Now comes the time to draw together these two divergent themes. Returning to the reputational method, we'll find out in detail how our case study city responds to the survey questions and back-up interviews our method employs. After a brief overview of power in San Jose, based on the *Mercury News* study of 1979 using the reputational technique, we'll go beyond foundations into intimate portraits of the powerful in that community. We could instead have delved into the movements and institutions that have risen and fallen in our case-study community. But the most fascinating details are revealed through the people who commanded those institutions and led those movements. What follows shortly is a detailed look at each of the ten people who made up the top tier of power in San Jose in 1979, including how they got their power and how they used it.

Overview of Findings

During the power structure study, most of San Jose leaders maintained that there was no formal or informal power bloc that acted in concert to shape public policy, determine the course of civic projects, or in any other way rule the city. Yet they recognized that certain individuals and their institutions exerted far greater influence and wielded more extensive power than others. As part of the study, leaders were asked a series of questions designed to provide greater clarity about the extent and dimensions of power for which certain persons had reputations. These were detailed in chapter 3.

One question the study posed is particularly effective at pinpointing the consensus among leaders about the most powerful in their circle. Respondents were asked, "If a project were before the community that required decision by a group of leaders, which four could put it over?" The answer from 32 of the top 40 leaders interviewed: Halsey Burke, David Packard, Tony Ridder, and Al Ruffo. These four men, it was felt, could encompass such a broad network of contacts and support that if they were to work in concert, they could virtually assure the success of any project they chose. Interestingly, Burke, Packard, and Ridder had become leading voices in the Santa Clara County Manufacturing Group, which had itself grown into one of the most powerful forces in San Jose. And Packard, Ridder, and Ruffo all had been instrumental in expansion of the Spartan Stadium, a project near and dear to the hearts of the local elite.

The leaders also were asked to name "the four persons most effective at initiating projects." They were Burke, Frank Fiscalini, Ron James, Norman Mineta, Ridder, and Leo Ruth (there was a three-way tie). Ruth, who was not a member of the top ten, had been one of the city's most effective organizers of fund-raising events for the cancer society, Alexian Brothers Hospital, Serra Club, and a number of other civic projects. He also had been one of the key leaders in the drive to build the Center for the Performing Arts.

The "four persons most effective at stopping projects" were Mayor Janet Gray Hayes, James, Ridder, and Ruffo. Mayor Hayes received low marks from other leaders as a political coalition builder, yet most felt that because of her position, she could, if she wanted, make it extremely difficult for a project to go forward.

There was no consensus on San Jose's "most underrated leader." Burke and Christensen received an equal number of votes—more than others but not enough to award them the title.

Mayor Hayes received the title of "most overrated leader." Typical comments included these: "I don't think she understands how to use her power." "Her public relations skills exceed her leadership ability." "You'd think people would jump when she calls but they don't."

There also was no consensus on San Jose's "most trusted leader." Ruffo received the most votes but not nearly a plurality and U.S. Representative Don Edwards and Fiscalini each received just one vote fewer than the former mayor.

The consensus on the "least trusted leader," however, was quite profound. Rod Diridon, a county supervisor, was chosen. Typical comments included these: "You shouldn't wear your ambition on your sleeve. Raw ambition, constantly exposed, scares people." "He's only interested in Rod Diridon and furthering himself." "He represents all the elements of political cant and blind ambition." To Diridon's dismay, these comments were picked up in the spring of 1980 and used against him when he ran for an open seat in the State Senate, losing nearly 3 to 1 to an extreme, right-wing conservative.

In response to the questions, "Who has the most power?," "Who exercises the most power?," and "Who is the most influential person in San Jose?," publisher Tony Ridder was the clear choice. Not only did Ridder command the greatest resources, but he used those resources to an extent that made him a greater influence than any other individual in San Jose, according to the leaders themselves. Ridder also was named San Jose's "top leader," although the margin was slight.

This, then, was the overview of power in San Jose found by the

Mercury News study in 1979. Now let's take an in-depth look at the top ten persons identified in the power study. In doing so we'll discover the wealth of solid, useful information a properly administered reputational survey can dig up on power in any urban community. Our starting point, because of its extraordinary role in San Jose, is the *Mercury News* itself and the two men who ran it.

POWER OF THE PRESS:
P. Anthony Ridder

"San Jose used to be run by Dutch Hamann [the former city manager] walking through the doors of Joe Ridder's office," said one leading politician, reflecting on the way things were during the 1950s and 1960s. A 1971 study of Bay Area media made the following observations about the paper under the elder Ridder's control:

> The mere mention of the *Mercury* and *News* to other Bay Area publishers is enough to set dollar signs dancing. The morning *Mercury* and the afternoon *News* (plus the combined Sunday *Mercury News*) are the most profitable papers in the Bay Area and among the biggest moneymakers in the country. . . . There is by the way an editorial side to this commercial operation, and that is where the problems are found. . . . The refusal of the *Mercury News* management to permit any real investigation into local business or politics is only one of the reasons for superficial local coverage. . . . It is currently the voice of the retailers and the industrial establishment.[1]

This harsh assessment was not entirely fair to the reporters and editors who were forbidden to write or publish articles that ran counter to the aims of the paper's executives and their political and business cronies. "The lid was on all the time," one long-time *Mercury News* staff member recalled. Said another: "We were the boosters. Anything attached to scandal or wrongdoing in government that would embarrass the city manager was almost impossible to get in."

In his book *Reporting: An Inside View*, Lou Cannon, who later became West Coast bureau chief for the *Washington Post*, tells the story of how he and *Mercury News* political writer Harry Farrell once uncovered evidence that a state legislator had been involved in a scandal but because the politician was a Republican, the article was never allowed to run.[2] Farrell is fond of describing how he once was assigned to write articles specifically intended to keep a meat-packing plant—labeled a "slaughterhouse"—from locating in San Jose (on a site upwind of the newspaper's plant).

Vehement editorials and slanted news stories promoted everything from sewer bonds and water projects to the community theater and new housing tracts. Freeways, particularly a section of Highway 101 which the paper wanted built to bypass a dangerous area referred to in print as "Blood Alley," were also favorite causes. This, of course, not only reflected the desire to expand the size and therefore the markets of the city, but also the paper's own need to move delivery trucks more quickly about the expansive area.

"Joe [Ridder] never made any bones about it," one old-timer fondly recalled. "He believed that what was good for San Jose was good for the paper and that what was good for the paper was good for San Jose." Said another, "Joe Ridder would get immersed in a community project if he was sold on it. He'd call people, he'd give a dinner, he'd put the full force of his influence plus very positive editorial comment into it."

This was not an unusual course for publishers of the 1950s and 1960s. Similar patterns occurred throughout the country, from cities as large as Philadelphia and Los Angeles to the smallest hamlets. Joe Ridder, like others of his era, believed that it was a newspaper's duty—its obligation—to promote what it believed was right for the city and the region. These were the actions of a man dedicated to San Jose—albeit his own vision of it.

In 1974, a corporate merger occurred which was to change the role of the newspaper in San Jose. Knight Newspapers Inc., a highly respected newspaper chain (including the *Miami Herald*, the *Philadelphia Inquirer*, the *Charlotte Observer*, and the *Detroit Free Press*), merged with Ridder Publications Inc., the parent company of the *Mercury News* and a number of other undistinguished newspapers. The marriage of unequal partners—each share of Ridder stock was worth about a half-share of Knight stock—created the nation's largest newspaper group, measured by the number of papers published each week (by 1980 it owned thirty-two newspapers outright and half-interests in two others).

Controlling interest in the new company—Knight-Ridder Newspapers, Inc.—was held by John S. and James L. Knight. Their 30-percent stock ownership dominated the Ridder-family holdings of slightly less than 15 percent. So, with the Knight-Ridder merger, management of the *Mercury News* became the concern of corporate officials in Miami, where the firm was headquartered. Joe Ridder, who had voted against the merger, continued as publisher for a few more years. But in 1977, the top executives of Knight-Ridder Newspapers named Tony Ridder, Joe's nephew, publisher, and eased Joe into the titular position of president. Two years later, stripped of responsibility and authority, Joe Ridder retired.

This was a drastic change in the structure of power in San Jose, wrought by corporate executives in Miami. Tony Ridder, then just 37 years old, suddenly took command of 1,400 employees who wrote, produced, sold, and circulated more than 225,000 newspapers a day to most of the homes in the county. But Tony Ridder was no stranger to leaders of business and industry in San Jose. In fact, he had been one of their number for some time already. Coming to the *Mercury News* in 1964, he started in the circulation department. He began rising through the ranks in 1969 when he was named business manager, and by 1975 he was general manager.

In short order, he joined the right clubs. (See Table 5.2.) He was the Jaycees' Outstanding Young Man of the Year in 1970 and was elected to the board of the Association of Metropolitan San Jose (the forerunner of the Chamber of Commerce) that same year. He became a member of the San Jose Civic Improvement Association, treasurer of the Spartan Foundation at San Jose State University, a member of the San Jose City Sports Commission, a trustee of Good Samaritan Hospital, and a founder of the Intergovernmental Council of Santa Clara County.

Uncharacteristic of the later Tony Ridder, his most visible personal crusade, in the tradition of his uncle Joe, were the drives in 1972 and 1973 to gain county funding for the abortive sports arena. Although he had been instrumental in other important issues—notably the building of the Center for the Performing Arts and the expansion of Spartan Stadium—the campaigns for the sports arena displayed some of the most overt boosterism in the history of the *Mercury News*. Even though as general manager he had no day-to-day responsibility for news and editorials, his enthusiasm for the stadium was injected directly into the paper through newsroom executives who answered to his uncle Joe.

The 1972 ballot measure was advisory only, authorizing no money, no specific plan, and no location for the arena. There was little opposition and none that received coverage in the newspaper. In November, county voters approved the concept of an arena by a vote of 256,189 to 180,282. The next effort, much more difficult, was the selling of a bond measure to *pay* for a sports arena. To this, there was considerable opposition, especially from minorities who argued that county funds should be spent on increased services to the poor rather than a sports palace, but again none of those arguments was given serious display in the newspaper.

For two months before the 1973 bond election on the $26-million arena, the *Mercury* and *News* ran a stream of articles boosting the facility, coupled with proarena editorials. For six days prior to the vote, both papers ran photographs of "Yes on Arena" bumper stickers as part of a contest offering an all-expense-paid trip to Hawaii to readers who could identify the car in the photos. Reporters' stories often bypassed normal newsroom channels, were read and altered by editorial executives, and run in the paper without a reporter's by-line.

But Tony Ridder's enthusiasm wasn't enough. County voters turned down the sports arena measure by a whopping plurality. Years later, Ridder said he had learned from the experience that it was improper for the newspaper's business executives to use the paper for their own ends. After Tony Ridder became publisher, the newspaper ceased to boost an arena in its news columns. Nor could the business and industrial elite depend on the *Mercury News* to smother opposition to their initiatives by keeping news out of the paper— though, as we discussed earlier in this chapter, they certainly wanted to. "He certainly doesn't support the business establishment like the newspaper has in the past," said one businessman. The newspapers seemed to want to "exploit the negative and not accentuate the positive," added a leading lawyer.

The first indicator that Ridder would actively go against the old game plan occurred in September 1977, in an editorial headlined "More Orderly

Growth," which came out in favor of ending continued urbanization of the agricultural areas of the south county. It wasn't long before editorials were knocking the Chamber of Commerce, various pro-growth plans, and other former sacred cows. As one politician observed, "When Tony allowed the paper to attack the Chamber of Commerce they were crushed. They had a loss of power." Articles discussed minority dissatisfaction with United Way, gave both sides on land-use issues, detailed troubles at City Hall, examined growth-induced transportation and housing problems, and investigated politicians and businessmen. At the same time, lavish displays on society dinners and elite club news were being squeezed out of the paper. In 1978, the paper endorsed a Democratic candidate for governor (Jerry Brown) for the first time in its history and editorially opposed shifting the balance of power on the city council back to the pro-development forces. Mayor Janet Gray Hayes was endorsed for re-election; her challenger, Al Garza, was properly labeled as the pro-growth candidate; district elections proponents received as much attention as opponents; and the concerns of the poor and minorities began to receive more sensitive, balanced coverage.

These kinds of stances and articles are routine on large metropolitan daily newspapers. In San Jose, they were revolutionary. To the old guard, loss of the dependable *Mercury News* was a loss of power.

But Ridder was resolved that the paper would not be used as a mouthpiece for civic projects. That stance irked his peers in the power structure and brought Ridder more than a little criticism. Ironically, it in no way reduced his power or that of the newspaper. In fact, some leaders believed, it enhanced the paper's influence because its news columns and editorials were increasingly credible. "I think Tony's a lot more powerful than he realizes," said one of the top forty. "He's a very modest guy," said another. "If you told him he's got the city at his feet he'd say, 'Oh bull.' "

"I don't try to exercise power," Ridder said. "I want our editorial pages to be respected, but I don't want to exercise any power that I have other than to publish an excellent newspaper." This was a man very different from his predecessor at the reins of the newspaper. So different, in fact, that many business leaders in San Jose who were allied with Joe Ridder in the 1950s and 1960s suspected that the *Mercury News* was "run by Miami." They simply could not believe that one of their own would fail to use such a powerful tool to its fullest advantage if he really were calling the shots.

Miami is not only the home of Knight-Ridder Newspapers, Inc., it also is where Larry Jinks, editor of the *Mercury News* at the time of our study, spent nearly seventeen years on the *Miami Herald*, six of those as top executive in the newsroom. Even before his promotion in 1977, Tony Ridder had arranged to bring Jinks from Miami to reshape the *Mercury News*. Ridder and Jinks described the change as a matter of mutual respect and common commitment to a massive challenge—transforming a strident and undistinguished newspaper into a thoughtful and respected one. But from the outside, especially to some of the old-guard businessmen and professionals in San Jose, it looked as if Knight-Ridder had taken the *Mercury News* away from the Ridders and installed their own man. As one politician saw it, "I don't think he [Ridder] is the dominant personality over there. I think Jinks is running the show, or maybe Tony lets himself be run by Jinks."

Ridder, however, insisted that, "I'm the chief executive officer of the newspaper, and I'm ultimately responsible for what happens. But there isn't a good editor in the country who would work where the publisher was constantly directing the day-to-day operation." Enough community leaders recognized that fact to consider Ridder the most influential person in San Jose. And accepting that Jinks did in fact determine what went in the news columns, they ranked the editor as well among the ten most influential individuals in the city.

The influence of the newspaper in promoting growth, pushing bond issues, campaigning for local charities, redevelopment, community projects, or conservative politicians and policies, and the use of news columns to define issues and prevent others from arising, still was fresh in the minds of many San Jose leaders. Some, generally more liberal, anti-growth leaders, were grateful for the changes Ridder and Jinks had brought about. "The paper is incredibly better. It has a more responsible approach to reporting," said one. "[Ridder] is dedicated to the community," said another. "He could sit on the hill and watch the cash register work but he doesn't do that. He uses his power judiciously—with reserve, with class, and with style."

But some of the old guard found the changes abhorrent—Joe Ridder himself was said to feel that Tony was allowing the paper to deteriorate—and others were simply dismayed. "He's not aware of his impact. It's almost as if he has a fear of the power," said one businessman. "Tony, having been raised with a silver spoon in his mouth, doesn't really understand power and how to use it," said another. "He runs around with his little group of contemporaries and everybody lionizes him. But Tony doesn't have any burning desire to get out there and rectify the problems we have in our society."

"I think for a publisher to do a good job he can't remain completely neutral," said one contemporary. "Some of the business leaders are mad at the paper. The paper actually generated the growth around here and in that sense the paper has an obligation to the city. It's incumbent on the paper to promote things that are in the public interest."

Tony's uncle Joe used to give money generously to community projects and campaigns. It was, however, usually *Mercury News* money given in the name of Joseph B. Ridder. Tony, on the other hand, ended the practice of newspaper contributions to anything other than purely philanthropic causes such as United Way or the symphony. In the political arena this change was important: the newspaper, which reports on political campaigns, no longer could be touted as a financial backer of a candidate or cause. Tony Ridder continued the family tradition as munificent benefactor, but in a new, more honest approach.

"When Tony picks up the phone, the guy at the other end is going to be listening unless he's a damn fool," said one businessman. When the mayor wanted help on a downtown cultural project, she sought Ridder's aid. When expansion of Spartan Stadium ran into financial difficulties, Ridder was among the group that tackled the problem. Politicians, city staff members, and developers have routinely sought Ridder to plead their cause, hoping for his support. Often the visits have preceded public debate, an attempt to avoid taking a public position and find later that Ridder and the newspaper are against them.

Ridder was unaffected by those who complained, as one businessman did, that the paper had lost its community touch, or for others whose enmity he had stirred. "We've grown up," he said. "In small communities people can get in the paper whatever they want and the newspapers don't make a judgment on whether something's newsworthy or not. They're used to a small town operation here."

A PUBLISHER'S EDITOR:
Larry Jinks

When the *Mercury News* set out to study power in San Jose, Larry Jinks expected his boss, Tony Ridder, to appear in the top level of the power structure. But he didn't suspect that he would be named there too. This was not something a modern, professional journalist covets. He wants to be influential through his work, of course, but he does not want to be considered one of the primary molders and shapers of events in the community. He's supposed to be an observer, not a participant. In most large cities, the editor of the newspaper probably would not be ranked alongside the publisher as one of the ten most powerful people. But, as we have said, San Jose is a *new* large city, like many in the Sunbelt. Its old guard is on the wane, new corporate forces have developed, and the power of public opinion has intensified: all this in a city with a tradition of a newspaper accustomed to throwing its weight around.

"San Jose has always been somewhat provincial," observed one leading businessman. "There was a group who used to run things. It's not an isolated city like it used to be and the new leadership hasn't coalesced yet." The reaction among San Jose's leaders to the arrival of Jinks underscored that assessment. Some felt he had done wonders for the paper. Others said he was running it into the ground. Not only did Jinks represent Miami, "silly" environmentalism, and "fuzzy" liberalism, he had these pesky notions about fair play, objectivity, and thorough reporting as well. Those who had lunched at the Sainte Claire Club with *Mercury News* executive editor Paul Conroy, Joe Ridder's editorial hit man, were uncomfortable with Jinks. He had the gall to decline an invitation to join that club. He didn't play serious golf. And worst of all, he wouldn't order his reporters to shape their stories to fit certain preconceived notions about reality.

Said one politician: "He's too concerned with sensationalism. He'll smear inconsequential items across the front pages as if they were major news stories. He's turning the paper into something like the *National Enquirer*. He tends to be overcritical of government at all levels." The offended respondent was taking exception to articles that exposed illegal land dealings by a mayor of a nearby city ("they blew that all out of proportion") and others that detailed charges that a health service operator was running a scam ("they smeared her").

Others found such stories just what the doctor ordered for San Jose. "The changes in the editorial policy of the *Mercury* have been dramatic," said one lawyer. "They're getting into issues they never got into before. There's more fact-finding, which is more influential than saying we're with this group and everybody else can go to hell."

If Jinks's efforts were hotly debated among San Jose leaders, they were welcomed by critics of journalism. William Rivers, who had written so unflatteringly about the *Mercury News* in that aforementioned 1971 study of Bay Area media, called the paper the "second best newspaper published in California" (behind the *Los Angeles Times*), and Ben Bagdikian, a Berkeley journalism professor and former national editor of the *Washington Post*, observed that "for the first time in my acquaintance with it, [the *Mercury News*] is performing serious and enterprising journalism."

This was little comfort to some of the city's business elite. They were not interested in the views of college professors and press critics. "You should do more showing the positive things about a community than you do digging up garbage," was one prescription. "A lot of people are displeased with some of the negative articles about business and especially the residential-building industry," said another. "They [the papers] portray them [developers] as the profit-hungry builders who cut down the orchards."

Some said the paper was "timid" for failing to campaign against district elections. Others were angry that United Way wasn't getting sufficient play or that the Chamber of Commerce wasn't getting adequate support. Yet these criticisms in no way contradicted the notion that Jinks was in a position of great influence and that he clearly understood the power at his disposal. As one businessman observed, "What Larry perceives as important problems, the newspaper treats as important problems." This was indeed great power. As Todd Gitlin observed in *The Whole World Is Watching*, "Media are mobile spotlights, not passive mirrors of the society; selectivity is the instrument of their action."[3] Even while Jinks refused to interfere in his reporters' stories, his conceptions of what was significant, his commitment to examine community issues seriously, his beliefs in balanced reporting and the kinds of editors and writers he was hiring and turning loose, were dramatically affecting the role of the newspaper in San Jose.

It was Jinks and his editors and political reporters who resolved that the 1978 take-over of the city council by the pro-development "Gang of Four" and their firing of controlled-growth City Manager Ted Tedesco were worthy of massive, definitive coverage. This was unlike anything that had been seen in San Jose journalism in the past. And the impact was devastating. David Runyon, one of the four, buckled in the glare of the mobile spotlight. Shortly after firing Tedesco, Runyon was arrested in a curbside brawl with police, the second in a year, and charged with public drunkenness. He soon resigned. Al Garza, whose role as a leader of the four-man majority had been detailed in the paper, was buried in the November election by Mayor Hayes, losing more than 4,000 votes he had won during the primary in June. Joe Colla, a third member, also lost in November to Hayes's ally, Jerry Estruth. "The paper did it," said one influential lawyer, shaking his head in dismay. "It was the paper that beat Al Garza and Joe Colla."

Although it occurred more than a year after the *Mercury News* study of power in San Jose, one other example of the paper's impact stands clear. After months of simmering dissent by his staff, continuing displays of mismanagement and lack of leadership, City Manager Jim Alloway was in trouble. Under fire from two city councilmen already, he hung on with the backing of Mayor Hayes and five others who had hired him after Tedesco's demise. His troubles were detailed in news stories but little changed. But when the *Mercury News*, on Easter Sunday in 1980, called for Alloway's resignation, the council's backing began to erode. Suddenly it was legitimate for members of the council who had hired Alloway to think of asking him to go. It was clear that the newspaper would support them, or at least would not attack them. Within a month, Alloway, whose backing had withered to, at best, Mayor Hayes and two others, resigned his position.

"The politicians are all scared of the *Mercury*," said one elected official. "They're tremendously worried how the *Mercury's* going to look at something." In a transitory era when old centers of power—the Book of the Month Club, the Chamber of Commerce, and others—were on the wane or had seen their influence gradually diminished, and when new sources of influence such as the Santa Clara County Manufacturing Group, which represented the high-technology industries, still were establishing their power base, the ability of the *Mercury News* and its publisher and editor to frame public discussion of major issues lent them inordinate power.

About a year after the *Mercury News* study, Jinks, who had consistently asserted that he had no ambitions of leaving San Jose, was made an offer he could not refuse by the corporate management of Knight-Ridder Newspapers. He became vice-president for news for the corporation, returning to Miami. His replacement was Robert D. Ingle, former managing editor of the *Miami Herald*.

MAYORS MAY COME AND MAYORS MAY GO (BUT THE POWER OF THE OFFICE REMAINS):
Janet Gray Hayes

A month after taking office in 1975 as San Jose's first woman mayor, Janet Gray Hayes proposed that the city should study how many illegal aliens were living in San Jose. Large numbers of illegals, she said, could drain city services, aggravate unemployment, and lead to substandard wages. She was promptly denounced by the American Civil Liberties Union and La Confederacion de la Raza Unida. One Chicano leader called her a "panicked racist."

The mayor's reply? "Sticks and stones may break my bones." She later apologized for the juvenile remark and, despite a 7 to 0 vote by the city council supporting the proposal, announced that plans for the illegal-alien tally would be dropped. It was an inauspicious christening for a new mayor who had narrowly defeated her opponent on her pledge to "make San Jose better before we make it bigger."

Some of San Jose's most influential leaders believed in 1979 that Hayes had come a long way since then. "She's enormously more mature," said one lawyer. "She's learning to lead," added a businessman. "She won a tough campaign [against Councilman Al Garza in 1978]. She displayed some debating skills. She's deeply dedicated."

Others weren't convinced. "She's just inept," said an influential lawyer. "She's a nice charming housewife. She ought to go back to being one. She's not a leader qualified to head a major city." Snapped one politician, "She's just an opportunist who's simply there by persistence in the women's movement. She has a superficial knowledge of what she's doing and not an original idea in her head."

Despite such acrid criticism, Hayes, who (with the aid of out-of-town media) built something of a national reputation as a woman mayor, was rated one of San Jose's ten most powerful people in the 1979 study. She also was named the city's "most overrated leader"—a dubious distinction that, she said, didn't bother her, but which, according to her confidants, she found deeply disturbing.

It was her position as mayor, not her personal abilities, wealth, or political acumen, that led others to place her at the top rank of power. *Anyone* in the office, most leaders said, would have to be considered a center of influence in San Jose, even though the position is largely ceremonial.

Hayes and her husband Kenneth, a physician, moved to San Jose in 1956. She worked for a while as a volunteer at the Adult and Child Guidance Clinic and became involved in various conservation, parks, neighborhood, housing, and arts projects. She began in the PTA, moved into the League of Women Voters (eventually becoming president for the entire San Francisco Bay Area), was vice-president of her neighborhood association, a member of various council-appointed citizen committees, and, in 1966, was named to the Redevelopment Agency, the independent body charged with revitalizing downtown San Jose in the wake of its collapse in the 1950s. As an agency member, she was a participant in the drives to obtain funding for the Center for the Performing Arts. Other activities included managing a 1968 city-housing referendum, chairing a city-goals committee, participation in a county open-space committee, and other environmental causes.

In 1971 she ran for city council, easily winning in a large field of candidates. In 1974, when Mayor Norman Mineta stepped aside to run for Congress, Hayes went after the city's top elected post. Drawing on her ties with schools, environmentalists, women's organizations, and neighborhood groups, she managed to narrowly defeat former police detective Bart Collins.

During her first term, she advocated safety improvements for the "Blood Alley" portion of Highway 101, completion of Guadalupe Freeway, controlling city spending, encouraging industrial development, and keeping expansion of residential tracts within existing city boundaries. Exactly how much impact she had on these issues was anything but clear. Except for her voice as the city's spokesperson, she had no greater real power under San Jose's weak-mayor form of government than any other council member. She did not want credit for the fact that in the decade of the 1970s, San Jose was the nation's fastest growing major city. Nor did she want blame for the city's failure to develop a downtown convention hotel, "affordable" housing, or inner-city business. She was happy to note, on the other hand, that various studies had deemed San Jose one of the most livable cities in the country, that it was a leader in industrial growth, and that since 1976, population growth had slackened somewhat. She claimed as accomplishments the passage, in 1975, of the city's first controlled-growth general plan, obtaining federal funds for the Highway 101 bypass, cutting property taxes by $5 million before Proposition 13, securing $3 million in grants for neighborhood health centers, and pushing for federal regulations that made the city eligible for redevelopment funding in "pockets of poverty."

On the other hand, several of the policies she personally recommended—strengthening the powers of the mayor, state legislation to redistribute sales taxes, strengthening the city auditor's office, and greater ties between City Hall and the neighborhoods—were never adopted. In the meantime, she was responsible for the city's hiring of City Manager James Alloway in 1979, and it was not until she had seen him humiliated by his own staff and other council members that she reluctantly agreed that he should step down. And despite her own reputation for honesty, she had the misfortune of presiding over city government during a period when one councilman was indicted for bribery, improprieties were alleged against staff members, and the public's confidence in local government plummetted.

Yet as mayor, she was the leading political figurehead in the city, and other leaders respected that fact—as long as she was in office. While many said she was less effective at leading the council and the community than her predecessor, Norman Mineta, they nevertheless agreed that her office itself was powerful. "She was no greater power in City Hall than any other person down there," said one leading lawyer. "If she said, 'Let's get this together,' maybe she could and maybe she couldn't." Said another: "She'll make you think she can accomplish anything. But she isn't actually the one who says, 'Here's what we're going to do.' She appears to exercise power. Anyone in that position would appear to, I don't care who it is. It could be an idiot."

Others gave her greater credit. They recognized that Hayes presided over the city at a time of great upheaval in the balance of power; her own survival in office was made possible by the shift away from the stranglehold the developers and construction industry once held on City Hall. "She's been able to slow down land use," said one lawyer. "And every person affected by that decision has called her a numbskull and a nitwit." Or as another leader observed, "She embodies the appropriate symbolic leadership of the new San Jose. She's populist-based. She came out of the League of Women Voters and the school system. She governs by her perceived honesty and goodwill rather than by her power."

True as that may have been, Hayes was by no means an anti-establishment political figure. In her 1978 primary and general-election campaigns, she received ten times the contributions from San Jose's power structure than did her opponent, Al Garza. Seven of the elite either loaned or directly contributed to her campaign amounts ranging up to $3,000. And hefty contributions came from about a dozen others.

Her political confidants included Charles W. Davidson, a developer, and Philip and Susan Hammer, presidents of the local bar association and the art museum respectively. (When Vice-mayor Jim Self resigned from the council in July 1980 and a caretaker member was needed whom the mayor could trust, Susan Hammer was chosen to fill out Self's term. No other candidates were interviewed by the council, so sure was the appointment.)

Hayes also was instrumental in appointing Iola Williams (at the urging of Davidson), the city's first black council member. And she was a key factor in selecting Tom McEnery, a young downtown businessman, in 1978 to fill the seat that David Runyon left when he resigned in the wake of the Tedesco firing. She also helped stockbroker Jerry Estruth in his city council campaign against her arch nemesis Councilman Joe Colla in 1978. When she was sworn in for her second term in January 1979, she was expected to head a firm coalition of slow-growth advocates, holding at her command five of seven council votes. Although she never managed to provide clear leadership to that majority, the basic philosophy she embodied seemed to prevail. In 1979, only two significant general-plan changes were approved—one for an IBM research facility on 500 acres in the pristine Santa Teresa foothills, and another for a condominium project south of the city's service area in the Almaden Valley. The developer of that project, coincidentally, was Charles W. Davidson, Hayes's associate.

Although Hayes represented the city in Washington at the United States Conference of Mayors or the National League of Cities, she had a difficult time at home maintaining the respect she wanted. "The mayor really ought not have very much trouble getting things going in this community," said one elected official. "If she understood power, leverage, manipulation, she'd have a lot of things happening." Said one businessman: "You'd think people would jump when she calls them, but they don't. She should have more clout than she does."

Most of all, she was a survivor in a town that was traditionally ruled by men with close ties to business, industry, and development. She was successful at turning up on the right side of issues at the right time, seldom being called to task when she changed her stance to meet current political demands. A 1976 delegate to the Democratic National Convention, she was pledged to Gov. Edmund G. Brown, Jr., but when Jimmy Carter won the nomination, she suddenly became one of his faithful. The rewards were personal rather than municipal—Rosalynn Carter spoke at Hayes's 1977 campaign fund-raiser, and Hayes was later named to the Department of Housing and Urban Development's mayors task force on housing. She argued for increased taxes on new buildings to pay for new streets in 1976, but she fought *against* using the same taxes in 1978, when her political foes wanted them for more new city streets. Then, in 1980, she argued once again *for* using the taxes to finance sewer-line reconstruction. She opposed Proposition 13, the state's tax-cutting measure at the same time she ran on a platform calling for reductions in city spending, and, as we have noted above, she portrayed herself as the foremost spokeswoman against urban sprawl while drawing huge campaign contributions from leaders in the development industry and occasionally voting in favor of development proposals that the most control-minded planners had opposed. Perhaps, as some suggested, a candidate stronger than Garza would have been able to unseat Hayes in 1978. But none tried. In the end, other leaders concluded, looking at the mayor's 72-point electoral victory, "You cannot ignore that many votes for whatever reason she got them."

THE LAND-USE PATRIARCH:
Albert J. Ruffo

The year was 1944. The city's most influential businessmen wanted roads, sewers, water, and power that would bring San Jose into the twentieth century. They formed the Progress Committee, pledged, as former-mayor George Starbird recalled, "to build something they all wanted, a new metropolis, in the place of sleepy San Jose." One of their soldiers was a young attorney and former football coach at the University of Santa Clara, the Jesuit school where many of the local elite were groomed. His name was Albert J. Ruffo—a good Italian boy on the make, but not so much as to seem unctuous. A little rough on the edges—he had played guard at SCU—and he was a Democrat, but most of all he was a team player.

In his six years on the new council, including a two-year stretch as mayor, Ruffo helped develop the city's airport, hire a new city manager (A. P. "Dutch" Hamann), widen streets, move City Hall, extend sewer lines, kill rent control, quash public housing, attract new industry, institute a sales tax, and begin the annexation battles that would spread San Jose across the map like a Rorschach pattern. Beginning then, and continuing into the 1980s as head of one of the city's most influential law firms, Al Ruffo's career was testimony itself to how well he could sell the logic of development to city council after city council. From the extension of sewers on First Street to serve General Electric Co. in the mid-1940s, to the rezoning for the first commercial development near IBM's huge facility in South San Jose in the mid-1950s, to the voracious swallowing of orchards for housing tracts in the 1960s and 1970s, Ruffo's finesse had played a crucial role.

Vallco Fashion Plaza and the PruneYard, Eastridge, and Santa Teresa shopping centers, each of which drove another nail into the coffin of downtown San Jose's retail business, were just a few of the commercial developments in which he played a major role. Spartan Stadium, the Center for the Performing Arts, San Jose Municipal Golf Course, San Jose State University, and the University of Santa Clara were among the many projects and institutions he boosted and steered.

"More than any other single person he has enjoyed a major piece of the action over a long period of time," said one San Jose leader. In fact, for more than a quarter of a century, Ruffo had been a player in nearly every major project in the city of San Jose. He lost his share of battles before the city council and the planning commission. But during his reign as the patriarch of the land-use attorneys, the king of zoning, Al Ruffo won many more times than not. He was identified, alongside Hamann and a handful of others, with the rapid-growth ethic that created modern San Jose. And despite his age—he was born July 1, 1908—he continued to represent clients before the city council, sometimes waiting hours for his turn at the microphone, just as he had done for nearly thirty years. He received $5,000 to $10,000 per appearance in 1979, but there were many senior attorneys who would not have played supplicant to the city council for ten times that amount. Said one political activist: "He doesn't perceive himself as an elite. He'll still go down to the council and argue for his projects, and he'll sit on the Charter Review Committee, and he works hard at it. I have a lot of respect for his relatively democratic approach to power."

Some said he was over the hill—especially in light of changes on the city council that have made nonconforming development proposals much more difficult to sell. "He's a bit on the wane but he's still extremely powerful. And tactfully so. He knows just how hard to push and when not to push. He never makes threats. He just asks you to respond to his logic. But the old logic of development isn't as accepted as it used to be." Still, Ruffo popped up in connection with many of the most significant projects the city considered in the late 1970s. At the time of the power structure study, he was the attorney for Corwin Booth, a San Francisco developer who had contracted with the Redevelopment Agency to build a 500-room hotel in downtown San Jose. The contract not only was overly generous to Booth, but because of a clause Ruffo had worked in, made it possible for Booth to delay construction as long as interest rates were above ten percent. Rates never dropped even near that level, and finally, in 1980, after several years of negotiation and procrastination, Ruffo and the city dissolved the contract, with considerable benefits ceded to Booth, including rights to build two office buildings on part of the land on which he had done nothing.

"Ruffo is personally and single-handedly responsible for delaying the downtown by pushing that [the original] contract down Ted Tedesco's throat," said one businessman. "Corwin Booth's got a contract with the city that stinks," said another. "I'm disappointed Al would be a party to that." Mayor Janet Gray Hayes even admitted that because of Ruffo's long history as a leading citizen—a sort of a city father—she naively trusted that he would not help Booth obtain a contract that would hurt the city.

Nor was this the only instance in which Ruffo's own interests conflicted with what some considered best for the city. Ruffo's son-in-law and legal partner, Thomas P. O'Donnel, was attorney for the Civic Improvement Association, the group that built the Center for the Performing Arts and on which Ruffo served. And his son John, an architect, was consultant for the expansion of Spartan Stadium, another project in which Ruffo had been instrumental. Such nepotism, other leaders said, was unseemly at best.

It was not as if Ruffo, his family, or his law firm were desperate for work. Ruffo's legal firm represented some of the largest landowners, developers, and businesses in the Santa Clara Valley, specializing in land use, zoning, and environmental control litigation.

Ruffo's social and service-organization connections were many. A former part-owner of the San Francisco Forty-Niners, he was a member of the numerous hospital, foundation, university, and club boards. (See Tables 5.2 and 5.3.) He was a former regent of the University of Santa Clara, former governor of the State Bar of California, and past president of the San Jose Civic Club. Although never invited to join the Sainte Claire Club (he was too rough-cut, too Italian Catholic for the WASPs), he was a member of the San Jose Country Club and the University Club.

His connections extended throughout government. Two of his former junior associates became state legislators—Assemblyman John Vasconcellos and State Senator Jerry Smith, later named state-appeals court judge—and another junior partner was one of the brightest stars in the Mexican-American political movement. Through a university booster group, the "Bronco Bench," Ruffo retained close ties with the old guard at City Hall, especially in public works, where an old-boy network had held—key posts in the city administration for three decades. "He represents the person who has best made the transition from the old San Jose to the new San Jose—from the predominance of the University of Santa Clara and the agricultural bunch who pretty much ran things in government," to today, said one lawyer.

MONEY (AND AN INTERNATIONAL REPUTATION) TALKS, AND SAN JOSE LISTENS:
David Packard

Best known for his Washington years as President Nixon's deputy secretary of defense and his national and international connections, industrialist David Packard has always been keenly aware of his interests on the regional and local level as well. As we saw in chapter 4, he was the seminal force behind the formation of the Santa Clara County Manufacturing Group. Packard, chairman of Hewlett-Packard, located about twenty miles north of San Jose in Palo Alto, got the ball rolling by calling upon his friend Robert C. Wilson, then-chairman of Memorex which was located next door to San Jose in Santa Clara, to help him bring together the county's largest manufacturing and banking firms into an umbrella association that would become the voice for industry in Silicon Valley.

We've already glimpsed Packard's impatience with the somewhat provincial San Jose Chamber of Commerce. Packard and other big corporate leaders in the valley wanted an organization that could wield a bigger stick, that wasn't tied to city funding, and that would involve top-level executives in analyzing social and political problems that affected business.

In short order, the Manufacturing Group was formed, and business analyst Peter B. Giles was hired to serve as executive director. By 1980, the group represented 65 member companies with more than 160,000 employees. With its chairman as the president of Lockheed Missiles, the county's largest employer, and its principal officers composed of a host of names familiar from our power study—Packard himself, Halsey Burke, and McKenzie Moss, among others—the organization had obvious clout. Other companies whose top executives eagerly joined included General Electric, Syntex, Owens Corning Fiberglas, IBM, GTE Sylvania, Bank of America, Ford Aerospace, Varian Associates, American Microsystems, National Semiconductor, and the *San Jose Mercury News.*

The group, which meets regularly with city and county executives, has taught both San Jose and Santa Clara County governments how to cut costs. It also quickly became involved in a number of issues, including transportation, housing, employment, and taxation; it has published and circulated reports to key decision makers throughout the county, and has lobbied in Sacramento for specific legislation affecting the region's industries. Within a year of its formation, the Manufacturing Group had, according to most leaders interviewed in San Jose, outstripped the San Jose Chamber of Commerce as a power center and promised to become the single most important source of influence in the county in the coming decade.

And Packard created it almost as an afterthought to long years of activity, first in his business but later in state and national politics. In 1979, Packard's company employed about 42,000 worldwide and had sales of $1.7 billion. He personally was worth about $700 million (most of that in Hewlett-Packard stock), and his family philanthropy, the David and Lucile Packard Foundation, was worth another $18.4 million. One of the wealthiest men in America, and one of the world's most powerful businessmen, it was no wonder that when Hewlett-Packard talked, everybody in Santa Clara County listened.

It was 1961 when Packard resolved that, henceforth, Hewlett-Packard would locate any new facilities outside of Palo Alto in other Santa Clara County cities; he wanted both to preserve the residential character of Palo Alto that made employment there so attractive and to encourage wider distribution of industry throughout the county. Nearly twenty years later Santa Clara would discover what became known as the "jobs-housing imbalance," characterized by too great a concentration of industry in the county's north, especially in Palo Alto, and too much of the housing in the south, especially in San Jose. Packard had foreseen it, warned against it, and relocated his company's new plants to the south in hopes of avoiding the crisis. But the inevitable occurred. Creation of the Manufacturing Group sixteen years later was an attempt, in the face of growing public hostility against industrial development, to keep the crisis from undermining the economic base Packard had helped to build and to assure industry a voice in finding solutions to the problems that it had created itself.

"He doesn't do much down here [in San Jose], but he can win almost any issue he chooses," said one civic leader in San Jose. "He's big time and people are impressed with him. He can have enormous influence over whether this valley continues to develop and where it develops." Said another: "The influence of his company extends throughout the county. He's the leading industrialist, and he has a deep dedication to improving the county." Even those who belittled Packard's influence in San Jose, since he spent little time there and cared less about city politics, had to admit his decisions had impact. For example, when his company chose to put a $17-million plant on a 100-acre site in North San Jose and hire 630 employees to run it, Packard, through his corporation, was clearly exercising impact on the city that few locals could equal. And the plant was just the first phase of a long-range building program.

Others noted that despite all the years of wrangling and haggling over expansion of San Jose State's Spartan Stadium, when push came to shove in the summer of 1978 and $1.5 million was needed to underwrite construction costs, it was Packard who came to the rescue with a $750,000 interest-free loan. Sure, County Supervisor Rod Diridon and Mayor Janet Gray Hayes made the pitch. So did Tony Ridder and Al Ruffo. But it was Packard who came up with the cash, making the expansion program possible.

"He bailed out Spartan Stadium," said one opponent of the expansion. "If his money and influence hadn't been there it would have collapsed." Others, however, were less impressed. "He's going to get paid back for that money," said one businessman. "When you're worth $700 million, that's not much."

Packard, a long-time Republican, maintained cordial if not close relations with several of the county's Democratic but nonpartisan officeholders. Mayor Hayes, one leader said, "invited [Packard] into the San Jose power structure" shortly after she was elected mayor of San Jose in 1974. Hayes drove up to Palo Alto for a two hour audience with Packard and [William] Hewlett at their corporate headquarters. She wanted advice on running the city's bureaucratic machinery and thought their corporate experience might help. They told her to trust her chief operating officer (the city manager) and to let him run the city. They also told her they thought the Chamber of Commerce ought not to be funded by the city but should stand on its own. "Packard," said one leader, "is an advisor to Janet Gray, but he doesn't push his views on her. But if he said, 'I'll build a plant in San Jose if you build [a] light rail [transport system],' he'd get it." Another remembered that when the city and the Chamber of Commerce were having trouble selling tickets for a nationally advertised banquet to honor recipients of the Congressional Medal of Honor in 1977, a call went out to Packard, chairman of the Bay Area Host Committee. "All of a sudden guys who'd said they couldn't come were buying two, three, and four tables for hundreds of dollars."

In San Jose, where major projects are few and far between, displays of influence add up over time. And Packard has been building that perception about himself for more than 30 years. Back in their Stanford days, he and Hewlett started their partnership with a $538 investment in a Palo Alto garage; today, Hewlett-Packard is one of the world's leading manufacturers of electronic, biomedical, analytical, and computing equipment. Many consider its products the top-of-the-line in their fields.

Packard was the political activist. Hewlett, though he gave liberally to philanthropic projects, was personally more interested in running the business. It was Packard who hankered for social and political involvement. His first venture began with a term on the Palo Alto Board of Education from 1948 to 1956. He served on the university board from 1954 to 1969, including two years as president. He also became a member of the advisory board of the Hoover Institution, Stanford's right-wing think tank, and a director of Stanford Research Institute, which until 1970 was an official arm of the university, performing research for corporations and governments throughout the world.

In 1969, Packard was named deputy secretary of defense, but not until after a series of congressional hearings which investigated the propriety of hiring the chairman of a firm doing $94 million in defense work, and after he agreed to place his millions of Hewlett-Packard stock in a blind trust. He ran the Pentagon's day-to-day operations for Melvin Laird until 1971, returning to private life and distributing to charities the $21.6 million his stocks had earned while he worked for Uncle Sam. He then served as Bay Area chairman of the Nixon re-election effort and was later picked by Nixon to be the Secretary of Defense. But noting that he would have to take huge financial losses, Packard turned the job down.

As an illustration of interlocking directorships, Packard's high-powered board memberships are instructive. Before joining government in 1969, Packard had been on the boards of United States Steel, Crocker National Bank, General Dynamics, Pacific Gas and Electric, and Equitable Life Insurance. He quit them when he joined the defense department, but in 1972 he took seats on the boards of Standard Oil of California, Caterpillar Tractor, and Boeing. From these companies and Hewlett-Packard, his combined income, including stock dividends, salary, and director's fees, was about $3.5 million in 1978. In addition, he and Hewlett operated Rancho San Felipe as a private business, with cattle on 25,000 acres in Santa Clara County, another 25,000 in California's Central Valley, and 12,000 in Idaho.

In addition to Packard's corporate-boardroom connections, he was a member of numerous highly influential international and national commissions. His power link-ups through several very exclusive Northern California social clubs were also significant. The list below briefly outlines some of Packard's affiliations in 1979 with elite power groups outside the immediate region of Santa Clara:

Trilateral Commission, member
Business Roundtable, member
U.S.-U.S.S.R. Trade and Economic Council, member
Advertising Council, member
Business Council, member
Woodrow Wilson International Center for Scholars, chairman, advisory committee
California Roundtable (a California business lobby with great clout), co-chairman
Pacific Union Club, member
Bohemian Club, member
San Francisco Commonwealth Club, member
Engineers Club, member

Packard also acknowledged in the survey that he was a member of San Jose's Sainte Claire Club (although he said he had only been there once).

These were the credentials of a man of power—not just in San Jose but in the United States. In Santa Clara County alone, his family foundation parceled out $491,000 in 1978—41 percent of the $1.2 million in grants the foundation made to charitable causes. San Jose grants, trifles in the scheme of the Packard foundation but huge for a town full of "cheap millionaires," included $5,000 for the symphony, $7,500 to the Women's Alliance, $3,125 to West Valley Chicano Neighborhood Enterprises, $11,380 to the San Jose State Mountain Lion Study, and $2,500 to the Youth Science Institute.

Packard himself said he thought it was an error for others to name him as one of San Jose's most influential leaders:

> They don't know any better. I've had no desire to be influential in San Jose except when I've seen an issue that has some impact on the company. I have some interest in the city and our company has a very large stake in this area right now. Our success and progress is dependent on being located in a community that's attractive for all our employees.

But as others pointed out, Packard's influence, based on his corporate standing, extended throughout the county. Because San Jose was the largest city in the county, the financial and professional center, and was becoming the geographic center as well, the decisions made by San Jose were crucial to companies like Hewlett-Packard. Therefore, if Packard were interested only in those decisions which affected his firm, he would be deeply concerned about San Jose's role in industrial development, housing, and transportation. And these were precisely the issues in which his Manufacturing Group had taken a keen interest and begun to play a major role.

"He has political influence and money. He has influence on all aspects of our lives—land use, transportation, you name it," said one leader. "He's the one who everybody checks with," said another. "The point is to get David Packard on your side and the battle is half won."

As San Jose continues its trend toward attracting electronics industries, the influence of the Manufacturing Group—what one leader called "Packard's alter ego"—and Packard's own company will continue to grow in San Jose. To most leaders in 1979, his interests were synonymous with those of the high-technology firms on which the area's economy depends, and although he neither lived nor worked in San Jose, he was indeed one of the city's most powerful figures. "He has an international reputation," one businessman observed. "There are very few national figures who could wield a lot of power here. But he's one."

MR. CHAMBER OF COMMERCE:
Ronald R. James

If creation of the Santa Clara County Manufacturing Group doubled David Packard's influence in San Jose, it equally diminished the standing of the San Jose Chamber of Commerce and, by extension, its director, Ron James. "The creation of the Manufacturing Group was a blow to his prestige," said one businessman. "That thing [the Manufacturing Group] should have been run right out of the San Jose Chamber," said another. A third businessman had this enlightening commentary:

> It's easy to sell. It's hard to close a deal. Ron's good at public relations. He's good if he's given direction. But he doesn't give much direction. We'd like to see a little more chief-executiving over there. He likes to reign but he doesn't like to rule. He's "Mr. San Jose." He's representative of that place where San Jose is right now. But his executive talent is something else.

Some said it would have been impossible for the Chamber of Commerce to prevent the rise of the Manufacturing Group—that the high-technology firms needed their own organization—or that it would have weakened the influence of San Jose companies had the chamber become controlled by electronics companies from Palo Alto, Mountain View, Sunnyvale, and Santa Clara.

And there were many in San Jose who perceived James as a major leader, albeit not in a class with some of the others. "Ron has done a fantastic job with the Chamber of Commerce," said one businessman. "They're really a lobbyist group and Ron's done that well. He's built the chamber up in terms of numbers, he's got that [new headquarters] building built, he has good people working for him. Packard was probably concerned with the growth of his company and felt he could best achieve that through a small cohesive group of large employers. He wanted a separate group that could be readily identified as a power center."

"With all due respect to David Packard," said another, "he wanted some organization in Santa Clara County that he could run, so he set up the Manufacturing Group. I don't think there was anything that James or anybody else could have done to prevent it."

So views on Ron James were divided. Being "Mr. San Jose" at a time when the city was still trying to decide if it was an overgrown farm town or a major metropolis was a double-edged sobriquet. But as chief executive officer of an organization that represented the interests of more than 2,000 businesses and businessmen on a budget of $1.2 million (half funded from the city's hotel/motel room tax), James was considered one of San Jose's most influential leaders.

Following the lead of the Manufacturing Group, the chamber had become more involved in land use, transportation, and government efficiency. It still was the chief spokesman for San Jose businessmen, particularly on issues affecting downtown San Jose where the chamber's Metropolitan Associates Trust

Fund could invest large sums on chosen projects. Besides maintaining its city subsidy, it continued to successfully lobby the council on significant issues such as expanding the sewage system. Because James was at the helm, "He is in a position to pull economic interests around issues. When he speaks, the council listens."

In early 1979, the city council showed just how well it listened. The city's general plan mandated that high-rise office buildings should be placed in the downtown area and discouraged elsewhere. At the same time, the city was desperately trying to bring a 500-room convention hotel into downtown to complement its convention center and to help revitalize the central business district. But it was presented in late 1978 with a proposal for a 500-room hotel and office complex on cheap land near the San Jose Municipal Airport. The battle lines were clearly drawn. On one side were councilmen Jim Self and Tom McEnery, downtown developer Lewis Wolff, and others, who argued that if the city wanted its policy to be effective, it would have to say "no" to the massive airport-hotel complex. Not only would giving in be regarded as a sign that the council was not seriously committed to the inner city, but chances of obtaining financing for a downtown convention hotel would be seriously undermined by the existence of another like-sized facility at the airport.

On the other side stood the development interests who didn't want to see the council telling builders where they could and could not place their projects. And leading the charge for the airport hotel was Ron James and the Chamber of Commerce. James argued that if San Jose didn't allow the project, then neighboring Santa Clara would gobble it up and the city would lose a potential economic boost (and the chamber a source of income). James produced a study citing a massive shortage of hotel rooms that even the airport project could not make up. His double-edged argument was successful, and the council voted approval. The incongruity with city policy was solved quite simply: The definition of "downtown" was altered to include the airport—several miles to the north.

James, whose great-grandfather worked the Almaden Quicksilver Mines in the 1860s and later founded the City Drayage Company, was one of a handful of San Jose leaders identified in 1979 with long-time roots in the city. Reared in San Jose and a graduate from Stanford University in 1950, he started work at the family business, then known as James Transfer & Storage. He joined the "right" organizations and clubs, attending Rotary for nine years straight without once missing a meeting, and in 1961 was named San Jose's Outstanding Young Man by the Junior Chamber of Commerce. (See Table 3.2.)

Already he had served as area chairman of the Boy Scouts, group chairman of the YMCA capital improvements drive, as a member of the Urban Renewal Committee, United Fund drives, Better Business Bureau, and the Shallenberger School PTA. A year later, he was appointed to an opening on the city's planning commission, then a rubber-stamp outfit with no general plan to guide or restrict it, and in 1964 he was elected its chairman. A few months later, the young conservative announced his intention to run for a city council seat.

His family connections and his own community involvement paid off immediately. Roger Williams of IBM served as his campaign chairman, Gordon Levy of Dean, Witter & Co. and Ernest Zumbrunner of Ernst, Ernst & Ernst signed on as financial co-chairmen. He outspent everyone else in the race with $10,345, having received major contributions from the Santa Clara County Homebuilders Committee and the ultraconservative Citizens for Responsible Government. Elected easily, he joined a council which was then the willing intermediary of the local development industry.

In 1966, on a 4 to 3 vote, James, then 38, was elected mayor by the council, a job with little authority other than chairing council meetings. Then, under provisions of a 1967 charter amendment that mandated general election of the mayor, he promptly announced he would seek to become San Jose's first popularly elected mayor. In April, with industrialist Halsey Burke and IBM's Williams raising more than $19,000 (including $5,000 from the Homebuilders Committee), James outspent Councilman Robert Welch and defeated him with 79 percent of the vote.

Upon his inauguration, James observed that despite a "tremendous wave of population which we have experienced, it is nothing to what we will experience in the future." Transportation, sewage, industrial development, and housing would be the key issues of the future, he predicted. One of his first major moves was to create a "Committee on Low-Cost Housing" to study ways of providing more homes to meet the growing demand. His administrative assistant, James O'Brien, who later became director of the Associated Building Industry trade group, was named housing coordinator. James went on to preside over four more years of growth.

Although James had a reputation as one of San Jose's upstanding bluebloods, charges surfaced in 1969 that threw a cloud over his image. Councilwoman Virginia Shaffer, a persistent thorn in the side of the old-guard business establishment, charged that in 1965, while James was chairman of the planning commission, the Transamerica Title Insurance Company bought 9,650 square feet of James-family property for $965,000 and later resold it to the city to provide parking for the Pacific Telephone headquarters office building. The city manager had issued a report to the council declaring that the James family faced a "financial hardship" because they could not develop the land which lay in the path of an unfunded expressway. Nothing ever came of the charges. No investigation was made by city or county officials, and the newspaper told of the incident almost entirely through James's denials.

During James's tenure, the rate of expansion of the local economy and increase in population slowed slightly because of regional and even worldwide pressures, and the pace of annexation cooled as well. But residential builders found James and his council eager to please. "The council will not even discuss such basic questions as whether further growth should be encouraged or discouraged," the Stanford Environmental Law Society wrote in 1970.[4]

James returned to the family business in 1971 rather than seeking a second term as mayor. A few years later, about the same time his family sold its moving and storage business, James was named president of the Chamber of Commerce, then "a hand-shaking and ribbon-cutting" group with about 900 members.

Under James's leadership, the chamber grew in size and clout. But at a time when grassroots forces throughout the city were making inroads on the city council, James was not as successful at shaping public policy as many of his peers thought he should have been. "He's not as powerful as some," said one civic leader. "A person like Tony Ridder, with one phone call, could exercise more power than Ron. But Ron can put the pieces together. He's a good 'go-for.' He was the moving force behind the Spartan Stadium, he's pushing the chamber into getting downtown in order, and he's been active in encouraging international trade."

Indeed, James retained an active hand in those government issues that affected business, as a participant in the Industry and Housing Management Task Force that outlined the need to control industrial expansion in the county, and on other committees concerned with transportation and taxation. He was a director of the California Automobile Association and San Jose Water Works (the largest locally owned utility) and a member of the San Jose Country Club, San Jose State University's advisory board, and the local YMCA board.

With the Manufacturing Group drawing the attention of San Jose's most powerful businessmen and bankers, some San Jose leaders wondered if James would continue to maintain the reputation for influence he appeared to have in 1979. "He's degenerated into a Chamber of Commerce guy who's interested only in preserving his chamber position," said one harshly critical businessman. "He's been a part of the power structure around here for a long time," said another leader. "But he doesn't strike me as a strong personality. He's not really a tough-minded man who sees what basic decisions need to be made."

To James's credit, he seemed at the time of the study to be attempting a widening of chamber horizons. He began drawing electronics firms into the Chamber of Commerce and, despite considerable objection from some board members, to involve the chamber in countywide issues. He and Manufacturing Group president Peter Giles began to meet on a regular basis, and the chamber still had the ear of politicians of all stripes. As San Jose's old guard seemed to fade and new forces appeared to take hold, James attempted to make the transition. "Under the new council and board of supervisors, I wonder how much influence he'll have," said one political insider. "I imagine that because of his position, they'll probably have to listen to him and consult him. But I just don't know."

THE CLASSIC
BEHIND-THE-SCENES
INFLUENTIAL:
Halsey C. Burke

More than any other San Jose leader, Halsey C. Burke, president of Burke Industries, represented the interconnections among major business, financial, and philanthropic interests classically associated with the power elite. Not only was he chairman of a firm that in 1978 sold $21 million in rubber products and floor coverings, he was a director of the San Jose Water Works, Bank of the West, Santa Clara County Manufacturing Group, United Way, San Jose State University, and the San Jose Chamber of Commerce Advisory Board. (See Table 5.3.)

Although he had never held elective office, he was one of San Jose's most influential citizens, wielding behind-the-scenes political clout as a donor, fund-raiser, adviser, and major figure in the Republican Party. "He's on everybody's list," said one civic leader. "He belongs to the right clubs and community boards. He gives his name. And he has influence with the establishment."

It was Burke who put together the series of luncheons throughout 1978 at which San Jose business and professional executives discussed and counseled City Manager Ted Tedesco on a variety of pressing issues. "He's a man who does things behind the scenes," said one businessman. "He spends a great deal of time contributing." Said another, "Because we're in a city where business leaders tend to be transitory, Halsey stands out."

As president of United Way in 1977 and 1978, Burke deftly handled two major crises that threatened to tear the philanthropy apart: a $1.2-million damage suit filed by a combined health agency charity charging United Way with unfair restraint of competition (by using alleged arm-twisting to steer contributions toward United Way); and an eight-month battle with Minorities for a Fair Share and the County Human Relations Commission charging dis-crimination in grant allocations and inadequate minority representation on the agency's board.

United Way won the unfair restraint suit. After Burke enlisted the county board of supervisors in negotiations, the agency signed an agreement with seventeen minority organizations that included creation of an affirmative action committee, technical assistance guarantees, an appeals process, uni-form criteria listings, a seed-money program, and other concessions. Despite the legal struggles and unfavorable publicity, United Way contributions in-creased 22.6 percent during Burke's tenure as president. "United Way was about to fall apart last year and he held it together," said a leading politician whose own governmental body would have been pressed for funds had United Way been unable to meet the needs of minority and low-income groups.

Burke also had been a major figure in the Rotary Club, which, as we've seen, continued to be a principal meeting place for San Jose businessmen. He was Ronald Reagan's county chairman in the 1970 governor's race and was co-chairman of Gerald Ford's Santa Clara County campaign in 1976. When Ford visited the city during the campaign, his tour guide came not from gov-ernment but from industry—it was Burke.

Like David Packard, Burke had extensive civic and club connections and held several simultaneous seats on various corporate boards. Where Packard was solidly linked to the national power structure through his institutional associations, Burke was just as solidly linked to the local and regional interlock-ing power network. A brief glance at some of his past affiliations makes the point clear:

San Jose Community College, member
San Jose Chamber of Commerce, president
San Francisco Bay Area Council, vice-president
Music & Fine Arts Foundation, director
Industrial Management Club, director
Retirement Jobs, Inc., director
Good Samaritan Hospital, director
American Red Cross, director
San Jose Water Works, director
Bank of the West, director
Standard Insurance Co., director
Sainte Claire Club, member
Almaden Country Club, member
St. Francis Yacht Club, member

He had been involved in virtually every major civic project in San Jose in the past quarter century, from bond issues, to the performing arts center, to the stadium expansion efforts in the 1970s. As the 1980s unfolded, he had moved into leadership of the Santa Clara County Manufacturing Group, being one of the two or three San Jose leaders whose views David Packard sought on issues.

Some leaders thought Burke had spread himself too thin. "He tends to do an adequate job on all of them rather than a super job on any one." "Halsey is a figurehead rather than an actual doer." Said one businessman, "He tends to be cheap. He could put more money back into the community than he does." Such comments, frequent as they were, did not dissuade even the speakers from considering Burke a key leader in San Jose. Some noted that former mayor Norman Mineta relied heavily on Burke for advice from the business community. Others observed that Janet Gray Hayes also sought Burke's advice consistently.

This was another anomoly of San Jose politics. Because mayoral races are nonpartisan, Burke had no problem working for and advising Democrats who held the office. Burke supported Mineta and Hayes and, according to one insider, helped "neutralize candidates against [Councilman] Al Garza" during the 1974 council campaign. But when Mineta decided in 1974 to seek a seat in Congress as a Democrat, all he got from Burke was his best wishes.

Burke, a native San Josean, was a graduate of King's Point maritime academy, and veteran of the Merchant Marines. When Tedesco was city manager, one of his favorite pastimes was sailing aboard Burke's 54-foot ketch, setting out from her berth at Bellena Bay Marina in Alameda.

INHERITED POWER AND PRESTIGE
—AND KNOWING HOW TO USE THEM:
Glenn George

Of those named to the top ranks of influence in San Jose, only Glenn George qualified as a bona fide second-generation power. Chairman of Joseph George

Distributor, the largest liquor wholesaler between San Francisco to the north and Monterey to the south, George inherited his position in the city's power structure from his father, Joe, one of the area's most active philanthropists. Yet while many sons and grandsons of former local power brokers never moved into the power elite, George, as one leader put it, "trades on his father's reputation" and, in doing so, has built his own reputation as an influential leader.

"People always seem to think you gotta get Glenn George working for you," explained one important leader. "He has a heritage," said another. "His father was a very charitable individual—maybe one of the most charitable ever here—a tough son of a bitch but very humane. Glenn has taken his place pretty well."

Joe George bought a liquor distribution business in 1940, an opportune time. Soon the region boomed. With the growth (spurred by George and the Progress Committee) came increasing demand for beer, wine, and liquor. By the time of his death in 1972, Joe George left an estate of $2.6 million.

George continued to build the business. In 1979, it had sales of more than $60 million. Like his father before him, George had served as a regent of the University of Santa Clara, president of the old Community Chest, foreman of the county Grand Jury, and had been active in the Heart Association, Rotary Club, and several other civic causes.

Glenn, like Joe, was a Republican who supported and raised money for candidates from either party in local elections. He was co-chairman of Janet Gray Hayes's 1974 campaign for mayor and was finance co-chairman for County Supervisor Rod Diridon's 1980 run at the state senate. Both were Democrats, but George backed them anyway.

More than any other local issue, George was identified with the campaign to expand San Jose State University's Spartan Stadium. Local sports boosters envisioned it as the potential location for a professional team of some sort. And George had good reason to want to expand the stadium—he was a part-owner of the San Jose Earthquakes soccer team which played its home games there. He was also a San Jose State graduate who had kept close to the school, as a member of its president's council, advisory board, and a director of its Spartan Foundation. He was chairman of the Spartan Stadium Campaign Committee, which, along with thousands of dollars in donations, had secured loan pledges of $750,000 each from the San Jose City Council and industrialist David Packard.

Expansion of the stadium required not only a good fundraiser with strong political connections; it called for a leader, backed by a group with staying power, who could overcome years of objections from neighborhood residents and others that the city should not subsidize expansion of the stadium just for the university and private sports teams. This was an issue very close to the hearts of the city's power structure. Of the city's forty most influential persons, nine were members of the campaign's executive committee, and nearly all the others supported it with their money, influence, or votes on governmental bodies.

The drive to expand the stadium—which had been going on for about a decade, juggling one potential public-financing method after another—reached a partial victory in 1979 with the pledges of support from the city and Packard. But rising costs had eaten deeply into the planned expansion budget. It was George who vowed to raise another $700,000 that would finish the job.

"Glenn is one of the first people that all the politicians turn to when they're looking for help," said one leading businessman. "He has the ability and contacts in the right circles, and he has the ability to produce money." Said another, "He's an influential guy in many ways. He's the kind of guy who can always be counted on to raise money." He led successful fundraising drives for the Red Cross and the Camp Fire Girls. He was a major figure in the wholesale-liquor business as an executive-committee member of the California Beer Wholesalers, and a director of the Northern California Liquor Dealers Association.

His business had had its troubles with state regulatory agencies. In 1974, the company was named by the Department of Alcoholic Beverage Control as one of 450 California liquor dealers charged with giving kickbacks of free goods and cash to retailers. It was a nasty slur on the reputation of a local business-man whose most cherished honor was that his father, a "booze salesman," had a school named after him in the Alum Rock School District.

George, unlike some of the city's top leaders, was actively involved in the San Jose social scene. It was not nearly so exclusive a set as one could have found in old Midwestern and Eastern cities, but for San Jose, George ran with a select crowd. His poker game—a weekly affair started in 1958 at a Rotary Club barbecue—included Max Bloom, stock broker, arts patron, and sometime adviser to Mayor Hayes, and a number of other wealthy businessmen and professionals. The group, players insisted, was just a card game, not a political caucus. But Bloom, George, and another in the group—grandson of the founder of the FMC Corp.—had been active lobbyists on behalf of several cardrooms before the city council and county supervisors. One of the principal beneficiaries of their lobbying efforts had been Nick Dalis, owner of Garden City Card Club and a major financial contributor to local political campaigns, including Mayor Hayes's, for whom both George and Bloom had worked.

A MOVER FROM CITY HALL TO CONGRESS, BUT STILL A SHAKER IN SAN JOSE:
Norman Y. Mineta

"Norm Mineta," said one leading San Jose businessman, "could quit Congress tomorrow, come back home, and he'd still be one of the most influential people in town." Not just another Democratic politician, it was not simply Mineta's position that made him—unlike so many legislators whose influence withers when they move away—one of the city's most powerful people. Rather, it was his confident (almost arrogant) style, his persistence and blunt ambition, and his vast connections. The first Japanese-American mayor of a major U.S. city, and next a rising star in Congress, many felt that it was Mineta who quietly, carefully, and without creating bitter enemies first reversed the pattern of urban sprawl that for thirty years had splattered San Jose all over the county map.

Because he had moved to Washington following his election to Congress, some San Jose leaders believed Mineta's influence in the area had waned. "He's not the person I'd go to to get something done in San Jose," said one. "He pretty much stays out of city political issues," said another. "Partly because it's not his role and partly because it's safer." Still others said he had hurt himself by developing a reputation for exploiting people to get what he wanted, discarding former allies and friends when they no longer were useful. As one political insider said, "He chews people up."

But one politician, with whom many other leaders agreed, explained Mineta this way: "He's back here a lot. He has a solid base in the community, and he's generally the most significant political figure in the valley." That Mineta was perceived this way was no accident. He spent a total of approximately eight weeks a year in the district, visiting at least every other weekend, about two or three times more than most other congressmen. Besides putting in about an hour at his insurance agency (from which he received roughly $18,000 a year "mostly for his name," as an aide explained, he primarily met with small groups, spoke at well-publicized breakfasts, luncheons, and dinners, received constituents at his district office, and held heavily attended, issue-oriented public meetings.

In short, Mineta worked hard at ensuring re-election and, at the same time, retaining an image as a major force in the community. He was especially careful to nurture his contacts with industrial, financial, and business leaders, most of whom were Republican but whose interests in Congress he faithfully represented. "He's a local boy that made good," said one politician. "He can bring influential people together. He's the top leader around here," said another.

Born in San Jose in 1931, the son of a Japanese immigrant, Mineta, his parents, and 110,000 other Japanese Americans were rounded up and sent by train to wartime detention camps in 1942. The Minetas were shipped from camp to camp, until his father landed a job at the University of Chicago. Following the war, the family returned to San Jose, where Mineta finished high school and attended the University of California at Berkeley, serving on the student council for four years. He joined the Army after graduation, became an intelligence officer in Japan and Korea, and returned to San Jose to work in his father's fledgling insurance business in 1956. In the staid and proper Japanese community, Mineta was recognized as one of the bright young men, and in 1959 he was named president of the Japanese American Citizens League.

In 1962, he was named to the city's Human Relations Commission. He was picked for the county grand jury in 1964 and in 1966 was appointed to the city's Housing Authority board. His political career well under way, he began to take a public role in February 1967, when, as chairman of the Citizens Committee for City Health Services, he led a drive to obtain a subsidy from the county Board of Supervisors for the city's health department. The proposal had been engineered by City Manager "Dutch" Hamann and although it was unsuccessful, Mineta, by leading the charge, garnered publicity and the gratitude of Hamann, then perhaps the single most influential leader in San Jose. Just a month later, Mineta was elected to the Central Committee of the County Democratic Party. The rules of the game were becoming quite clear.

Four months later, Mineta was appointed to fill a vacancy on the city council. It was the first time in the council's 117-year history that a non-Caucasian
had been chosen for a council seat. An important role he had played earlier, he
later observed, was a key element in his selection to the council: Mineta had
been the precinct chairman—the one responsible for getting out the vote—
during the 1964 bond drive to fund the community theater. While garnering a
difficult 65-percent approval vote (which fell short of the needed two-thirds),
he had time to cement close ties with influential business and civic leaders.
Later, their support was essential to his rise in politics. In 1968, the council
selected Mineta vice-mayor, and in the next year's primary election he was
elected to the council without a run-off.

When Mayor Ron James retired in 1971, few were surprised that Mineta
entered the race. With backing from his friends in the Japanese community,
large numbers of Chicanos, an array of neighborhood groups, and some of the
top movers and shakers, Mineta won a staggering 62 percent of the vote
against a field of 32 candidates. He had pointed to a "paralysis of the will" that
gripped San Jose and he promised to provide leadership that would push the
city forward. He was no firebrand, but he was believable. He held the support
of the grassroots with backing for low-income housing, increased federal aid to
the cities, greater minority representation in government, and a slower city
residential growth rate.

He also endeared himself to local businessmen, pushing for expansion of
the city's airport, greater industrial growth, downtown development, and, in a
move especially pleasing to the electronics firms, an inventory tax-free international trade zone. During his tenure as mayor, San Jose, for the first time since
the end of World War II, established mechanisms to control the runaway
growth that had earned the city a national reputation as a model of urban
sprawl. After years of mayors and managers who had pushed for more and
more growth, Mineta brought to San Jose a new manager with a reputation for
controlling growth—Ted Tedesco. In his 1972 State of the City speech, Mineta
observed that as a result of rapid industrialization "the city of San Jose and
other local government agencies have experienced great difficulty in providing
all citizens with adequate services and public facilities." This would have an-
tagonized developers had Mineta not underplayed the issue. Yet he was able to
help adopt an urban-development policy that promised, in his words, "to ensure containment of future growth within the urban area where municipal
services already exist."

"No longer will the city extend its services over great distances to reach new
developments at a substantial cost to existing San Jose taxpayers," he said.
Meanwhile, Mineta exploited the officially powerless position of mayor with
flair, making frequent, high-profile trips to Sacramento and Washington to
lobby for urban legislation, becoming a member of the Legislative Action Committee of the U.S. Conference of Mayors and a director of the National League
of Cities. San Jose became known as the "West Coast King of municipal grants-
manship," drawing huge sums of federal revenue-sharing and employment-de-
velopment money for which Mineta never hesitated to take credit.

Mineta also had the good fortune of serving in office when major redevelopment projects, long in the pipeline, began to take shape, lending the appearance that it was the mayor who had made new buildings rise from empty parking lots.

When Congressman Charles Gubser decided not to run for reelection, Mineta, who had been gearing up for the 1974 mayor's race, jumped at the opportunity to seek higher office. It was the year the Watergate Class matriculated to Congress, when nearly any Democrat who had never been indicted could win a seat, and Mineta parlayed his apparent accomplishments in San Jose into a 53-percent plurality over the Republican George Milias.

In June 1975, Mineta scored an impressive victory: he was elected caucus chairman of the freshman congressional representatives; at that time a particularly effective body, they had collectively vowed to reform outdated House rules and had ousted several senior members from powerful committee chairmanships. By 1977, Mineta had been tagged a House liberal, earning a 95-percent rating from Americans for Democratic Action. He was appointed to the House Budget Committee, the Select Committee on Intelligence, and the House Public Works and Transportation Committee (a prime spot for pork-barrel measures). He also was named deputy-whip-at-large. (In 1980, Mineta's close friend and former administrative assistant, Les Francis, was named executive director of the Democratic National Committee, further increasing Mineta's ties to the White House and the Democratic Party leadership.)

As the power of the electronics companies grew in Santa Clara County, Mineta's liberalism began to fade, even before the rise of the Reagan Right. ADA gave him only an 80-percent rating in 1979. As a member of the Public Works Committee, Mineta guided legislation through that included $34.5 million for a federal building in downtown San Jose. He personally guarded the funding, maintained contact with local officials, led government inspection tours of the site, and made angry phone calls to local bureaucrats when problems arose. He also fought a rear-guard battle against legislation on jet aircraft noise that would have forced San Jose to buy $110 million in residential property as part of a noise buffer zone.

"He still has people who look to him instead of [Mayor] Janet Gray [Hayes] for leadership on urban issues," said one politician. "Even city planners, bureaucrats, and some of the council." Said an important lawyer: "Sometimes having lunch with Janet Gray is a waste of time. But [Mineta] controlled his council. You'd get to Norm and say, 'I have this problem,' and he'd say he'd have four votes. Janet Gray won't know."

Mineta, as one businessman said, "seems to have a finger on whatever's happening—like a freeway off-ramp for downtown, the proposal to expand the Willow Glen post office, downtown buildings, and other local issues." Or as another observed: "He could still get four votes out of the city council if he wanted to."

IT'S THE MAN AND HIS NETWORK, NOT THE JOB:
Frank Fiscalini

In December 1960, it looked as if Frank Fiscalini, the 38-year-old superintendent of the East Side Union High School District, was finished as a top administrator. His rise to the top of the sprawling East Side school district, from teacher in 1950 to superintendent in 1956, had been meteoric, and it appeared his fall would be likewise. Following a series of controversial incidents, including a book-burning episode, the transfer of a vocal teacher, investigations by the California Teachers Association, and a teachers' strike, the school board ousted Fiscalini, adding to the list of complaints charges that he fostered an out-of-date educational philosophy, developed a school program that was too expensive for the results it achieved, and operated a patronage system in the administration.

The response from the community was fast and furious. The president of the James Lick High School PTA angrily told the board, "We will declare war. There will be no peace in this district until all of you trustees are gone." The James Lick student-body president told the board, "I have a feeling that all I have learned about democracy is not true." In less than two months, Fiscalini and his supporters organized a recall of the school trustees, and, in February 1961, the four trustees who had dumped Fiscalini were themselves thrown out of office. Two weeks later, the new board reinstated their man, and in June they offered a "welcome back" pay raise for their embattled hero, despite a funding shortage in the district that year.

The message—don't mess with Frank on his home turf—was not lost on the city's establishment, which over the years embraced Fiscalini as one of their own. More than a few of the city's most influential leaders remained permanently impressed with his stunning electoral vindication and its testimony to the power base that Fiscalini had created, nurtured, and enjoyed for more than two decades.

By 1979, Fiscalini, czar of the school district, had become the single most important leader in any of the county's school systems and was considered by many the key to the city's East Side. "Frank is a powerhouse. I see him all over the place," said one businessman, whose interest in schools was otherwise non-existent. "He's a very level-headed guy—serious and down to earth. He's at every function. If you're trying to do something that requires political clout on the East Side, you'd see Frank," the businessman said.

Naturally, Fiscalini had developed a host of enemies. Some parents and teachers on the East Side believed he had made their school district his personal political instrument, installing board members and administrators who would not challenge his rule. In 1978 and 1979, a coalition of twelve minority organizations fought Fiscalini, charging that even with three minority group school-board members, the district still had too few minority teachers, that parents were shut out of decision making, and that various policies were discriminatory.

But even his opponents recognized that in his tenure as superintendent, Fiscalini maintained a base of support unrivaled in local politics and built facilities unique in the county. The crown jewel of Fiscalini's empire was a $27-million educational park, with 52 separate buildings, including a 575-seat theater and 4,700-seat gymnasium—the second largest in the county and the home court for San Jose State University basketball. And this was a *high school*. Called Independence High School, its name reflected not only its patriotic 1976 completion date but offered a warning to those who would challenge Fiscalini.

The construction of this educational dominion began in 1966 when Fiscalini applied for an $88,000 federal-study grant aimed at creating alternatives to segregation. Faced with one of Northern California's largest school districts, and with one-third of the student population Hispanic, Fiscalini hoped to create a campus that would be not only available to the poor, Mexican-Americans, and other minority pupils, but also so attractive that it would draw the brightest, wealthiest white children from throughout the district as well. He set up a blue ribbon advisory committee to support and sell bonds for the plan. Members included then-mayor Ron James, County Counsel Howard Campen (a wealthy, downtown property owner), City Manager "Dutch" Hamann, State Senator Al Alquist, Assemblyman Walter Curry, and assorted other bankers, lawyers, civic leaders, educators, and politicians. Their 1970 bond drive overcame charges that the planned educational park would be an extravagant squandering of tax dollars, and the needed $41 million for land, construction, and interest was raised.

In 1979, Fiscalini's realm included 20,000 high-school students; 1,500 adult, vocational, and occupational students; 1,475 employees; and a $44.8-million budget. He was not the highest-ranking public school administrator in the area—a state university and three junior colleges are in the county—but he was the highest paid—earning nearly $60,000 annually. Not only had he secured his own power base, but he had branched into other areas, having come to be regarded as essential to the success of nearly any serious political initiative on the East Side.

Through his contacts in the Hispanic community, Fiscalini maintained strong ties to rising Mexican-American politicians. He was for years regarded as City Councilman Al Garza's political godfather, although he and Garza reportedly had a falling out when the councilman ousted Ted Tedesco from the city manager's office. Still, Fiscalini, whose politics were quite conservative, maintained Garza's ear. "Anything Al does in terms of running as a candidate is with Uncle Frank's advice," said one political leader. "If I wanted to get to Al and I thought he'd do it, I'd go to Frank—that would be a good tactic. I think he could deliver that vote." Fiscalini also aided Assemblyman Alister McAlister, a former member of Fiscalini's school board, in his early races for state office. And he retained close relations with another former board member, Edward Alvarez, a highly respected tax attorney in former mayor Al Ruffo's law firm.

Fiscalini was chairman of the board of Alexian Brothers Hospital, probably the second most significant institution (after the school district) on San Jose's East Side—an area that was growing rapidly and becoming increasingly important in citywide political matters. He was also a member of the San Jose Police Department advisory board—another sensitive position because of the fragile peace in the streets between police and Chicano youths—as well as many other boards. (See Table 3.3.) In 1980, Mayor Janet Gray Hayes named Fiscalini chairman of a citizen's commission designed to plan for the development and redevelopment of downtown San Jose.

Following adoption of district elections in San Jose, Fiscalini maintained a low profile in the Alum Rock district where his school was based. Both of the leading contenders sought his support in 1980, but with his involvement in Alexian Brothers Hospital and the downtown task force, Fiscalini remained noncommittal, claiming to be "too busy" to get involved. As he approached his twenty-fifth year as the East Side school chief, Fiscalini began to consider other jobs—mayor of San Jose or state schools superintendent, to name two. "He's an aggressive fellow," observed one leader. "He's come to speak for the East Side, and he's not afraid to stick his neck out. There aren't a lot of rugged-individual civic activists like him around."

Observations

As we might have expected from the foregoing observations about Sunbelt cities, in 1979 San Jose's power structure was dominated by businessmen. Specifically, six of the top ten leaders—Ridder, Ruffo, Packard, James, Burke, and George—represented the interests of industry and commerce. Ridder, the most influential leader of all, held a special role because he commanded a major business establishment that was also the dominant news medium in the county.

Ruffo, James, Burke, and George are the kinds of local business elites commonly found in community power structures throughout the country. The term *local* should be emphasized here: the interests of these four leaders were almost wholly local, or, at their widest scope, regional. On the other hand, this term is showing some signs of a change of meaning: Packard not only governed an important *local* industry, but his interests and connections were regional, national, and even international. Ridder too was linked to a national network through the parent corporation of his *local* newspaper. Thus, as we have seen in chapter 4, whereas two decades ago San Jose's power structure would have been self-contained and unconnected beyond the region, by 1979 two of the top ten movers and shakers were tied to a national elite. Further, when Jinks, a corporate nomad, and Mineta, a congressional leader, also are considered, it is clear that San Jose's power structure in 1979 showed even more signs of growing increasingly national in scope, as are many Sunbelt cities throughout the country.

The presence of a number of government officials in the top ten is a Sunbelt characteristic as well. Of the three that appeared, only Hayes, the mayor, would be *expected* to appear in the top eschelon of community power. In fact, any mayor would, because of the perceived, if not real, power of the office itself. But the presence of Mineta and Fiscalini—a congressman and a school administrator—at the top of the power structure can best be explained by the lack of local, corporate power centers in San Jose and by the nature of California politics, which allow politicians with personal constituencies to attain high rankings in the local power structure.

Most community power structures find at least one media executive in the top ranks. As publisher of the dominant newspaper, Ridder was the obvious candidate for such a position. That Jinks also was found in the top tier was illustrative of power in San Jose: It further underscored the strengthened role of the new media when other power centers were lacking, and it was testimony to the fluctuating character of San Jose that a corporate nomad could rise so quickly to the top of the power pyramid, a situation common in Sunbelt cities.

In the following chapter we'll analyze San Jose's power structure in the context of its political history and its relation to other cities, including those of the Frostbelt. We'll see that the study of power in one community reveals not only who dominates locally, but how that study may serve as a microcosm of power in communities generally.

Notes

1. William L. Rivers and David M. Rubin, *A Region's Press: Anatomy of Newspapers in the San Francisco Bay Area* (Berkeley: Institute of Governmental Studies, University of California, 1971), pp. 51–54.
2. Lou Cannon, *Reporting: An Inside View* (Sacramento: California Journal Press, 1977), pp. 284–286.
3. Todd Gitlin, *The Whole World is Watching* (Berkeley: University of California Press, 1980), p. 49.
4. Stanford Environmental Law Society, *San Jose: Sprawling City* (Stanford: Stanford University, 1971), p. 2.

6

The Changing of the Guard: Power in the Sunbelt and Frostbelt Today

The publication of a power study stirs up great interest and discussion in a community. People react intensely. Many dispute who belongs on the list and who doesn't. Others disdainfully point out those who were overlooked. Some quibble about rankings and methods. People who turn up on the list grow demure, if secretly smug, disclaiming their prominence or arguing that it's only temporary. Some who don't make the list resent being overlooked and others envy those who are deemed powerful. Whatever the argument, people are interested. They want and need to know who rules their communities.

A systematic community-power study provides that information, but it may also produce results that challenge popular assumptions about power. The political history of San Jose presented in chapter 4 is a somewhat impressionistic survey of power in the city, reflecting common conclusions of people who are reasonably well-informed on the subject. We can now return to those conclusions and the questions they raised and assess them in the light of a systematic study of power. Combining what we know about the political history of the city with what we have learned about its contemporary power structure, we can also make some projections about the future of power and politics in San Jose.

Similarly, we can return to the generalizations and hypotheses generated by the review of community power theories in chapter 2, using our findings to test these generalizations as well.

Finally, San Jose is one of the emerging cities of the Sunbelt and the findings of this study have implications for the other cities of the region. To understand these implications, we will compare San Jose to a city of the Frostbelt and to other cities of the Sunbelt.

SAN JOSE TODAY: A POWER STRUCTURE IN TRANSITION

The men and women found to be powerful in 1979 were a different group than might have been listed in an earlier era. Had a study been done in 1960, those named would have included some contractors, the newspaper publisher, the city manager, and other members of the Progress Committee and the Book of the Month Club. It would have been a hometown list, made up of people who had spent their lives in San Jose and who intended to stay. Few influentials who lived elsewhere in the region would have been included, and it is unlikely that grassroots, minority, or women leaders would have been identified among the powerful.

But the 1970s appear, at first glance, to have been an era of grassroots insurgency. San Jose's old guard certainly suffered several tactical defeats. Voters ceased to approve capital improvement bonds, curtailing local subsidies to growth. City Manager Hamann, recognizing the shifting public mood, resigned before he could be fired. Mayoral and city council candidates who espoused controlled growth were elected, although once in office some backed away from their promises. Still, enough remained committed to managed growth that various mechanisms for more responsible development were adopted.

Although the gap between whites and minorities continued to widen, Hispanics and other minorities made some absolute gains in economic status and political influence. As the decade came to a close, they succeeded, together with emerging neighborhood and other activist groups, in replacing at-large city council elections with district elections. Meanwhile, women candidates emerged from such traditional organizations as the League of Women Voters and the Parent-Teacher Associations. Enough were elected to earn San Jose the pop title, "Feminist Capital of the Nation."

Grassroots Gains: How Deep Are They?

Yet despite the defeats of the old guard, the apparent victories of the grassroots seem to have been insufficient to place their leaders

Table 6.1
POWER STRUCTURE BY INSTITUTION

Business[a]	Government	Media[b]	Neighborhoods	Labor	Minorities
X					
X					
X					
X					
X					
X					
X	X				
X	X				
X	X				
X	X				
X	X				
X	X				
X	X				
X	X				
X	X				
X	X				
X	X				
X	X	X			
X	X	X			
X	X	X	X	X	X

X=one individual
N=40

[a]Included in Business are three bankers and three lawyers whose practice is almost entirely in corporate law.
[b]Included in Media is the publisher of the local newspaper, whose power is derived from his position as a businessman as much as it is from the editorial page.

among the city's power elite. Only two women—both elected officials—were named among the powerful in the 1979 study. Only one labor leader, one Chicano activist, and one other grassroots organizer (a professor) made the list—a rather meager showing for an ostensibly insurgent movement. In fact, the remnants of the old guard did better. Survivors or heirs of the old guard held five of the top ten positions and at least seven slots in the second and third tiers of power.

Table 6.1 shows how San Jose's power structure is divided along institutional lines. For the purpose of illustration, all counted here are considered to have equal power.

When the individuals named as powerful are given points based on their rank in the power structure (top tier, 3; middle, 2; bottom, 1), the picture changes very little, as seen in Table 6.2.

The weighted chart sharpens the focus on the dwarfing of neighborhood, minority, and labor leaders in relation to business and government powers.

The overwhelming power of business leaders is balanced somewhat by the eleven elected officials and three appointed administrators in the

Table 6.2
POWER STRUCTURE BY INSTITUTION: WEIGHTED

Business	Government	Media	Neighborhoods	Labor	Minorities
X					
X					
X					
X					
X					
X					
X	X				
X	X				
X	X				
XX	X				
XX	X				
XX	XX				
XX	XX				
XX	XX				
XX	XX				
XXX	XX				
XXX	XX				
XXX	XXX	X			
XXX	XXX	XXX			
XXX	XXX	XXX	X	X	X

XXX=top tier XX=middle tier X=bottom tier
N=40

top forty—a high number for a study using the reputational technique. Their presence indicates that more than one-third of the city's top leadership is formally accountable to the public. They are the people who, in the idealized vision of pluralism, are supposed to hold power in a representative democracy. They would have appeared on the list had we used either the traditional positional method or the decisional technique of studying power. Their presence also indicates a power structure that is not monolithically elitist, supporting the hypothesis that during the 1970s the grassroots forces made some gains on the old guard elite.

Still, combining the 3 grassroots leaders and 14 public officials (most of whom trace their roots to the old guard rather than the grassroots), we arrive at a total of 17. In other words, 23 of the 40 leaders represent private interests. Of the top ten, 7 are business leaders; only the mayor began her career with grassroots activity, though most San Joseans now think of her as a member of the city's social and political elite rather than as the housewife-activist she once was..

Apparently then, power in San Jose is concentrated where it always has been—among the economic elite. There has been some movement toward a more pluralistic power structure, but the redistribution of power is minimal and, as we shall see, perhaps at its peak.

Table 6.3
TOP TIER LEADERSHIP BY
INSTITUTION

X		
X		
X	X	
X	X	X
X	X	X
Business	Government	Media

X=one individual
N=10

What then of the grassroots electoral and policy victories in the 1970s? Have they any meaning? Are they indicators of movement toward genuine representative democracy? Can we expect to see further decline of the old guard and seizure of their positions in the local power structure by the grassroots? Or has a new elite begun to ascend in place of the old guard?

Two factors are apparent in analyzing what seem to be the successes of the grassroots in San Jose. First are the structural aspects of California politics that enhance grassroots activity. Secondly, as we have seen, San Jose has begun a transition during which new economic forces have replaced the old and, at the same time, shifted their interests to regional, state, and national politics. In the end, the grassroots victories themselves may have been single-issue successes that failed to significantly change the distribution of power. If the 1979 study of San Jose is accurate, we must conclude that the grassroots have won only modest power.

California's Political "Free-for-all"

California politics, like politics in other growing Sunbelt states, is volatile. This is partly because of the many new voters who hold no loyalties to traditions, leaders, organizations, or parties. In addition, the structure of electoral politics in California discourages the entrenchment of these loyalties through nonpartisan local elections and nominations by primaries rather than through party caucuses or conventions. The reformers also gave voters policy-making power through the initiative and referendum, whereby they can put legislation on the ballot themselves through a petition process.

The structural reforms designed to combat bossism also ensure that political parties remain weak, leaving the process open to insurgent candidates and movements. In local elections, and to a great extent in statewide races, it's every candidate for himself or herself, with no ostensible blessing by party or elite. The "cult of personality" reigns supreme in California elections, while parties, despite their pretentions, are vestigial organs. With a cadre of workers and the benign neglect of the media, a number of grassroots candidates in San Jose have overcome establishment-designated candidates.

The initiative and referendum processes also facilitate grassroots activity by preventing or at least making less likely the suppression of issues. Anyone with enough followers can force an issue onto the public agenda. Howard Jarvis and Paul Gann proved this in 1978 with Proposition 13 which, despite opposition from business and government elites, redesigned property tax law in California. San Jose's 1973 growth-controlling initiative was an earlier example. It became a turning point in the city's electoral politics. Although proponents of district elections did not have to resort to the initiative process to place their cause on the ballot, their credible threat to do so encouraged the city council to place the measure before the voters in 1978. In 1980, a referendum to repeal a gay rights ordinance, an initiative to provide binding arbitration for police and firefighters, and an advisory vote on military conscription all were ballot issues. With these mechanisms available, as is commonly the case in Sunbelt states, elites may have greater difficulty in trying to keep issues from getting out of the bag.

Changing Business Interests

In addition to the political structure of California politics, there are more contemporary forces, none of them controlled by the grassroots, that contribute to the modest pluralism found in San Jose.

By the late 1970s, the old guard was losing its grip. Many of the builders and developers and the politicians they colluded with were aging, retiring, and withdrawing. With few exceptions, they had no heirs to carry on for them. Their interests remained in development, a role in the economy and politics of the community that grew increasingly narrow as the city matured and new industries gained dominance. At the same time, the minority of people who knew who the old guard were and respected them was dwarfed by newcomers who didn't know them and didn't care to. All the new residents wanted was their schools, streets, and police and fire protection. If development meant less money for their neighborhoods, then development wasn't for them.

Yet on the specific issues about which they cared, the money and influence of the old guard still counted. Real estate and development

Table 6.4
BUSINESS LEADERSHIP BY ECONOMIC SECTOR: WEIGHTED

			X	
X		X	X	
XX		X	X	
XX	XX	X	X	
XX	XXX	XX	X	
XXX	XXX	XX	XXX	XXX
Development	Industry	Finance	Commerce	Chamber

XXX=top tier   XX=middle tier   X=bottom tier
N=20

interests still were a significant force in 1979, as Table 6.4 indicates. Their continued presence is due in part to the sheer weight of the old and in part to the lobbying skills and campaign contributions of the new corporate development firms.

Clearly, the real estate and development forces in San Jose retained standing in the structure of community power. But the trend is away from their dominance, as evidenced by a look at how the top tier of leadership is divided among various economic sectors, shown in Table 6.5.

In San Jose, and throughout the nation, nationally active corporations were attaining economic dominance, a trend that to some extent provided another opening for the grassroots. Instead of local ownership and resident managers with broad interests in local politics, the political economy came to be run by regional vice presidents and branch managers of large corporations headquartered elsewhere. The new corporate leaders came and went. Most took little interest in city politics and community affairs. Even some of those named prominently in the power structure because of their positions or their activities—such as James Miscoll of the Bank of America or Larry Jinks of the *Mercury News*—moved on quickly. These are men for whom San Jose was merely a step up in their corporate careers. The advent of the corporate nomad and the corporate economy provided an opening for the more stable elements of the grassroots.

As the old guard began to decline and the corporate economy expanded, another factor provided the grassroots a limited opportunity. Policy decisions were increasingly being made at the regional, state, and national levels. This was nothing new. Federal decisions about housing, transportation, and defense spending had as much to do with the development of "Silicon Valley" as did the decisions of local elites. But the trend accelerated. The federal government continued to make key decisions that affected the community in these and other areas.

Table 6.5
TOP TIER BUSINESS LEADERSHIP BY ECONOMIC SECTOR: WEIGHTED

	XXX			
XXX	XXX		XXX	XXX
Development	Industry	Finance	Commerce	Chamber

XXX=one top tier leader
N=5

The state repeatedly intervened in land use and fiscal policy, diminishing the autonomy of the cities. The county began to assume a broader role in transportation and land use. And a host of regional agencies asserted themselves in planning, transportation, air- and water-quality control, sewage treatment, and other matters. The economic elite, through organizations such as the Santa Clara Country Manufacturing Group, shifted its attention to these other levels of government. How did the grassroots benefit from this? Their influence on those decisions still left to the cities was enhanced at least partly because the powerful had focused their attention elsewhere. But the corporate elite had not shifted their concerns to a wider arena without purpose: this was where the broader, more significant decisions were being made. Those left to the cities, those upon which the grassroots had increased impact, no longer carried the significance they once had. Perhaps the economic elite thought district elections in San Jose too insignificant to oppose, allowing the grassroots a shallow victory.

While these factors—the decline of the old guard, the emergence of the corporate economy, and the regionalization of key decisions—opened up some opportunity for the grassroots, the activists created their own opportunities. They spent a decade organizing, and their victories on growth management, police practices, and district representation significantly affected the lives of San Joseans.

Measured against similar movements in other areas, particularly in Frostbelt cities, San Jose's grassroots successes may seem remarkable. But in the end, as the systematic power study shows, the grassroots did not win a major redistribution of power. They won victories on specific issues but did not forge coalitions that could render more substantial change. The battle for district elections was the only attempt to build a broad-based coalition to redistribute power, and it remains to be seen whether that redistribution will be substantive or merely symbolic. The victories of the grassroots were important, but they did not effect major social change. As in earlier eras, most of the power in San Jose still is concentrated among and exercised by the economic elite, although the composition of that elite has changed.

SAN JOSE'S FUTURE: WHAT THE SURVEY SUGGESTS

Testing Our Hypotheses

In chapter 2 we discussed the accumulation of theories and methodologies that laid the groundwork for the study of power. Reviewing the social science literature on power, we came to the point at which social scientists began hypothesizing that power structures could vary over time and among communities. Change ranged between the two poles of elitism and pluralism. According to Clark and Lineberry and Sharkansky, this variation could be explained by examining certain characteristics of communities that they found to be associated with the shaping of power structures. The characteristics or variables they discussed are illustrated in Table 2.1. Using San Jose as a model, the table matches each variable against actual developments in San Jose during the past decades, providing a prediction (hypothesis) of the shape of the city's power structure that would be found by the study.

Across the board, the cumulative effect of the characteristics indicated an increasingly pluralistic power structure, or at least a power structure in transition from relative elitism to relative pluralism. Virtually every change—increasing size, increasing diversity, the proliferation of community organizations, industrialization, a growing number of absentee-owned corporations—broadened participation in the model San Jose. Virtually every change, however, was also related to growth, which may be the single strongest summarizing factor in changing a community's power structure.

The San Jose study supports in part the predictions drawn from the work of Clark and Lineberry and Sharkansky. The power structure unveiled is indeed modestly pluralistic. Public officials comprise more than one-third of the top leaders. An additional three leaders were grassroots or labor activists. By most standards, this is a relatively pluralistic power structure.

This is a substantial vindication of the reputational technique, for critics have charged it can only identify behind-the-scenes economic influentials, not the power of those dependent on the institutional roles. Chapter 2 argued that the method is nevertheless valid and that elected officials would be revealed as the dominant force in community life if, in fact, they dominated. The study has shown them to be significant, although not dominant.

To a strong degree, then, both the reputational technique and the power structure variables of the researchers mentioned above are supported by these findings. Yet caution is necessary. The pluralism which the San Jose study revealed is highly relative. Twenty-three of the top forty leaders are business or professional people. They commanded seven positions in the top tier of ten. Despite a *tendency* to pluralism, they still dominate. Who these individuals are may vary over time and from community to community. Their institutional base of power may also vary. But the economic elite holds the greatest power. The institutions they command control their communities, even if only negatively, as many Frostbelt cities have learned when local industries failed or moved. Systematic reviews of the literature of community power have concluded that business leaders are "universally . . . prominent"[1] and that they provide the largest number of top influentials.[2] Even pluralist Frederick Wirt concluded that in San Francisco, the "batting average [was] relatively high for business."[3]

These power structure researchers were referring to the overt political activity of business leaders, but G. William Domhoff has argued that "it is not essential . . . that business leaders be directly involved in governmental decisions if it can be shown that they dominate the social context and shape governmental structures in which decisions are made."[4] Edward Hayes, a political scientist who has studied community power in Oakland, concurs, pointing out that business has both "systemic" and "specialized" influence. *Systemic influence* refers to how business "affects the basic structure of government" or "limits policy alternatives." *Specialized influence* applies to specific policies such as zonings, rent control, or redevelopment.[5] As we have seen, the top leaders in San Jose are active in both categories. And through their systemic influence, they keep some issues from arising, thus avoiding the need for active intervention.

The power of the economic leaders is not total. No theorist argues that they *always* win, just that they rarely lose. And because they need government assistance for their economic goals, they will always attempt to influence government. No other group in the community has such a permanent and tangible stake in what government does. No other group has such substantial resources to influence government. Is it any wonder that economic leaders so frequently appear in the top ranks of community power structures?

So while growth has brought some redistribution of power to our case study city, San Jose, the economic elite still holds more power than any other sector. Furthermore, as we have already seen, the relatively pluralistic power structure discovered by the 1979 San Jose study may be a product of a particular time. The situation may be the result of a transition between the demise of the old guard and the emergence of the new. It may also be a product of the declining autonomy of local government and the shifting of elite attention beyond local institutions.

Whatever the cause, the 1970s were a time of opportunity for the grassroots. The 1980s will test the limits of that opportunity. If the grassroot forces exceed limits tolerable to the elite, the economic leaders may reassert themselves. Efforts to redistribute power or halt residential and industrial growth might constitute such transgressions, although San Jose's new elites did not bother to seriously oppose district council elections. They are, however, growing more interested in the politics of growth.

There are signs of a reassertion of economic power in San Jose in the 1980s. There is a settling in of the new elite and a renewed interest in the actions of the city. If the San Jose study had been done ten years earlier, a substantially different power structure would have emerged. Done ten years later, the results would also be different. San Jose is just emerging as a modern, mature, corporate city of the Sunbelt. The elite of the Valley of the Heart's Delight is being replaced by the elite of Silicon Valley. Our study has captured an invaluable cross section of a power structure in the midst of intense transition.

San Jose in the 1980s

As San Jose enters the new decade, major economic interests are in a state of resurgence, more at the regional than the local level. The people named as powerful in the San Jose study indicate this trend. Typically, economic influentials dominate, but many of them represent new corporate interests with strong connections to regional and national institutions. As Floyd Hunter put it, "having [David] Packard on the list shows the change in San Jose; he's a national heavy hitter."[6] People like Packard, or their surrogate regional vice presidents and managers, are growing in influence in San Jose.

Santa Clara County Manufacturing Group. The emergence of the Santa Clara County Manufacturing Group, an example of this, may be the single most important recent development in community and regional politics. The 65 corporations that make up the Manufacturing Group previously seemed to win their battles in individual cities with little difficulty. But recently, they have grown concerned about problems of housing and transportation for their workers as well as the provision of adequate services for their plant expansions.

Local efforts to control growth have become an inconvenience that has led this corporate coalition to express a deeper interest in community politics, broadly defined, than its individual members have traditionally shown. Winning zoning approvals for plant expansions is no longer enough. City services, employee housing, an attractive quality of life, not to mention access to important markets, transfer points, and related industries, are all important factors today. To ensure more favorable conditions for local expansion, corporations have had to assert themselves on a wide range of issues being decided by San Jose and other cities, as well as by county and regional planning agencies. The enormous power of these economic institutions is recognized by public officials, who not only have great respect for the corporate leaders but fear the loss of jobs and tax revenues to other parts of the country (and world). In a period of only three years, the Santa Clara County Manufacturing Group has become a force to be reckoned with.

Redevelopment of downtown San Jose. The redevelopment of downtown San Jose may also facilitate the emergence of the new corporate elite. As we've seen, the suburban economic exodus left it a classic redevelopment wasteland. But suddenly, in 1980, interest in redevelopment grew intense, fed by the general economic expansion of Silicon Valley as well as the growing need for centralized regional headquarters, law offices, accounting firms, and brokerage houses. Rising transportation and housing costs made a redeveloped central district more economical. If this interest comes to fruition, San Jose could emerge as a regional center for banking and corporate headquarters. If so, these newly centralized interests will almost certainly make their influence felt in community politics, as they have elsewhere, thus enhancing the powers of the economic elite and making San Jose's power structure more like the traditional elites found in older cities.

Construction. The construction industry has also experienced a recent resurgence. Attitudes toward the builders grew more benign as a housing crisis hit San Jose. An average home cost $120,000 in 1980. Even families earning the city's median income of $27,000, high by national standards, were priced out of the housing market. Housing has become a central problem for residents, as well as for businesses recruiting new workers to the area.

As this more favorable attitude has grown, the builders themselves have learned to use their power with greater skill. They emphasize the need for "affordable" housing and present their work as a community service. Their professional lobbyists are persuasive, and, through their political action group, Citizens for Housing and Economic Stability (CHES), they have invested well in political campaigns. Nine of the ten council members elected by district in 1980 were endorsed and lavishly funded by CHES.

As the local contractors are displaced by corporate developers

(Exxon Enterprises is just one), their strength grows. The corporate builders not only have greater political skill, they also have the planning sophistication and financial wherewithal to meet whatever conditions the city imposes on them. Thus they frequently win approval for projects by tacking on extras like new roads or open space, something the local contractors could not or would not do.

As in the past, then, developers will be a formidable force in city politics, but as sophisticated members of the new corporate breed. Similarly, the *San Jose Mercury News* has exercised power in a more sophisticated manner since its rebirth as part of a national corporation. The publisher, perhaps the most powerful man in San Jose today, is well connected to regional and national elites, as are his editors. The combined newspapers are part of the Santa Clara County Manufacturing Group, sharing the concerns of the manufacturing, financial, and development interests in the continued growth of the area.

The Role of the Mercury News.   The *Mercury News* is no longer the growth-promoting, conservatively biased newspaper of the past. It has become responsible, professional, mildly liberal, and generally balanced. While it once suppressed information, it now provides broad coverage of issues. But it remains the dominant local news medium, operating virtually without competition. That gives the *Mercury News* enormous power to frame issues. The newspaper exposed the purge of City Manager Ted Tedesco during the era of the "Fearsome Foursome," contributing to the demise of the four. Later, the newspaper precipitated the firing of Tedesco's successor. It was crucial in the district election debate, where it provided neutral coverage, despite an editorial against the charter amendment. It has helped place the jobs-housing imbalance at the top of the public agenda. And on a number of minor issues, its positions have been pivotal. Local politicians, recognizing the power of the press, are attentive, even intimidated.

An example of the newspaper's power to frame issues—and of its subtle use of that power—are the seminars it organizes. Editors select a key issue, such as juvenile justice, redevelopment, or jobs and housing, and invite a panel of speakers for a discussion; the result is two or three pages of news coverage and usually an editorial. This, in the view of the *Mercury News,* is a community service. And it is. But it is the *Mercury News* that chooses the issues and panelists, and so sets the public agenda.

An Emphasis on Regional Planning.   If the manufacturing corporations, the financial institutions, the downtown and residential developers, and the *Mercury News* work together, they will be an even more formidable force in the future of San Jose than they are today. The Manufacturing Group, led by David Packard, could well put them all together. It seems likely it will dominate the community and regional power structure of 1990.

That common interest needed to bind them together is coming to the fore now: the need for better regional planning to facilitate their continued joint expansion. There are fourteen cities in Santa Clara County, besides San Jose, and they contain about half the population and more than half the jobs; competition among these jurisdictions makes for irrational planning and, largely, for the current job-housing imbalance. Every city wants revenue-producing industry. Few want service-demanding housing, particularly low-income or high-density housing. Yet individual cities are too small to plan for balanced growth in the area.

Not surprisingly, then, county government has already grown more important. In 1972, the county took over public transportation. During the 1970s, the county became more aggressive in land-use planning. In 1980, it wrote a general plan aimed at balancing growth in the entire county, even though the county government does not have land-use control within cities.

Moves to strengthen county government or to introduce some new form of regional government are on the agenda of some of the economic elites already. The Manufacturing Group has indicated some interest, and the *Mercury News* has taken an increasingly regional perspective in recent years, on both the news and editorial pages.

The Future of the Grassroots.   If the economic elites are on the rise and focusing on regional planning, what of the grassroots? These groups continue to be active. Their interests remain substantially unchanged from what they were in the 1960s and 1970s. Neighborhood and homeowner groups still work to improve basic services, concerns which could put them in direct confrontation with the elite if anger over straining already overextended services continues to be expressed as antagonism to growth. Minority groups are also concerned about services, but they are more sympathetic to growth, which they hope will bring them jobs and housing. And minority groups continue to be interested in affirmative action and police practices, issues that sometimes put them in confrontation with homeowner groups. Both homeowners and minority groups expect district election of city council members to improve their influence in the city.

Despite some continuing liberal grassroots activity, the most dynamic grassroots force in San Jose as the new decade began was the religious right. Concerned Citizens and the Moral Majority claim thousands of followers. They made their presence felt in the 1980 elections with their successful repeal of gay rights ordinances by a 3 to 1 majority. They went on to aid in the election of several city council candidates. But their broader impact on city politics is yet to be felt. If their social conservatism translates into economic conservatism, they may ally with development interests. Or, without inflammatory issues to exploit, they may be unable to sustain their activity.

There are signs, however, of a weakening among grassroots forces generally. The modest redistribution of power provided by district elections may be subverted by the successful intervention of the builders and developers in the campaign process. Community organizations and district representatives also will be less effective in a regional arena, the direction in which some economic leaders are moving. Fiscal limitations on cities, most notably the 1978 property tax cut brought about by Proposition 13, constitute yet another constraint on the ability of cities to meet the demands of community groups. Finally, there is a "burn-out" factor. Community organizing is on the decline in San Jose. In some cases, people just got tired or left town; in others, the leaders were coopted; and the happy few disbanded when their issues were resolved.

In short, as San Jose enters the 1980s, the days of the grassroots may be numbered. The corporate economic elites are on the rise, limited only by their own willingness to stay and fight. This trend suggests that San Jose is becoming more like other, older cities in the United States, especially those of the Frostbelt.

SUNBELT VERSUS FROSTBELT: DIVERGING OR MERGING?

Indianapolis, Indiana, is a classic city of the Frostbelt whose power structure has been examilned using the same methods as the San Jose study.[7] Briefly comparing the results of the two studies can help us understand the differences and similarities between Sunbelt and Frostbelt urban power structures. An example of the exercise of power in Indianapolis highlights the differences.

Power Politics in a Traditional Frostbelt City

In 1976, Indianapolis Mayor William H. Hudnut learned that federal money was available to finance a feasibility study for a city transit system. Many community leaders wanted to strengthen the connections between the central business district and the Indiana University-Purdue University campus just northwest of downtown. The mayor's staff envisioned a "people mover" linking the city to the university and its 20,000 students and faculty.

To obtain a needed federal grant, the city had to compete with other cities. Community support, especially from downtown businessmen, was crucial. So Hudnut told his planners to delay their application until he could rally the necessary backing. Hudnut called his friend Carl Dortch, president of the Indianapolis Chamber of Commerce, and explained that, although he wanted the appearance of providing leadership on the issue, he did not want to embark on a course of action without the backing of the top business leaders in the community. No problem, Dortch said. He would set up a meeting.

Within a week, a group of businessmen assembled in the conference room of the Chamber of Commerce. To those who attended, the setting seemed natural and appropriate, although the issue to be discussed was a major municipal improvement about which the public had yet to be informed.

In addition to Hudnut and Dortch, those in attendance included several bankers, major retailers and contractors, and the publisher of the *Indianapolis Star* and *News*. Enough business power had been assembled to render a decision. Hudnut explained that he wanted the city's leading businessmen to comment on the federal grant application. It was just a feasibility study, he assured them, but before he took even that step, he wanted to know what they thought.

Comments tended toward the negative. It would be ugly. Trash would collect under it. Hordes of commuters would block the entrances to businesses. It was a waste of money, and so on. One leader even objected that his bank was spending a huge sum to build a new combined headquarters and Hyatt Hotel and that the railway would ruin the architectural line of the new building.

Nevertheless, a consensus emerged that since it was only a feasibility study, and since the federal government would be paying for it, it couldn't hurt to apply. With more information, the gentlemen agreed, a better decision could be made. The overriding concern was, "What will it do to the area?"—what one participant later called "intelligent selfishness." With Mayor Hudnut's assurance that the details of location would be decided after the feasibility study had been granted, the businessmen offered their cautious support.

Hudnut thanked the business leaders for their time and consideration. He would take their comments under advisement when he made his decision. But this was really ritual, a perfunctory acknowledgement of his role as a political leader answerable to a broader constituency. In fact, a decision had been made.

By 1980, the feasibility study had been completed, Congress had authorized a $2-million preengineering contract, and the city was waiting to hear if it would receive a grant for the project itself—estimated to cost $65 to 85 million.*

This episode is but one example of the exercise of power by the ruling elite in the city of Indianapolis. The pattern is routine in Frostbelt cities where political, economic, and social power are easily assembled in a group of elite leaders. In Detroit, for example, there are three such elite groupings: New Detroit, Inc., Detroit Renaissance, and the Economic Growth Corp. Des Moines has the powerful Greater Des Moines Committee; Baltimore, the Greater Baltimore Committee.[8]

In Indianapolis, the Chamber of Commerce and the Greater Indianapolis Progress Committee are the formal centers of corporate power, one connected to business, the other attached to government. The Progress Committee is, quite simply, the public mechanism through which the ideas, energies, and interests of the city's business leaders are funneled. It was to that group that former Mayor Richard G. Lugar (later a Republican senator) took a proposal, concocted by a handful of business and political elites, for consolidation of city and county government in 1968. Although a benign-sounding idea on the surface, a closer look at this meeting will show why it represents one of the most dramatic examples of the exercise of elite power ever seen in an American city.

In the mid-1960s, Indianapolis politics were changing. Since the 1930s, Democrats had controlled elections in the central city, while Republicans controlled the Marion County offices and state legislative delegations. In addition, Republicans generally ran the suburban municipalities that ringed the city.

The old city, particularly Center Township (its heart), had grown poorer and blacker than the rest of the county. For example, in 1950, Indianapolis accounted for 77 percent of the assessed valuation in the county, but by 1977 the city's proportion had skidded to 47 percent.[9]

Non-whites accounted for 39 percent of the population of Center Township, 27 percent of the city itself, and just 17 percent of the county. Black leaders felt they had a good chance of controlling city elections, and they were confident that the 1970s would see the city's

*In early 1981, President Ronald Reagan's proposed budget cuts threatened the "people mover" project. If it should fall to the federal budget ax, that would not alter the fact that the local decisions on the project were made by a handful of powerful men, meeting privately. Furthermore, many of the same key leaders who decided the "people mover" issue later came up with an even more ambitious project—a domed sports stadium that was estimated to cost $65 to $68 million. Lilly Endowment pledged $25 million, another local foundation pledged $5 million, and the movers and shakers pushed a bill through the state legislature to fund the remainder from a tax on food and beverages sold in restaurants and bars.

first black mayor. Republicans and some white Democrats feared that same development. Partly in order to prevent this turn of events, Mayor Lugar, L. Keith Bulen (GOP county chairman), and a few leading businessmen developed a plan to consolidate the city and county governments. The mayor and four representatives would be elected by the whole county and the balance of the 29-member city-county council would represent separate districts. This scheme would greatly diffuse any impact from a concerted inner-city black vote.

Having swept electoral offices in the 1968 general election, the Republicans controlled the state legislature, the only body needed to approve the consolidation; in Indiana, even the largest cities do not enjoy home rule. To guarantee passage of their consolidation bills, Lugar, Bulen, and their associates specifically *excluded* from consolidation the most significant and politically explosive elements of local government—schools, sewers, local welfare relief, and police and fire service. What they did plan to consolidate was the political power structure.

Before these political operatives tried to enact their idea, however, they brought it first before the Greater Indianapolis Progress Committee. The reason was simple: without backing of the city's most powerful business and professional leaders, their blatantly political maneuver would have no chance. So Lugar called a meeting of the Progress Committee, outlined the plan and asked for support from the business establishment before he made a move in the political arena. The committee, dominated by Republican businessmen, embraced the plan as its own and, with the assistance of shrewd constitutional lawyers, guided the consolidation through the legislature. Any popular referendum on the measure that the state legislature might have used to test the public mood was assiduously avoided. As Carl Dortch, president of the Indianapolis Chamber of Commerce, later said, "Had there been a referendum on [consolidation], I don't think it would have been approved."

Two years later, the consolidation was found constitutional by the State Supreme Court in a sweetheart lawsuit brought by Dortch and defended by Harry T. Ice, the city's most powerful attorney, whom we already know from the top ten of the 1976 *Indianapolis Star* power study.

Why San Jose Lacks a Traditional Elite

Nothing in San Jose's history matches such typical political maneuvering in Indianapolis. Small groups have held power only for a limited time. Even since San Jose's emergence in the 1960s as a metropolitan center, the most powerful individual leaders have still failed to join in a single structure through which influence *that effective* could be exercised. (The potential power of the Santa Clara County Manufacturing Group remains, so far, relatively untested.)

The differences between the two cities are emblematic of the differences between Sunbelt and Frostbelt cities in general. First is the concentration of locally owned and operated corporate enterprises. The *Indianapolis Star* power study found among the top ten leaders three bank chairmen, two industrialists, a newspaper publisher, a development contractor, and the president of the Chamber of Commerce. Rounding out the field were a corporate attorney and the mayor. We have already seen in chapter 3 what that network of local corporate powers looked like pictured as a wheel of interlocking board memberships. (See Figures 3.2 and 3.3.) Many of the companies were of statewide or national significance in banking, manufacturing, real estate, and energy.

San Jose's top ten leaders were more evenly distributed, as our power study found, between corporate, government, and civic leaders. But the corporate leaders tended to have regional or even national significance. Only ten San Jose-based companies were represented in the entire power structure, and few had economic significance beyond the county.

With fewer local corporations of significant economic stature, San Jose does not have the concentrated industrial and financial leadership that most Frostbelt cities have. This is especially significant in development of downtown San Jose, the area that businesses fled in the 1950s when suburban expansion shifted markets to the city's outer neighborhoods. Left behind were small businessmen and shopkeepers whose political might was tiny compared to the residential builders and developers who were shaping the city. But downtown San Jose has simply not been a serious concern for the major corporate interests who have built their low-rise headquarters in Silicon Valley cities to the north such as Mountain View, Sunnyvale, Santa Clara, and Palo Alto.

In contrast, when businessmen in Indianapolis decided in the mid-1960s that they needed a major new downtown hotel, they pooled their financial and political resources and brought one to town. They remodeled the City Market, rebuilt the City-County Building, constructed a sports arena, built new skyscrapers, and began work on a transit system.

The power (and interests) of elite commitment can be simply drawn by contrasting the two downtowns and the roles of the two separate elites in each. In Indianapolis, every one of the first-tier leaders and most of their peers worked out of downtown offices. Of San Jose's top ten leaders, only two had downtown offices. No wonder one city's downtown was speedily developed while the other is only recently receiving attention.

Another difference between San Jose and Indianapolis is the importance of electoral politics. In Indianapolis, municipal elections were no serious concern for the ruling elite. Enough power could be assembled outside government to attain their goals, making it unnecessary to control specific public offices. As shown by the consolidation of city and county government, the elite could change even the structure of government without approval of the voting public.

In San Jose, on the other hand, without the finance and corporate capital to fund major projects, government was needed. The Center for the Performing Arts is but one example. District elections, a modest realignment of government, came to San Jose in 1978 independent of the power elite. Developers and builders were once the political kingmakers of San Jose, but they were voted out of office during the 1970s.

The power structure of Indianapolis, as in most Frostbelt cities and even some older Sunbelt ones, is rigid and entrenched compared to the structure of a city like San Jose; by Frostbelt standards, everyone in San Jose is a newcomer. In Indianapolis, for instance, half of the top ten leaders were born in the city; the other five had spent most of their lives there. In San Jose, on the other hand, only six had long-time connections to the city (by birth or residence); three others were relatively recent arrivals, and one had never lived or worked in San Jose.

In Indianapolis, social status is still important. The Dramatic Club, University Club, Columbia Club, Lamb's Club, Woodstock Country Club, Athletic Club, and the Crown Hill Cemetery Board of Executors are considered proper measures of one's credentials. The official social register no longer is used to determine if an individual is socially acceptable, but the vestiges of social elitism survive.

San Jose never has had a social register. The city grew so rapidly in the 1950s that membership in the few existing social institutions no longer impresses many people. Today, a rendezvous at Plateau 7, an undistinguished restaurant and bar across the street from City Hall, is more apt to produce an important business or political deal than is lunch at the Sainte Claire Club. Tennis and racquetball, not golf and duck hunting, are the sports of the city's movers and shakers. And these do not require prestigious memberships. Participation in events of the Museum of Art or support for the San Jose Symphony and United Way are not prerequisites for power.

A final possible constraint on the evolution of a traditional elite in San Jose may be that, despite its population of well over 600,000, it is only the fourth largest city in California. In most other states, a city this size would be the economic, social, and political center. Yet San Jose is not. Those honors go to Los Angeles and to San Francisco (only an hour away). Although San Jose nearly equals San Francisco in size, the northern city remains the focus of the region. The Bay Area's dominant media and financial institutions are headquartered in San Francisco, and the city is socially and culturally more traditional. San Jose has always existed in San Francisco's shadow, with a strong sense of inferiority. San Francisco, say the stereotypes, is where society and culture are the ultimate aspirations; San Jose is a place to make money and raise families.

POWER IN SUNBELT CITIES

San Jose and Indianapolis, reasonably typical of their regions, represent differences in power structures that are common among Sunbelt and Frostbelt cities. These differences are not, however, simply a product of geography. They are related to the timing of development, to changes in the economy, and to the unique characteristics of Sunbelt cities. These differences are not simply a matter of whether or not one region is run by power elites and another is free of them. Perhaps the key idea about Sunbelt cities, as we've learned in studying San Jose, is *change*. Power structures are less entrenched in them than in their Frostbelt counterparts—even *less* so in many today than they were fifteen or twenty years ago. But as we will see, this is not because elitism has withered away for good and pluralism has won the final victory. It is because internal and external forces have brought on transition. New elites have entered the picture, and old ones have achieved a new sophistication. Although Sunbelt cities have always had qualities unique to them, it is this dawn of a new power structure that makes their contrast with the more traditional Frostbelt cities so important. An understanding of power in the Sunbelt is essential to an understanding of the future of cities in the United States; the cities of the Sunbelt, more than of the Frostbelt, are reflections of contemporary America, and they may dominate our immediate future.

Yesterday: The Old Guard Elite

We know that, with some exceptions, Sunbelt cities are young. Most were small cities thirty years ago—dependent on agriculture, mining, or petroleum, with few manufacturing or service industries—that grew explosively in the 1950s, 1960s, and 1970s. Their growth, as we have already seen, was based in part on climate and space, but more significantly on the expansion of certain sectors of the economy, especially energy, electronics, aerospace, and defense. Federal spending and Sunbelt boosterism were important factors here. And, with its cheap land

and energy, its low taxes and construction costs, and its nonunion workers, the new, dynamic industries went where the cost factors were best: the Sunbelt.

Northern cities attracted less new development because they were priced out of the market. With elaborate and aging physical support systems, unionized labor forces, and costly demands for social services, they had to devote municipal resources to maintenance and social programs rather than to economic expansion. They became less profitable locations for industry; industry went elsewhere.

In chapter 4, we saw that San Jose's Progress Committee and Book of the Month Club ran the city from 1944 to about 1969. They recruited industry, raised the capital for necessary civic improvements, and stifled demands for social services. They were the men who made the city a successful growth machine, and they were among the primary beneficiaries of growth.

Although they never achieved the broad powers of Frostbelt elites (like Indianapolis), during that era, many Sunbelt cities seem to have been dominated by similar small, cohesive groups. "Local business elites have had close working relationships and actively underwritten elected and official public decision-makers," one study has shown, not only in Atlanta, but also in Albuquerque, Miami, Tucson, New Orleans, Dallas, and Phoenix.[10] Houston's rise has been ascribed to the entrepreneurial talents of local business leaders: "nature does not make cities; people make them."[11] To facilitate development, the entrepreneurs of Houston built a transportation system that overshadowed a nearby city with a better natural port and enticed the National Aerospace Agency to Houston with a gift of land. The same sort of booster elite operated in San Antonio through the Good Government League, building water and sewage systems, streets, a coliseum, highways, and an airport and implementing an annexation strategy that "out-maneuvered" adjacent cities and added 110 square miles to the city in twenty years.[12]

As in San Jose, newspapers were an important component of the growth machines in most Sunbelt cities. They sold the candidates and the capital-improvement bonds to the voters and suppressed dissent. Their "hallmark . . . has been peerless boosterism: congratulate growth rather than calculate its consequences; compliment development rather than criticize its impact."[13]

The reform structures of government common in Sunbelt cities were also effectively used by these booster elites. Such structures produce "somnambulistic government," fostering "a quiescent, acquiescent citizenry, where only the business community and property-owning middle class need be politicized."[14] Ironically, reform structures make it difficult for the electorate to hold elected officials accountable, for they are not responsible for administration nor, under an at-large election system, does any one elected official represent any one area. Reform structures also make it difficult for minority and grassroots groups to enter electoral politics because of the cost of elections, the absence of political parties as a legitimizing and support mechanism, and the tendency of candidates who appeal to the majority (rather than to particular ethnic groups or neighborhoods) to dominate. These victors usually have the blessing of local elites and newspapers, and they are usually boosters.

What has the Sunbelt wrought? Ultimately, some claim, growth machines, not communities. Political scientists Peter Lupsha and William Siembieda conclude that the emphasis on expansion, on the culture of profit that puts the economic well-being of the community above the needs of individuals and neighborhoods, and on reform structures of government that suppress demand and expectations have produced communities in which public services are minimal—a "poverty of public services in the land of plenty."[15]

Others have reached even more devastating conclusions on the sorts of cities the Sunbelt has produced:

> In the plastic, unadorned subdivisions, high rises, and slab office buildings of Los Angeles, Phoenix, Dallas and Houston eastward to Tampa and Miami, life and culture have been sacrificed to the most robotized forms of mass production, mass merchandizing, and mass culture. The faceless structures that sprawl across the "southern rim" lack the seasoning of history, of authentic cultural intercourse, or urban development and centering . . . . Homogeneity has effaced neighborhoods, regionalization has effaced municipalities, and immense enterprises, fed by the bequests of big government have effaced the existence of the socially active citizenry. The basic concerns of the Sunbelt cities are growth, not reform; the basic concerns of its citizens are services, not participation. Politically, the residents of the Sunbelt cities constitute a client population, bereft of citizenship and social activism by the very success of their economic growth. To the degree that meaningful politics is practiced in these cities, it is orchestrated by business and government . . . [16]

These are harsh judgments on cities so often blessed with "most liveable" awards, yet such views have been expressed by more than a few Sunbelt dwellers. Whatever the evaluation of the quality of cities the Sunbelt growth machines have produced, there seems to be unanimous agreement that the movers and shakers came mainly from the economic elites of the cities. The differences between Sunbelt boosterism and Frostbelt elitism are usually acknowledged, but the power structures are still seen as similar. Instructive as these conclusions once may have been, they are time-bound and of limited validity in today's Sunbelt cities, because power structures in Sunbelt cities are changing.

Today: Power in Flux

The work of Terry Clark and Lineberry and Sharkansky, which we have relied on heavily, suggests that as a city grows, its greater size, diversity, industrialization, and other developments lead to an increasingly pluralistic power structure. Thus the pattern of Sunbelt booster elites which Lupsha and Siembieda and others have observed, might break down over time. The San Jose case study demonstrated that to some extent this is true. We did find a power elite in San Jose, and it was dominated by business interests. But it was not omnipotent, and it was less commanding than we might have expected from reading the authors cited above.

Our research turned up large amounts of evidence which suggest that San Jose is not alone among Sunbelt cities in experiencing this change. To our surprise, our survey of ninety-five major metropolitan daily newspapers revealed that twenty-three (besides the San Jose and Indianapolis studies cited here) had published articles about power in their communities. Half of these were merely impressionistic studies, but half *attempted* a systematic approach and three of these were highly sophisticated. Interestingly, fourteen were studies of Sunbelt cities, suggesting a concern in those communities with finding out who has power. The fact that the answers weren't already known lends support to our thesis of changing power structures.

Throughout the Sunbelt—in Albuquerque, Austin, Dallas, El Paso, Fort Lauderdale, Los Angeles, Memphis, Orlando, Sacramento, San Antonio, San Diego, and Wichita—the common finding was a changing power structure. *Albuquerque:* leadership was "more diluted" than it had been in the past.[17] *Austin:* the power structure was "fragmented," and the "good old boys" were no longer dominant.[18] *Dallas:* "It's not that simple any more to name the real movers and shakers," a local leader said. "There was a time about fifteen years ago when a dozen or less called the shots, but you can't even narrow it to a dozen at this point," said another.[19] *El Paso:* although the old elite was still powerful, there was a notable "trend toward outside decision-making."[20] *Ft. Lauderdale:* "Anything that happened here before 1970 is ancient history," one observer noted.[21] *Los Angeles:* there, "power was passing into new [corporate] hands."[22] *Memphis:* the elite had been weakened by industrial diversification and minority organizing.[23] *Orlando:* "The old leaders are stepping aside and a vastly diffused power base is knocking elbows to fill the void."[24] *Sacramento:* it had become "a branch office town," with leadership "remote and ill-defined," largely because the national corporations with facilities in the city paid more attention to their "hometowns" then to the "hustings."[25] *San Diego:* a leader remarked it was also "a branch office town, a satellite of Los Angeles. . . . Decisions are made every day about San Diego matters that affect the city one way or another, but they are made in other cities, by people who have never been here and have no interest in the community." There was a "vacuum in leadership," as "important executives are too busy proving themselves to out-of-town bosses" to be active in local politics," and death and retirement had "decimated" the old leaders.[26] *San Antonio:* "By the mid-1970s, the boosterism of previous decades had begun to unravel, in part because of the birth of mass politics. . . . Discord within the progrowth coalition also developed as some boosters began to associate benefits *and* costs with the city's postwar growth patterns."[27] *Wichita:* power was "fluid and shifting," with no dynasties and no single, unified elite.[28] Repeatedly the studies remarked how "a decade ago the search for the establishment was relatively simple," but not today.[29]

Change had clearly come. Yet how much and in what way? As in San Jose: neighborhood groups emerged to challenge the growth coalitions in Albuquerque, Austin, El Paso, and San Antonio; minority groups organized to fight the old guard in these cities as well as Houston and Memphis; major reorganizations of government, usually including district elections (demanded by neighborhood and/or minority groups), were considered (and in most cases approved) in Albuquerque, Dallas, El Paso, Memphis, Sacramento, San Antonio, and San Diego. Yet despite the high profile and single-issue victories of the antigrowth, grassroots movements, few women, minority, or labor leaders and *no* environmentalist or neighborhood activists were named among the most powerful in these communities. They may have gained influence, but the scope of their power was clearly narrow in comparison to that of economic interests.

In every community, the top leaders were still businessmen (including editors and publishers of local newspapers). A handful of politicians also appeared on each list. But the business leaders that dominated were *not* the same as might have emerged from studies done ten or twenty years ago. The old elites were losing power not only to the grassroots but also to new economic leaders. Many of these leaders—especially in Albuquerque, Austin, El Paso, Ft. Lauderdale, Houston, Phoenix, San Diego, Tucson and Tulsa—were associated with the new aerospace, electronics, and defense industries, national corporations heavily dependent on federal contracts and lacking in local ties. Other new economic leaders emerged as national companies bought out local department stores, newspapers, television stations, banks, and industries. These changes meant that "a lot of the real decision-making power in" these communities "passed out of [them] altogether."[30]

In every community, the old style of growth by aggressive annexation and minimal planning had brought problems: traffic congestion, polluted air and water, inadequate sewage systems, insufficient public services. But as Mayor McConn of Houston said, "Our problems are related to growth, not to a mass exodus of people that troubles other cities [that is, the Frostbelt]. And amen, I'll take the problems of success anytime."[31] The problems of poverty and unemployment, however, were neither caused nor solved by growth. Most Sunbelt cities still have unemployment rates similar to many areas experiencing no growth,[32] and "the rising level of Sunbelt affluence has done little for the poor."[33] Those most left out, of course, are the burgeoning minority populations of the Sunbelt.

And in every community, it was growth that brought change. New people, new organizations, new economic powers, and new problems changed the face of these communities' power structures. The old guard—San Jose's Book of the Month Club, San Antonio's Good Government League, Dallas's Citizen's Charter Association, and the like— have faded or died or been absorbed. Our study of San Jose and those of our journalistic colleagues in other Sunbelt cities have caught these communities in a time of change in the distribution of power, a period of transition. Growth had brought new interests at both the grassroots and elite levels. Both challenged the old guard, largely due to the problems the old guard's *style* of growth had caused. But while the grassroots may be genuinely antigrowth, the new economic elites are not. Their interest in growth lies in the continued expansion of their industries, however, not simply in the construction of more and more housing and shopping centers which preoccupied the old guard. The new economic elites favor planned growth, not so much as environmentalists, but as pragmatists and as corporate professionals who know that maximum growth in the long run requires careful management of existing resources.

Tomorrow: The New Corporate Elites Versus the Grassroots

The Sunbelt cities are in the vanguard of what political economist David Gordon calls the "corporate" phase of capital accumulation and urban development.[34] The preceding commercial and industrial phases were characterized by strong, locally based elites. But in the corporate phase, much power is held by institutions and individuals outside the city, represented locally by managers and regional vice presidents. Sunbelt cities "reached maturity during the stage of corporate accumulation," according to Gordon. They were "constructed from scratch to fit the needs of a new period of accumulation in which factory and plant and equipment were themselves predicated on a decentralized model."[35] Yet, "much of the Sunbelt's industry and a significant portion of its finances remain under the control of outside economic actors," not only in terms of the location of corporate headquarters, but also in the dependence of Sunbelt industries on the banks, lawyers, and accounting firms of the Frostbelt states.[36] In San Jose, El Paso, Tampa, and most other Sunbelt cities, an increasing amount of power over the fate of the city is held elsewhere.

During the changeover, the grassroots had a moment in the sun. But as the dust settles, the new elites are emerging. For a time, they took little interest. They had no need to. The old guard took care of their minimal needs—favorable zoning, adequate infrastructures, housing for their workers, low taxes, minimal regulation. But the problems of growth—traffic congestion, overextended services, pollution, rising housing costs—reached the point where the old style of growth was no longer tolerable. The environmental and neighborhood activists raised the antigrowth banner in many Sunbelt communities. They turned on the old guard just as it was aging and weakening and replaced its electoral stooges with new elected officials committed to more responsible planning. Latino and black minorities, restive at having lagged behind economically, also grew more assertive, and made some gains.

But the corporate elites, like their predecessors, need growth. They must expand their markets and their plants. When the old guard could no longer deliver, or when the grassroots came too near to seizing power, the new elites grew more interested in politics in the "branch-plant" cities of the Sunbelt. They could just pack their files and move elsewhere, as industries have done in the Frostbelt. Some already have. But apparently, the corporate consensus on the Sunbelt cities is still favorable. Conditions have not yet sparked a mass exodus. Rather, they have grown more involved in local politics, especially in planning and especially on a regional scale. The activities of the Santa Clara Manufacturing Group are illustrative, as are the changing editorial policies of newspapers like the *Los Angeles Times* and the *San Jose Mercury News*. The corporations, including the press, now advocate "good planning," instead of the unrestrained growth of the past. But as Harvey Molotch observes, they "tend to support 'good planning' principles in some form because such good planning is a long-term force that makes for even more potential future growth."[37] Their increasingly responsible and seemingly liberal positions are, simply, good business planning.

The old local elites played their parts well. They built cities to suit the new people and the new industries. But they also produced two forces that turned on them. First was the population that suffered the consequences of growth in the form of inadequate services—the neighborhoods, the environmentalists, and the minorities. Second were the industries that dwarfed or absorbed the local economic institutions. *Electoral power* thus shifted in part to the masses who could no longer be controlled by the old guard, and *economic power* shifted to the corporations which displaced the aging elite.

In the 1980s, the grassroots will engage in struggle with the new corporate elites. We suspect the advantage is on the side of the economic forces. They have the wherewithal, the organization, and the staying power that the grassroots lack. They have learned, not only the rhetoric of controlled growth, but also the practical advantage to their own interests in managing growth. By attempting to shift the decision-making arena to a regional rather than local scale, they could enhance their power and weaken the grassroots correspondingly. That regionalism is high on the national corporate agenda is apparent in the advocacy role of the Committee on Economic Development, a coalition of the largest corporations in the country.[38]

> The bewildering multiplicity of small, piecemeal, duplicative, overlapping local jurisdictions cannot cope with the staggering difficulties encountered in managing modern urban affairs. The fiscal effects of duplicative suburban separatism create great difficulty in provision of costly central city services benefiting the whole urbanized area. If local governments are to function effectively in metropolitan areas, they must have sufficient size and authority to plan, administer, and provide significant financial support for solutions to area-wide problems.[39]

As they enter battle with the corporate elite, the grassroots forces need to recognize the threat that regionalism could pose to their influence. They must overcome the parochialism that has characterized relations among neighborhoods within cities and cities with regions. Affluent and protectionist neighborhoods and cities have benefited from competition and fragmentation, while low-income and minority neighborhoods have lagged behind in services and especially in schools. Unless both rich and poor neighborhoods and cities recognize their common interests, both could lose power as authority shifts to a regional scale beyond their reach. Unless regional planning is constructed from the bottom up, in such a way that representation is assured from the least powerful neighborhoods and cities, it surely will be imposed by the economic elites from the top down, and with no such consideration. There is nothing inherently evil in larger units of government and more comprehensive social planning. There is a great deal wrong, however, when the move to regionalism is made in order to disenfranchise the grassroots.

As the issue of regionalism demonstrates, the emergence of the corporate elite is making Sunbelt cities more like their Frostbelt sisters. Power is increasingly concentrated among economic elites. Local governments have become more involved in the management of their economies and containment of the socio-political fall-out of growth then they were in the 1960s and 1970s. But even as the Sunbelt cities mature and their power structures are realigned to correlate more closely with those in the Frostbelt, they are not likely soon to duplicate the structure of power in the old urban centers because their economic elites are transients and nomads. They are branch-office towns, a product of the corporate economy. If, however, the new elite succeeds at consolidating power, this too may change. Some Sunbelt cities may become centers of corporate power, rather than merely satellites, marking a new era in community power structures.

LAST WORDS

Nothing could better illustrate the benefits of cooperation between journalists and social scientists than the constructive interplay between journalistic power studies and social science theories described in the last section. As we have seen, social scientists can contribute ideas and a framework for general understanding and for comparison, but they need their journalistic colleagues to gather contemporary data widely. Journalists, on the other hand, can contribute timely, specific data, but they need the general and comparative framework the social scientists provide in order to give greater meaning and deeper understanding to their stories. The work of both disciplines, to which we have referred, would have been considerably strengthened by such an awareness. We hope that the collaboration of a social scientist and journalist in this book help make the case for more interchange between the professions.

As we have also seen, there is more work to be done. Some of the points in this chapter have been speculation based on the San Jose findings. Our thesis of transitional power structures in Sunbelt cities should be tested by other studies in other Sunbelt cities. If we are correct, studies done in the next decades will describe power structures that have begun to differ substantially from San Jose's in 1979. We hope our readers will be inspired to do such studies.

We also think it is time for another round of studies of Frostbelt cities. Such research will confirm or disprove our contention that Sunbelt power structures differ from those of the Frostbelt; or they may reveal that the structures, once different, are growing more alike. As the corporate economy develops, many Frostbelt cities are losing corporate headquarters and industry generally. Some may become branch-office towns like their Sunbelt counterparts, such as Sacramento and San Diego. There may be a redistribution of corporate headquarters into regional centers such as Los Angeles, Dallas, Atlanta, and Miami, making Sunbelt and Frostbelt cities more similar. The dominance of the monopoly corporations in the national economy makes the branch operation—be it finance or manufacturing or media—a common phenomenon in our society. A key question is whether corporate headquarters will be distributed among several regional centers or in only a few. If the latter is the case, both Sunbelt and Frostbelt cities may experience the branch-office syndrome.

But to document and understand these changes, we must continue to study. Not only must we continue the study of individual communities, we must shift our focus to the regional level. Some form of regional government already is in place in many communities, and it is on the agenda in many more. Corporate coalitions, too, like several we have examined in this book, need much closer scrutiny.

Finally, we should continue studying power and its structure because it is important not only to social scientists and journalists but to all people who live in cities. They want and need to know who rules. We doubt that studies themselves have much impact on the shape or duration of particular power structures. But nothing is so entrenched as the unknown, and nothing can be affected or altered unless it is first understood.

Notes

[1] Peter Rossi, "Power and Community Structure," in Terry Clark, ed., *Community Structure and Decision-Making* (Scranton: Chandler, 1968), p. 135.

[2] William D'Antonio, William Form, Charles Loomis, and Eugene Erickson, "Institutional and Occupation Representatives in Eleven Community Influence Systems," in Clark, ed.

[3] Frederick M. Wirt, *Power in the City* (Berkeley: University of California Press, 1974), p. 338.

[4] G. William Domhoff, *Who Really Rules* (Santa Monica: Goodyear, 1978), p. 39.

[5] Edward C. Hayes, *Power Structure and Urban Policy* (New York: McGraw-Hill, 1972), p. 189.

[6] Floyd Hunter, interview, March 4, 1980.

[7] Philip J. Trounstine, *Indianapolis Star*, November 28, 1976.

[8] *The Detroit News*, October 4, 1978; *The Des Moines Register*, 1976; Peter Bachrach, and Morton S. Baratz, *Power and Poverty* (New York: Oxford University Press, 1970).

[9] Philip J. Trounstine, *Indianapolis Star*, January 16, 1978.

[10] Peter Lupsha and William Siembieda, "The Poverty of Public Services in the Land of

Plenty: An Analysis and Interpretation," in David C. Perry and Alfred J. Watkins, *The Rise of the Sunbelt Cities* (Beverly Hills, Calif.: Sage, 1977), p. 185.

[11] William D. Angel, Jr., "To Make a City: Entrepreneurship on the Sunbelt Frontier," in Perry and Watkins, p. 125.

[12] Arnold Fleischmann, "Sunbelt Boosterism: The Politics of Postwar Growth and Annexation in San Antonio," in Perry and Watkins, pp. 153, 155, 167.

[13] Gene Burd, "The Selling of the Sunbelt: Civic Boosterism in the Media," in Perry and Watkins, p. 129.

[14] Lupsha and Siembieda, p. 186.

[15] Lupsha and Siembieda, pp. 176, 187.

[16] Murray Bookchin, "Toward a Vision of the Urban Future," in Perry and Watkins, pp. 262, 265.

[17] *Impact, Albuquerque Journal Magazine*, February 26, 1980.

[18] *Austin American-Statesman*, December 17, 1978.

[19] *Dallas Morning News*, December 10, 1978.

[20] *El Paso Times*, December 17–24, 1978.

[21] *Fort Lauderdale Sun-Sentinel*, February 19, 1979.

[22] Robert Gottlieb and Irene Wolt, *Thinking Big* (New York: Putnam's, 1977).

[23] *The Commercial Appeal*, Memphis, September 20, 1970.

[24] *Florida, Sunday Magazine of the Orlando Sentinel Star*, October 28, 1979.

[25] *Sacramento Bee*, April 1, 1979.

[26] *San Diego Union*, November 1–14, 1976.

[27] Fleischmann, p. 166.

[28] *Wichita Eagle-Beacon*, November 20, 1977.

[29] *San Antonio Express*, February 17, 1974.

[30] *El Paso Times*, December 17–24, 1978.

[31] *New York Times*, December 16, 1977.

[32] Harvey Molotch, "The City as a Growth Machine: Toward a Political Economy of Place," *American Journal of Sociology*, Vol. 82, No. 2 (1976), p. 321.

[33] Perry and Watkins, p. 296.

[34] David M. Gordon, "Class Struggle and the Stages of American Urban Development," in Perry and Watkins, p. 78.

[35] Gordon, p. 78.

[36] Robert B. Cohen, "Multinational Corporations, International Finance, and the Sunbelt," in Perry and Watkins, pp. 212, 225.

[37] Molotch, p. 316.

[38] Committee for Economic Development, *Reshaping Government in Metropolitan Areas* (New York: CED, 1970).

[39] *Modernizing Local Government*, a Statement on National Policy by the Research and Policy Committee, Committee for Economic Development, New York, July 1966, p. 44.

Index

Absentee ownership, 42–43, 47–48, 106
Advertising Council, 147
Aerospace industry, 9–10, 13, 90, 100, 184, 188
Albuquerque, 109, 185, 187–188
Albuquerque Journal, 194
Alloway, James A., 63–66, 115–117, 138, 140
Alquist, Alfred, 115, 126, 161
Ames Research Center, 90
American Civil Liberties Union, 138
American Fletcher National Bank, 74–76
American Microsystems, 145
American Telephone and Telegraph Company, 76
Annexation, 92–95, 97–98, 102–103, 105, 189
Anticipated response, 19
Associated Building Industry, 151
Atlanta, 26, 185
At-large elections, 83–84, 101, 186
Austin, 187–188
Austin American-Statesman, 194

Bachrach, Peter, and Morton Baratz, 15, 52–53, 193
Bagdikian, Ben, 137
Baltimore, 180

Baltimore Sun, 15
Bank of America, 57, 64, 76, 115–117, 123, 170
Bank of the West, 73, 121–122, 154
Bay Area Rapid Transit (BART), 99
Behavioralism, 23–24
Beritzhoff, Sigmund E., 115, 120, 122
Berliner, Sanford, 115, 124
Bernard, Frank, 115, 122
Bigley, Charles, 85–87
Blackmore, Ray, 86
Bloom, Maxwell H., 115, 120, 122, 156
Boccardo, James, 71, 115, 120
Boeing Aircraft Corporation, 86, 147
Bohemian Club, 147
Bonds (municipal), 69–70, 88, 95–96, 100, 105, 165
Bookchin, Murry, 15
Book-of-the-Month Club, 96–97, 100, 107, 124, 126, 138, 165, 185
Brown, Edmund G., Jr., 124, 134, 141
Bulen, L. Keith, 181
Bureaucracy, 39, 48
Burke, Halsey, 114, 120, 122, 124–126, 129–130, 145, 151–154, 162

Burke Industries, 114, 152
Business Council, 147
Business Roundtable, 147

California Automobile Association,
    152
California politics, 168–169
California Roundtable, 151
Campaign for Economic Democracy
    (CED), 115
Campus Community Improvement
    Association, 115
Canneries, 80–81, 86, 88, 92, 99
Cannon, Lou, 131, 163
Capital improvements, 95, 97
Carter, Jimmy, 141
Carter, Rosalyn, 141
Case study method, 37, 50
Caterpillar Tractor, 147
Center for the Performing Arts, 65,
    69–71, 116, 123, 130, 133,
    139, 142–143, 183
Chamber of Commerce (San Jose),
    71–73, 83, 87, 96, 114, 122–
    123, 134, 137–138, 144–145,
    149–152, 154, 170
Charter, 82, 87–88, 101
Charter Review Committee, 143
Chase Manhattan Bank, 76
Chicago Tribune, 15
Chrysler Corporation, 76
Christensen, Terry, 115, 130
Citizens for Housing and Economic
    Stability (CHES), 107, 175
Citizens for Responsible Government,
    151
Civic Improvement Association, 143
Civil service, 85
Clark, Terry, 20, 40–42, 51–53, 172,
    187
Cleveland, 8
Colla, Joe, 137, 141
Collins, Bart, 104
Commercial Appeal, 194
Committee for Economic Develop-
    ment (CED), 53, 191, 194

Community, as unit of analysis, 20–
    21, 56–57
Community characteristics and power
    structures, 40–50, 172
Community Power Structure, 25–27
Competitive bidding, 85
Concurrent elections, 104
Confederacion de la Raza Unida, 138
Concerned Citizens, 177–178
Conroy, Paul, 136
Continuum of community power,
    38–40
Controlled growth, 106
Corporate nomad, 64, 170
Corporations, 48–49, 174–175, 189–
    192
Council-manager form of govern-
    ment, 83
Crenson, Matthew, 34, 52
Crocker National Bank, 147

Dahl, Robert, 27, 30–32, 35–36, 51–
    52
Dallas, 109, 185–189
Dallas Morning News, 194
Davidson, Charles, 115, 118, 141
Decisional technique, 30–38, 167
Decline of elites, 47
Defense industry, 9–10, 13, 90, 184,
    188
Des Moines, 180
Des Moines Register, 15, 193
Detroit, 8, 76, 180
Detroit Edison, 76
Detroit Free Press, 4
Detroit News, 15, 76, 193
Developers, 118, 140, 142–144, 175–
    176, 182–183
Didion, Joan, 110
DiNapoli, J. Philip, 115, 120, 122
Diridon, Rod, 115, 120, 122, 130,
    146, 155
District elections, 101–102, 105–106,
    109, 115, 126–127, 165, 171,
    174–178, 183, 188
Diversity, 40–41, 47

Domhoff, G. William, 32, 38, 49, 50–53, 173, 193
Dortch, Carl, 179, 181
Dye, Thomas, 33, 152

Eakins, David, 109, 110
East Side Union School District, 114, 160–162
Economic diversification, 41, 47
Edwards, Don, 115, 122, 130
El Paso, 8, 109, 187–188, 190, 194
El Paso Times, 15, 193
Electronics industry, 9–10, 13, 90, 99, 100, 106, 184, 188
Eli Lilly and Company, 63, 74–76
Elite theory, 25–30, 36, 172
Engineers Club, 147
Equitable Life Insurance Company, 147
Estruth, Jerry, 137, 141
Exxon Enterprises, 176

Farrell, Harry, 136
Federal contracts, 10, 184, 188
Feminist groups, 104–105, 165
Fiscalini, Frank, 55, 114, 120, 130, 160–163
FMC, 87–88, 90, 101, 106, 116, 156
Ford Aerospace, 145
Ford Motor Company, 76
Ft. Lauderdale, 12, 187–188
Ft. Lauderdale Sun-Sentinel, 16, 194
Francis, Les, 159
Fullerton, Gail, 123
Frostbelt, 11–13, 15, 171, 173, 178, 180, 182, 184–186, 189–190, 192–193

Gary, Indiana, 34
Garza, Al, 104–105, 134, 137, 139, 140, 142, 154, 161
Gay rights, 178
General Dynamics, 147
General Electric, 88, 90, 116, 142, 145
General Motors Corporation, 48, 76

General plan, 94–95
George, Glenn, 114, 120, 122, 126, 154–156, 162
Giles, Peter B., 145, 152
Gitlin, Todd, 137, 163
Goldeen, Don, 66, 115, 120, 122
Good Government League, 82
Goodwin, Clarence, 85, 87, 88
Gordon, David, 78, 109, 189–190, 194
Greater Indianapolis Progress Committee, 74, 180–181
Growth, 46–47, 91–108, 135, 140, 142, 145, 151, 172, 174, 176–178, 189–191
Growth machine, 78, 86, 91, 97, 99–101, 109, 185–186, 194
GTE Sylvania, 145

Hamann, Anthony P. "Dutch," 89, 91–93, 96–97, 100–103, 131, 157, 161
Hammer, Philip, 115, 141
Hammer, Susan, 141
Hayes, Janet Gray, 71, 103–107, 114, 118–119, 137–142, 146, 162
Hayes, Kenneth, 139
Hewlett-Packard Company, 57, 90, 114, 123, 144–148
Hewlett, William, 90, 146
Hoover Institution, 147
Hosfeldt, Robert M., 115, 120, 122, 127
Housing, 91, 92, 107–109, 174–177, 190
Houston, 8, 185–186, 188–189
Hudnut, William H., 65, 175–179
Hunter, Floyd, 25–30, 51, 128, 174, 193

IBM, 86, 88, 90, 92, 103, 116, 141–142, 145
Ice, Harry T., 55, 181
Indiana Bell Telephone Company, 74–76
Indiana Gas and Coke Utility, 74–76

Indiana National Bank, 74–76
Indianapolis, 15, 55, 57, 61, 66–67,
    74–76, 178–185
Indianapolis Chamber of Commerce,
    74, 179–182
Indianapolis Power and Light Com-
    pany, 74–76
Indianapolis Star, 55, 77, 179, 181–
    182
Indianapolis Water Company, 74–76
Industrialization, 41, 47, 86
Industry and Housing Management
    Task Force, 152
Inertia, 36
Influence, 18
Ingle, Robert D., 138
Initiative, referendum and recall,
    168–169
Interview techniques, 70–72

James, Ronald R., 72, 101, 103, 114,
    120, 122, 126–127, 130, 149–
    152, 158, 161–162
James Transfer and Storage Com-
    pany, 150
Jarvis, Howard, 169
Jinks, Larry, 114, 120, 125, 127,
    134–138, 162–163, 170
Journalism and social science, 2–7,
    192
Journalistic power studies, 187–188

K-Mart, 76
Key issues, 31, 33
Knight, James L., 132
Knight, John S., 132
Knight-Ridder Newspapers, Inc.,
    106, 128, 132, 134, 138

Labor unions, 10, 22, 83, 87, 105,
    108, 115, 166–167, 172, 185,
    188
Laird, Melvin, 147
League of Women Voters, 139
Levine, Mort, 115
Levy, Gordon, 150

Liebling, A.J., 3, 15
Lilly, Eli, 63
Lilly Endowment, 180
Lineberry, Robert L., and Ira Shar-
    kansky, 16, 39–40, 42, 48, 52–
    53, 172, 187
Lippmann, Walter, 3, 15
Lockheed Missiles and Space Com-
    pany, 90, 145
Los Angeles, 183, 186–188
Los Angeles Times, 137, 190
Lugar, Richard G., 180–181
Lund, Arthur K., 66, 115, 120, 122
Lynd, Robert and Helen, 24–27, 48,
    51, 53

Machine, 22–23, 80–87
Mandich, Mitchell, 110
McAlister, Alister, 161
McCorquodale, Dan, 115
McEnery, Tom, 115, 141, 150
McLoughlin, James P., 115
Memorex, 144
Memphis, 187–188
Merchants National Bank, 74–76
Metropolitan Associates Trust Fund,
    122, 149
Meyer, Philip, 3, 15
Miami, 132, 185–186
Miami Herald, 134
Middletown, 24–26, 48
Miller, Delbert, 52–53
Mills, C. W., 27–28, 30, 51
Mineta, Norman Y., 66, 101, 103–
    104, 114, 120, 126, 130, 139,
    154, 156–160
Minority groups, 48, 60, 101, 102,
    104, 109, 116, 158, 161, 165–
    167, 177, 186, 188–191
Miscoll, James, 64, 66, 115, 116, 120,
    122, 127, 170
Mobility of industry, 43, 47
Mobilization of bias, 34–35
Molotch, Harvey, 109, 190, 194
Moss, McKenzie, 115, 120, 122, 145
Moral majority, 177–178

National Bank of Detroit, 76
National Semiconductor Company, 145
Neighborhood groups, 48, 104–105, 109, 165–167, 177, 188, 190–191
Network analysis, 29, 49, 73–76
New Haven, 31–32, 49
New Orleans, 185
New York Times, 194
Nixon, Richard M., 144, 147
Nondecisions, 33
Nonpartisan elections, 43, 84, 168

Oakland, 42, 173
O'Brien, James, 151
Orlando, 187
Orlando Sentinel Star, 194
Owens-Corning Fiberglas, 145

Pacific Gas and Electric Company, 147
Pacific Studies Center, 110
Pacific Telephone Company, 151
Pacific Union Club, 147
Packard, David, 57, 66, 71–72, 90, 114, 119, 120, 122, 123, 129, 144–148, 154–155, 162, 174, 177
Packard Foundation, David and Lucille, 145
Park Center Plaza, 65
Pegram, Larry, 115
Philadelphia Inquirer, 4
Phoenix, 8, 185–186, 188
Pittsburgh, 8
Pluralism, 30–36, 167, 169, 172–173
criticized, 32–36
Political culture, 45–47
Political science and the study of power, 21–24, 27–36
Positional approach, 21–22, 167
Polsby, Nelson, 52
Population growth, San Jose and Santa Clara County, 79
Power, defined, 56

Power elite, 27
President's Commission for a National Agenda for the Eighties, 8, 11, 15–16
Proctor and Gamble, 76
Progress Committee, 87–89, 100, 142, 155, 165, 185
Progressive movement, 22–23, 83, 109
Proposition 13, 107, 140, 141, 169, 178

Questionnaire, 61–69
scoring, 65–69

Rancho San Felipe, 147
Railroad, 80–83
Rand Corporation, 101
Reagan, Ronald, 180
Redevelopment, 143, 150, 175–176
Reed, Thomas, 83–85
Reform movement, 22–23, 168–169
Reformed structures of government, 12, 43–44, 168–169, 185–186
Regionalism, 174–178, 191–192
Reputational technique, 26–31, 37–38, 51, 54–77, 167, 172
criticized, 28–30
Ridder, Joseph B., 64–65, 89, 97, 101, 103, 106, 131–132, 134–136
Ridder, P. Anthony, 63–64, 66, 106, 114, 116, 120, 122, 125–127, 129, 129–136, 146, 152, 162
Right-to-work laws, 10
Rinconada Country Club, 120, 121
Rivers, William, 137, 163
Rotary Club of San Jose, 73, 120, 121, 150, 155–156
Ruffo, Albert J., 89, 115–116, 120, 122–123, 126–127, 129–130, 142–144, 146, 162
Runyon, David, 137, 141
Rushing, Conrad, 115
Ruth, Leo, 66, 115, 120, 122, 127, 130

Sacramento, 109, 187
Sacramento Bee, 194
St. Louis, 8
Sainte Claire Club, 73, 112, 119, 120–121, 136, 144, 148, 154, 183
San Antonio, 8, 109, 185, 187–189
San Antonio Express, 194
San Diego, 8, 187–188
San Diego Union, 194
San Francisco, 9, 31, 39, 49, 90, 173, 183–184
San Francisco Commonwealth Club, 147
San Jose Chamber of Commerce. See Chamber of Commerce (San Jose)
San Jose Country Club, 120, 121, 144, 152
San Jose Mercury News, 12, 55, 57, 63–64, 77, 89, 92, 96–98, 100–101, 103–106, 110, 112–114, 116, 123, 125, 127–129, 131–138, 145, 170, 176, 190
San Jose State University, 73, 115, 122–123, 142, 152, 161
San Jose Water Works, 73, 101, 121, 122, 152, 154
Santa Clara County, 13, 79, 90
Santa Clara County Homebuilders Committee, 151
Santa Clara County Manufacturing Group, 71–73, 122, 129, 138, 144–152, 154, 171, 182, 190
Schools, 94, 100, 103–105
Seattle, 38, 45
Self, Jim, 141, 150
Sewage, 88, 91, 94–98, 100, 107, 171, 185, 189
Schaffer, Virginia, 99–100, 151
Silicon chip, 13
Silicon Valley, 13, 92, 110, 171, 174–175, 182
Size, 40, 47
Smith, Jerry, 115, 144

Social science and journalism, 2–7, 192
Socialization, 18–19, 34
Sociology and the study of power, 24–27
Sociometric analysis, 29, 73–76
Spartan Stadium, 65, 116, 122, 123, 133, 135, 142–143, 146, 152, 155
Standard Oil of California, 147
Stanford Environmental Law Society, 110, 111, 163
Stanford Research Institute, 90, 147
Stanford University, 90, 147, 150
Starbird, George, 92, 96, 99, 103, 110–111
Stratification theory, 24–27, 29
Structures of government, 43–44, 47
Sunbelt, 7–15, 44, 46–48, 78–79, 81, 84, 86, 91, 108–109, 136, 174, 178, 182–194
Swenson, Cliff, 66, 115, 120, 122, 127
Syntex, 145

Tampa, 186, 190
Tedesco, Ted, 103, 113, 116, 124–127, 137, 154, 158, 176
Terman, Frederick, 90
Transamerica Title Insurance Company, 151
Trilateral Commission, 147
Trounstine, Philip J., 16, 77, 193
Tucson, 185, 188
Tulsa, 188

Unionization, 41–42, 47
United States Steel, 147
U.S.-U.S.S.R. Trade and Economic Council, 147
United Way, 73, 118, 121, 122, 134, 137, 183
University of Santa Clara, 89, 122–123, 142, 144, 154
University Club, 120–121, 144
Urban Development Policy, 103

Urban renewal, 98
Utility companies, 80–81

Varian Associates, 145
Vasconcellos, John, 144
Villa, Jose, 115
Vote of confidence, city manager, 87–89, 101
Voter turnout, 104

Wards, 83
Washington Post, 137
Water, 88, 91, 98, 100, 101, 121, 152
Welch, Robert, 151

Wichita, 187–188
Wichita Eagle-Beacon, 194
Williams, Iola, 141
Williams, Roger, 150–151
Wilson, Robert C., 144
Wilson, Susanne, 115
Wirt, Frederick, 51, 53, 173
Wolff, Lewis N., 66, 115, 122, 150
Wolfinger, Raymond, 15, 52
Woodrow Wilson International Center, 147

Zoning, 91, 95, 97, 174, 190
Zumbrunner, Ernest, 151